COMMENDATIONS

The following commendations have been gratefully received for Ishmael and his ministry:

I'm convinced no one has had more of an impact on children's work in the UK (and further afield) than Ishmael. So many of us owe so much to him. He and Irene have been a source of inspiration and encouragement, as well as great friends to Belinda and myself. We certainly wouldn't be doing what we're doing now without them.

– *Doug Horley*
Energise, UK

Ishmael has made a huge and lasting impression on my personal life and on the ministry of Kingdom Kids and Kingdom Creative. He has been an inspiration and guide in my understanding of children and spirituality. He is the father of modern children's worship music and has pushed back the barriers and boundaries of traditional preconceptions of children's work. His radical passion for Jesus and children is infectious, as he continues to impart fatherly wisdom and love to all of those who dare to follow in his pioneering footsteps. He has been a father to me.

– *Jim Bailey*
Kingdom Kids, UK

I have known Ishmael for many years and consider him a dear friend. Ish has spoken and ministered at several of our international conferences on children's ministry. Few people have impacted my attitudes and thinking about how God works through children more than

Ishmael. His passion for God, his childlike spirit and enthusiasm have provoked and encouraged me in my own zeal to see children encounter God in marvellous and intimate ways.

– David W. Welday III
Vice President/Product Development
Strang Communications Company, USA

Ishmael is an advocate for the cause of the children within the body of Christ. He has chosen to look at things from the perspective of a child. Out of this position he shares his observations, often in the form of a confrontation, yet intended in a non-accusing way, leading his audience to receive a revelation of God's plan for children. Ishmael's life is dedicated to making room for children to be what God wants them to be and what he made them for.

– Jurgen Gerber
School leader of Principles of Child and Youth Ministries,
YWAM, Switzerland

Ishmael's unwavering devotion to kids, as well as his music, has been a personal inspiration to me. Having seen on many occasions his energy, enthusiasm, and special kind of lunacy with the kids, I can only describe him as an unsung hero! His example was certainly important when I started Rocky Kids, and I now see how difficult it is to get people to understand the importance of working with children.

– Dave Cooke
Rocky Kids, UK
Producer and composer

God has equipped Ishmael with gifts that help us all to better understand the Lord's work through us and those around us ... I pray that readers will take the wisdom printed on each page and apply it to their ministry, allowing God and his power to complete his desired work through them.

– Jeff Hilbert
Pastor, California

We have had the privilege of having Ishmael join us at our church week-aways for several years. Over these years we have been extremely impressed with his vision, style, enthusiasm and love for ministry with children. He brings young lives into the presence of God through worship, praise and heaps of fun, and therefore I'm convinced inspires life-long worshippers. Ishmael has led us in times of prayer and ministry, where children are ministering to each other and calling out for the Holy Spirit's power – that's what I call an effective and powerful ministry!

– *Greta Greenwood*
HTB Children's Work Director, UK

I feel honoured to have this opportunity to write a few lines for Ishmael's new book, because many children in our country have been greatly blessed by his ministry. Ishmael combines a special love for Jesus and for children with skills that not many people have. He can bring children into the presence of the Lord and encourage children's workers to do the same. I am very grateful to Ishmael for having shared his time, his teachings and his anointing for children with me. I am sure this new book will have a great impact on all those who really want to make a difference in children's ministry.

– *Marianne Buitenhuis*
Royal Kids Praise, The Netherlands

God called Ishmael and Irene to pioneer children's ministry years before many of us understood what God was longing to do through the new generation. Now a wave of children's leaders is following in the wake of their example. Ishmael's ministry always stays fresh, as he allows God to reshape what he does and what he teaches. His books are a must for children's workers trying to hear God's heartbeat for children.

– *Graham Reed*
Children Worldwide, UK

For those of us who have put away childish things, Ishmael brings a breath of fresh air – a challenge to our adult world with its inconsistencies, its traditions and trappings. He does not require us to agree with everything he says or does, but he demands that we rethink WHY we behave as we do – for the sake of our children. Ishmael's radical approach to children, his belief in them and their potential as spiritual beings, with a real contribution to make to the church, is a challenge and inspiration that has transformed my approach to children's work.

– Denise Baines
Children's worker, Brussels, Belgium

We were delighted when Ishmael agreed to be one of our patrons, because we share similar ideals when it comes to children and young people. Ishmael is much more than a conventional children's worker. He has a well thought-out biblical, practical and radical approach which is actually quite revolutionary in today's church.

– Keith Holder
Director, Educación Plus, Costa Rica

Ishmael's ministry and books have made me laugh a lot, weep, grow and think!

– Zezita (Maria José Pinheiro)
Children's leader, Portugal

Ish is a loyal friend and a real man of God, who hates religion, loves the Lord and loves the lost.

–Steve Legg
Breakout Trust, UK

It's hard to think of anyone who's done more in modern times to disciple a generation than Ishmael.

– Pete Greig
Revelation Youth Church Leader

When we think of children's ministry that is radical, effective and God-inspired we immediately think of Ishmael! We know of no other ministry that carries such a passionate heart in reaching and reclaiming this generation for God.

– Ray & Nancy Goudie

Reclaiming
a Generation

ISHMAEL

EASTBOURNE

Published by
KINGSWAY PUBLICATIONS
Lottbridge Drove, Eastbourne, BN23 6NT, England.
Email: books@kingsway.co.uk

Designed and produced for the publishers by
Bookprint Creative Services, P.O. Box 827, BN21 3YJ, England.
Printed in Great Britain.

Contents

Dedication

Dedicated to any children's worker who feels unnoticed, unsupported, isolated and unappreciated. Be encouraged – you have the most exciting job in the church!

Special thanks to all those wonderful people that have worked alongside me and been part of my numerous teams over the past 30 years. I really do appreciate all of you.

* * *

Ishmael is a consultant for both Children's Ministry and the Evangelical Alliance.

To contact him please write to the following address:

Revelation Centre
PO Box 38
Chichester
PO19 2UD

Visit the website on www.ishmael.org.uk

Introduction

You can please some of the people some of the time. . . .

For over 30 years my life has seemed to be surrounded by controversy. After my first 'preach' in my home church, I ran the wrath of the elders and was never invited back into the pulpit because I innocently included a Roger McGough poem. A few years later I remember singing at a concert in a prison, where my audience was composed of hardened criminals serving life sentences. I will never forget that one of my songs upset them and they all walked out *en masse,* offended.

While serving a term at Bible college the principal stormed out of the lecture hall, shouting that I had insulted his intelligence when I did an evangelistic, illustrated children's talk in my sermon critique, instead of the expected biblical exposition. Leaving college behind, I became an ordained minister, but I was also the lead singer in what was looked upon as a Christian punk rock band. Just as I thought things were going well I was summoned to my denomination's HQ for an informal 'chat' with one of the main leaders, where he informed me that he had received complaints from some of the young people at one of our concerts. The complaint was that they couldn't hear all the words, which didn't surprise me as I didn't know all the words!

I once caused an uproar at my denomination's conference by

using flashing lights to accompany my songs. I was told later that what made things worse was that they had spotted a young couple kissing in the back row. I had one of my albums banned by a large chain of shops because in one tongue-in-cheek song I sang that to attain church unity by leaving out Jesus could be likened to the Laodicean Church and the Antichrist.

I was banished by all the local church leaders in a large town for over ten years for encouraging them to dance at an inter-church gathering. I was labelled as a 'tasteless blasphemer' by a national Christian newspaper for leaping around and wearing a multicoloured wig while praising God on stage. I have had listeners completely lose control of their tempers and rush out screaming during teaching seminars.

I have sung about Jesus in bars where I have been spat at and had beer glasses thrown at me, but I tended not to mind this too much because – unlike the majority of the above – my audience was not made up of tolerant, loving Christians! And I have been taken off a leadership team when the leading elder found it impossible to lead the church while I was around because 'my character was stronger than his'. And so I could go on.

So it's been an interesting life so far: I have never ever been bored, and all the little difficulties I've mentioned above I like to think have done me good, taught me lessons, and helped to shape my character. I can honestly say that I have no real enemies, but I think I may have a few very close friends who don't like me much!

But, believe it or not, and I may sound totally naïve, in all the above I never meant to be controversial, cause trouble or deliber-ately offend anyone. I can't understand why ministers with self-confessed charismatic tendencies would leave a platform or liter-ally hide in their pulpits while I've encouraged their congrega-tions to dance around their building. I can't understand how I have upset leaders who invited me to their 'lively' churches, and afterwards why they refused to even say goodbye. Surely before they considered inviting me, they researched what I believe in and what I do?

Please don't misunderstand me. I am not saying everyone else is wrong and I am perfect – far from it. Saint Ishmael is a few years away yet, but I try and do my best to be as perfect as I can be. On each of these occasions I honestly believed I was doing and saying things that Jesus wanted me to do and say. I had no idea that I was even being contentious or offensive.

Why have I told you all the above little secrets? Because you may be about to start reading this book.

This book

I am aware that the book you are about to read could get me in even more trouble than all the above put together. I have deliberately hacked into religious traditions that some hold dear, and slaughtered every sacred cow I could think of. I know too well how touchy we Christians can be when someone disagrees with our way of thinking and seems to be bringing down a big hammer on conventions, customs and rituals that we and our forefathers have bowed down to and followed for hundreds of years.

I have not written this book to unthinkingly destroy and offend; it is written because I believe it's time to stop living in the past, blindly accepting certain things that we have inherited without even bothering to check out if they are biblical. Everyone keeps telling me that we must not offend the older ones, but now I am rapidly becoming one of those older ones – so please stop just thinking about us and start thinking about our children and their futures. It's for their sake that I am willing to stick my neck out and try to face up to some major issues that many Christians for centuries have happily swallowed without even looking at the ingredients, while our younger generation are regurgitating them and finding them totally unpalatable.

I have written this book because I believe it is time to reevaluate our many traditions, and as we do so, I pray it will give us a better understanding of what the Bible teaches is expected of our children. To be a Christian in today's godless, materialistic, immoral society is hard enough for our young ones, without us adding even more regulations to make it so impossible for them that they lose faith altogether.

Hopefully in time, both in the home and the church, we will be in a position to bring about the major changes that may be necessary to help our children stay close to Jesus, but release them from all the man-made rules. This book is not about compromising with the world's values and dropping godly standards; it's just written to set us thinking about being the church Jesus wants us to be and living the life that he wants us to live.

Please try and read it with an open mind, discuss it and pray about what I am saying, and then, before you make up your mind to agree or disagree, just look outside your window and ask yourself honestly how the thousands of lost little ones around you will ever get to know Jesus, or get to love church, if we just stay as we are for the next 2,000 years.

1

Ministry Begins at Home

After '*Angels*'

Years ago I wrote my first book about children in the kingdom of God, called *Angels with Dirty Faces*. Well, here I am again, a little older, a little wider(!) and a lot greyer. Many of the things I wrote twelve years ago were fundamental teaching, interesting anecdotes and exciting true stories. For this reason I have included most of the old book in this book for new readers to enjoy and previous readers to be reminded of. However, if you read my previous book, it will not take you long before you notice that I have added new thoughts and even taken away some old ones from every chapter.

In *Angels with Dirty Faces* I mainly concentrated on the children: how to teach them, pray for them and release them into life with the Holy Spirit. In this book I have added that effective children's ministry is not dependent on just Spirit-filled children but, more to the point, Spirit-led adults.

We lead, they follow ... sometimes

Children do not make up the rules and regulations. Children do not lead our churches and are not in a position to run the home and the family. Children are just instructed to listen to adults' guidance and follow – often blindly – adults' teaching and example, both in the home and church gatherings.

I believe we automatically (consciously and subconsciously) pass on so much that we have never examined or thought about, let alone checked out with Scripture. The instruction we often give finds its foundations in traditions and hearsay. Our children are not convinced by our arguments. To say we are not to do something because it's wrong, or we are to do something because it's right, gives no explanation and nothing for a child's mind to think through. As they grow older it seems so many of them have no idea what makes something right or wrong. If we really love children, we owe it to them to rediscover what we believe and our reasons for believing it, and then to sit down with them – with our Bibles open – to talk these things through.

We are losing children from church life, not because they do not love Jesus but because they cannot cope with what we call church and the regulations that surround it. Our children are not in a position to change things, but we are.

Some may wonder why I have included certain issues that would not normally be found in a book on children's ministry. The reason I have included them is twofold. First, having spent so much of my life with children and young people, I know that these are some of the topics they face and question every day, and I think it's time these issues were brought out and openly discussed. The second reason is that children will be leading church tomorrow: they don't just need little stories; they need our wisdom on why we do what we do as church today.

I am hoping that after research we adults will be able to form some rational, scriptural, though maybe not conclusive opinions to pass on to the next generation. Although it's easy to guess my opinions while reading this book, I have tried to resist making dogmatic statements, and know I have not got all the answers for your children and your individual situation.

Many teachers love to lay their deliberations down in a black and white fashion so that the reader is only left with two choices: agree or disagree. It's much easier when others do your thinking for you. I do not have the right to tell you what you should think, teach or portray to those in your care. Yes, I can advise, but if you disagree with my advice then I must still respect your right to decide for yourself. You, like I, are answerable to God for those entrusted to you.

We encourage our children to do their homework, so now it's time for us adults to do ours. Dig deep and study hard, because it's only when we are sure of what we believe and why we believe it that our children will find a new freedom in their walk with Jesus and a new security in church and the Christian life.

Effective children's ministry can only happen when what we teach is not based on popular or unpopular religious opinion, but finds its foundation in the Bible, is rooted in Jesus, and is anointed by the Holy Spirit.

Humble beginnings

'Never work with children or animals' the old saying goes. I appreciate that is not a biblical quotation, but I know many Christians who treat it as though it were. In fact, some go to extremes by treating their animals like children or, worse still, treating their children like animals. As for me, well, up until a few years ago the only animals that I really liked were farm animals, because of my agricultural background. Even today I keep three chickens in my back garden – named Suzy, Emily and Catherine, after the three girls living in my house.

But I must confess that the reason I liked most of these animals and birds was because I saw their potential on a nice hot plate, to keep the gravy and potatoes company. My reasons for liking children were very different, you will be relieved to hear. For my younger readers I need to make something very clear: I too was once your age. I know many of you, having seen me, may find that impossible to believe, but I want you to use your imagination. With this in mind, it should also come as no great shock to you that in my early years I learned a lot about children, because, naturally enough, a lot of my friends were children.

But as the years passed by, I matured. I wouldn't say that I put away childish things; I just renamed them. Now they were not called toys; they were called pastimes and hobbies, which of course were vital to help me relax and unwind. During this period of my life I never really thought about children much at all. Obviously, they must have been around, but except for visiting the odd Sunday school meeting or going, 'Coochie coochie coo!' to some little baby in a pram outside a church meeting (who would invariably cry in horror when he saw my face) they never seemed to be around me.

Great expectations

But then came Irene and, alongside her, love and marriage. Due to my being an overworked travelling evangelist, there were only four months between our first date and our wedding day. The reason for this was that I had only one free Saturday for the next year. Although this may sound rather speedy, irresponsible, and not the recommended norm, I would also say in our defence that we did know the voice of God, and knew that not only were we meant for each other, but also that God was happy about the date. We also talked it over with our minister, who I am pleased to say was happy about it too.

It was during these very fast-moving weeks preceding the wedding that the subject of children was approached. We quizzed each other on such things as when we would start a family and how many children we would like to have. It's at this stage that you fail to consider fertility, maturity, the enormous responsibility, and, more to the point, when or even if God wants you to have the little patter of footsteps running around your house.

But we were both of one mind: we wanted to have children as soon as possible after we got married. I was convinced that this would happen. After all, I had read all the right Christian pre-marriage books, watched the educational films about it on telly, and spent many years on a farm where the facts of life had been revealed to me in graphic detail. Because of my experience, I felt that I was way above Mr Average in these matters.

That is why I was so disappointed and surprised when I discovered that we hadn't conceived on our honeymoon. All sorts of thoughts and questions went through my mind over the next few months. Maybe we were unable to have children. Should we get checked out? How would we cope if it was revealed who the infertile partner was? How would I cope if it was me? Of course, this was all showing me as I really was: immature, selfish, naïve and totally impatient.

Family man

It was in our sixth month of connubial bliss that at last Irene became pregnant. Why on earth did it take so long? I'm sure I did everything correctly! Never mind, I was ecstatic. I remember rushing around telling everyone that I was going to be a dad, and I loved it when everyone came up to me, shook me by the hand and then said that lovely word, 'Congratulations'. To this I would reply with the usual old cliché, 'Oh, there was nothing to it.'

In a reasonably short time, the initial euphoria wore off. It may have been because fewer people were congratulating me, or it may have been the awesome responsibility ahead that was making me feel rather ambivalent about it all. Or was it waking up to the sound of morning sickness in the bathroom every day? Whatever it was, I was becoming a lot more thoughtful about the new little life that was going to come and invade our marriage.

The main problem was, having not had anything to do with

babies and children, I had somehow got it into my mind that Irene was going to give birth to a teenager, because this was the age that I was working with at the time, and this was the age that I knew most about. I kept thinking about all the fantastic things that my offspring and I could do together, things like touring and concerts. Maybe he or she would, unlike me, really be able to play an instrument and sing. Either way, I was convinced that he or she would be an excellent preacher and that God was going to use them in a far greater way than he had used me.

Being observant, I soon noticed that Irene was getting larger and larger, and being the lovely little, petite, four-foot-ten-inch lady that she is, I feared that there may come a time when she would be as wide as she was tall. I well remember that long hot summer when she was eight months pregnant. We had gone to the West Country for a holiday, after doing about six weeks of non-stop missions and living in a different house each week. I was beginning to discover just how uncomfortable it must have been for her, carrying around such a weight, tiring quickly, and getting cravings for the strangest types of food at the strangest times. It was also very embarrassing for her because, although we had just celebrated her twenty-first birthday, she looked so young and it could have been misinterpreted as a schoolgirl pregnancy. I remember taking a coach somewhere and the man in the ticket office innocently asked her if she wanted half-fare. At this she indignantly took a couple of steps backwards, pointed at the large lump and said, 'No I do not.' On reflection, he should have made her pay for two.

So, although both of us had seen the pictures and read much about the effects on the developing body in pregnancy, when it came to the real thing we were learning new and exciting things all the time. I found it wonderful to hear the little one's heart beating away like a bass drum, but there was always the inevitable fear about babies being deformed or suffering some mental illness. My fear was there because this would have been an area that I knew nothing about, and although I knew there would be no question of my love for my little one, I still, being totally inexperienced in such things, was frightened by the very thought. I should add that in my work with children since then, I have spent a lot of time with some of these little ones that our society has called 'not normal' and they have been some of the most beautiful children I have met. They have the same potential to love, serve, and be used by the Lord Jesus, albeit in different ways, as any child born with a perfect body and mind. What they lack in some areas, they have a double portion of in others.

Happy birthdays

The big day eventually came, eight months and one week after conception. I was walking up and down the corridor of the maternity hospital like a caged lion, along with other expectant fathers. They were smoking to calm down their nerves, while I was praying and trying to keep out of their line of fire as they breathed out the foul-smelling fumes. I had no intention of walking into a sterilized room to see a brand new life, smelling like something that had fallen out of an incinerator.

Soon a large lady dressed in a blue uniform informed me that I could be with my wife during the birth if I wished. This I did, and it was a tremendous experience. I clearly remember being told I was now the proud owner of a 1973, mint condition son. I remember shouting out, 'Praise the Lord!', and Irene and I thanked God for the wonderful gift of this lovely little boy, and for being together during the birth. We were totally elated.

I have always been the sort of person who loves to share good news, especially if it's an 'exclusive'. The phone bill soared as I rang everyone I could think of. Most, of course, were as happy as I was. Some were a little bit more subdued as, in my excitement, I rang a few wrong numbers and they didn't quite seem to share my enthusiasm.

I was very proud, and within ten days Irene and baby Joseph Gideon were released from the hospital. Both arrived home and we began our family life as a threesome. As I mentioned earlier, I had no idea what babies did, or how to relate to and communicate with them, so it came as rather a shock to me when I discovered that all this little thing seemed to be able to do was cry, eat, dirty his nappy and sort of smile if he had wind problems. This was not quite the man of God that I was anticipating.

From that time on, though, I watched with interest as young Joseph developed from sitting to walking (as, unlike most babies, he never seemed to crawl) then from gurgling to talking, and while all this was going on we were blessed with another little baby boy, whom we called Daniel Jonathan.

Having one child was interesting enough, but two children were fascinating. The two boys were as different as Laurel and Hardy. Their personalities and whole way of life seemed totally opposite. Joseph was cool and calm and, as the years went by, I could see that he seemed to achieve a lot without really having to try; a natural, you could say. Daniel, on the other hand, tended to be much more nervous and excitable, and through sheer hard work and great effort would attain similar results to that of his older brother. It was also interesting to note that Joseph was never a child that demanded a lot of kisses and cuddles; in fact, from a very young age he seemed to be embarrassed by this. But Daniel, with his opposite temperament, would always respond to a bit of outward affection.

It puzzled me how two such different children, with different needs and qualities, could come from one set of parents, but after pondering this for a short while I realized how different Irene and I were and how many of our traits, both good and bad, were being mirrored by our children. When the children were quiet and well-behaved, people commented how like their mother they were. I can't understand why, whenever they were the opposite, it was attributed to good old Dad.

Four years after Daniel, yet another bundle of joy joined the Smale family, this time of the female variety. We decided to call our little girl Suzannah Joy.

Claim it ... then name it

Just as an aside, never underestimate the turmoil that can be caused by selecting a name. Every parent invests in one of those little books that tells you every conceivable name that mankind has ever chosen to embarrass a child with. At first everyone wants a name from a heroic biblical character and they think that there are plenty to choose from, until they realize that all the best ones have already been pinched by their relations and friends.

It's worth mentioning that my first-born was named after two of my favourite Bible characters. It is also worth mentioning that later on in life Joseph did not share my taste in names or Bible heroes; he has now renamed himself 'Joss' and, needless to say, the name Gideon is never mentioned.

Rather than just choosing our favourite names that may have wonderful spiritual significance to us now, with major aspirations that we would love our child to achieve in future years, may I suggest to parents that unless we have an angelic visitation, let's consider the long-term consequences seriously! It will take a lot of thought and prayer to find a name that a child will be happy to own when they reach eight, let alone fourteen.

While on names, I heard a wonderful story about singer/songwriter Martin Smith's two-and-a-half-year-old daughter. While listening to adults discussing what to name a pregnant lady's baby, she approached the lady concerned saying, 'I know a good name for it if it's a boy.'

'What is that?' replied the pregnant lady.

'God,' said the little girl. 'That's a nice name.'

Why Ishmael?

On a personal note, I as usual am opposite to the norm. My parents gave me the lovely name Ian, and I guess back in 1949 that was quite a popular name. It was also Scottish for John, which is what everyone called my dad, even though his first name was William. Confused? Let's move on.

Although I should have been a 'child obeying my parents' and loved their choice of name, between you and me, as from the age of eleven I never really liked it. It did not seem to fit into my approaching teenage character. But I shouldn't have worried because, with the advent of the swinging sixties, my appearance soon changed – and so did my name. My friends who were not Christians nicknamed me 'Flower Power Fred', while my Christian friends made a sort of anagram out of Ian Stuart Smale and came up with 'Ishmael'.

As the sixties and flower power came to an end, so did 'Fred', but I am pleased to say that for some reason the Ishmael stuck. I liked being called Ishmael, not because I ever saw any similarities between me and a rather wild, hairy, rebellious character from Genesis, but because it was a fun name which means 'God hears'. Over my many years of what sometimes has been a lonely and misjudged ministry, that strange nickname has been a wonderful reminder of God's closeness. I was never going to allow it to become just a stage name, because I never wanted to be a different person off the stage than on it. And nowadays all the children I have sung to around the world, all my best friends, and even Irene and my children call me Ishmael or Ishy – and I love it. Only my mother is different: she often calls me Tim, getting me confused with my tall and thin little brother.

We decided on Suzannah for our daughter simply because we liked the name and we thought it would hopefully not be too much of an embarrassment when she was 16. Choosing names can be a nightmare, but by the time we reached our third child, we had learned our lesson.

Girls are different to boys

As the boys were growing older I found it easier to relate to them, but how would I cope with a little girl? In the past I'd never been very good with the female sex. It was never that I didn't like or respect them; no, it was more that in my own family, without question, the ladies, if not stronger, were far more vocal than their male counterparts or husbands. This usually incensed me to argue with them. In fact, the best disagreements and debates I've ever had have been with the fairer sex, and at the end of our heated verbals either they would end up in tears or I would end up in tears, or they would hit me over the head with their handbags. Our Suzy was no exception to the female family tradition. Her character was very different from the boys'. She was an extrovert, loved talking and was fearless in front of large audiences; quite a chip off the old block, you might say. She was also very caring, sensitive and considerate of others.

I kept my eyes glued to the children as the years passed by, knowing that childhood is short, and I started seeing more and more how God was using them. Joseph's prayers were solid and confident, as he prayed for me to be healed, or had words from the Lord for me, and they came with sincere conviction. Daniel was always asking questions about life's little enigmas, always seeking to know the real meaning behind truths and statements, never over confident, but always full of energetic excitement and enthusiasm as God began to use him. Suzy, who was a very feminine, frilly, demonstrative little girl, went to ballet lessons. Yes, whatever you may have heard, Ishmael does not just enforce bouncing! On one occasion, in front of her teacher and the other pupils, she began to sing and dance to a praise song with her hands in the air. After this, the amazed tutor and class didn't know what to say, except, 'Thank you, Suzy, that was very nice.' She was full of enthusiasm, sharing the good news of the Lord Jesus with any friends she made.

Ishmaelites

All three children had been fully involved with my work since the day they were born. When they were younger, they were keen to volunteer and eager to do anything for me. Nowadays they still accompany me to the odd gig, but understandably are not quite so keen to do everything I ask.

I have never favoured one child above the other. Just as all three have individual failings and weaknesses, so too they have wonderful God-given qualities, all unique to them, and I have deliberately taken time over their growing years to discover, promote and encourage these. I don't want them to be replicas of me, or even just fulfil my aims and ambitions. I just want them to discover God's will in their separate lives and then go on to see it fulfilled. John Wesley's mother, when asked which of her 19 children she loved the best, had a great answer: 'I love the sick one till he's well and the one that is away until she's back.'

Pastor's progress

If I could leave my little tribe just for a moment, it needs to be said that outside of my rapidly growing family, I still gave very little thought to the younger generation. I had been taught that this was the church of tomorrow, so it was logical to assume that tomorrow would be the time when I would think of them; but, as we all know, tomorrow never comes.

For a few years I was pastor of a church in Lancashire. We had a large number of teenagers and a very capable lady looking after the children's work, so again I chose to put all my efforts into the teens and older ones, not being too concerned about what happened to the children. In time they would, of course, become teenagers, and so, to my badly educated mind, would become of some value in the church. What I failed to understand at the time was that due to attitudes like mine, many of the children never realized their value and hence never stayed in the church long enough to even become teenagers.

Another of my failures was that I was under the impression that if important things had to be done well, it was much quicker and easier to do them yourself, rather than train up others. The children's work at this time was not on my priority list of important things. But God was about to change my way of thinking.

It happened on a Wednesday night, when we held our weekly prayer-meeting-cum-Bible-study and as usual I had arranged that I would unlock the church, set out the chairs, convene the meeting, lead the singing, open in prayer, preach the sermon, give the appeal, close in prayer, make the coffee, do the washing up, then lock up the building. Just the usual things you expect from a one-man ministry. However, on this evening things were not right. I had left home after having a blazing row – sorry, heated disagreement of views – with Irene, and the last thing I felt like doing was going to a meeting, let alone doing all the odd jobs that I had lumbered myself with. But of course I had to be there. I couldn't leave the sheep without a shepherd, even if he was a bad-tempered, grumpy one, which they probably would have been better off without.

I had a few professional secrets up my sleeve for rare disasters like this. The first dodge was to drop the praise and thanksgiving because you had to look happy for that. The secret was to go straight into some serious, gentle, slow songs. With this, people either kept their eyes closed, or those that were gazing around generally looked miserable or expected to see others looking miserable. I always find it strange how, when I move from praise into what many call worship, people's facial expressions change: one minute they are smiling, the next minute they are not. There must be a link somewhere between worship and a miserable face, but as hard as I try I cannot seem to find it anywhere in the Bible. With the way I was feeling I had no problem pulling that sort of face. I assumed that people must have thought I looked very 'worshipful'.

But this was going nowhere, so dodge number two came into force: I simply told the folk that we would have a time of open prayer. This meant that I could sit down and let them get on with it. At this point, I could just about overhear a couple of my deacons whispering things like, 'Pastor isn't his usual self tonight.' They would not have needed a word of knowledge to come to this conclusion.

Enter . . . a child

It was at this stage that everyone looked up, including me, as a child started walking to the front of the building. He walked straight into the little wooden box that I was hiding behind, put his hand on my shoulder and started to pray for me. Wow! I don't know what he prayed, but that was unimportant. I immediately leapt to my feet, thinking, 'Somebody cares and is not too scared to come and pray for me.' I felt great. In no time at all, the old springs had regained their bounce. I apologized to the Lord, and later to Irene, and was back in top gear. It was then that I noticed a deacon flipping through his Bible to see if it was scriptural for a child to lay hands on and pray for his pastor. Without meaning to sound unspiritual, I didn't care; I was just delighted. This was my first major shake-up as far as children were concerned. God could actually use them. They were not just little things to be seen and not heard; God wanted them to be seen and heard. I allowed these thoughts to lie dormant in my mind for a couple of years, as I was not quite sure how to develop them.

The commission

A few years later I was in a band, and we were doing a tour in Europe of venues where no Christians had gone before. One morning we played in a girls' school, to a class full of twelve-year-old girls. They were great, although they didn't speak very good English, and by the time we had sung a song through twice, they were joining in as if we were giving a rendition of 'Tulips from Amsterdam'. Then came the evening, and we were playing in a nightclub called the Golden Sunflower, which was an open display for everything that is evil and everything you would pray that no child of yours would ever get involved in. It was then that I noticed a few innocent little faces I recognized. Yes, there were some of the little girls we had been singing to earlier that day in school, but now they were being handled by old men before being taken outside to fulfil their duty as prostitutes. It takes a lot to turn my stomach, but this did. I had mixed emotions of tears and rage, and I knew that I would never forget that night.

Soon after this, God spoke to me directly for the first time regarding children. He said, 'What you have seen in Holland is already happening in England, and it's going to get worse.' He told me that his Spirit had come in power upon many people in churches around Britain, regardless of what denomination or stream of new church they came from. He then asked me this question: 'Why is it that this move has failed to touch or influence the children, and why is it that, even with all this going on, still the drop-off rate of children leaving church in their early teens is as high if not higher than it has ever been?'

I was led to that well-known scripture in Matthew chapter 18, when the disciples were asking who was to be the greatest in the kingdom of heaven. Jesus had a little child stand in front of the disciples, and told them to learn from him. That was my commission; not so much to go and teach the children, but more to go and learn from them. Throughout this book I want to share with you some of my initial discoveries, which are not just theory or an amateur's guide to child psychology, nor is it a book giving all the answers for every individual child. It is really just my first-hand account of what I have learned and experienced by working with and watching these dynamic little troopers.

I hope that this will shake up church leaders, wake up parents and excite our children as they read. I also pray that it will open the eyes of your local church community to see the potential and importance of their children, and also to take their God-given responsibilities seriously.

Matthew 18 states it loud and clear. Jesus said,

> And whoever welcomes a little child like this in my name welcomes me. But if anyone causes one of these little ones who believe in me to sin, it would be better for him to have a large millstone hung around his neck and to be drowned in the depths of the sea. (Matthew 18:5–6)

Irene's vision

I would like to share with you a vision my wife Irene had at Spring Harvest several years ago. I believe, looking back, that not only was it prophetic, but it was also a powerful demonstration through the children of what the future holds for the church.

Every day we would go on a march with the children round the campsite, singing, waving banners and proclaiming that we were in God's army. As we did this, people would rush out with cameras, and either stand and watch or join in. It was the highlight of the day for us, as well as for the children, and also a very moving experience as the vast marching crowd drew vast crowds to watch. Many a time has God's little army marched through meetings where thousands of adults have been assembled. Far from causing a disruption, many of the leaders of these meetings have told me that as the children arrived, a special anointing came upon the meeting, which stayed even after the children had left.

Here's Irene's vision:

As I watched the children marching around the campsite, the Lord very clearly showed me, as they began to march in a tight unit together, that they were following their leaders. I walked alongside them for a little way, then stood back. I closed my eyes for a moment and could hear their voices above everything else, loudly proclaiming around the buildings.

As I stood in the square, they came round, and I could see our daughter Suzy at the front line holding hands with a friend. It was Abigail Kendrick. I felt tears in my eyes at the sight of this little army marching for God, and I thought, 'Lord, I'm sure there are tears in your eyes watching this.' A little boy tripped over, and maybe it was his sister or a friend who helped him up, and they held hands and continued to march, catching up with the others. I felt God was saying, 'Now, can't you see? This is what I want for my body, my church.' I could picture regiments coming together all over the nation; they could be churches, fellowships, anything. They were helping each other put on their armour, and some regiments were already formed with their armour on, linking hands. Loving, caring, looking after each other, encouraging each other and their leaders, they were ready to march.

God said, 'Now march, and claim the villages, towns, cities and the nation. Fight for me and my kingdom, because all together we can stand.' I can still hear the voices of the children echoing; it was so powerful.

I am sure it is no coincidence that a few years later Abigail's dad was inspired to produce the concept of 'Make Way' and 'March for Jesus', encouraging thousands of men, women, boys and girls from all nations to join together. This grew to be the greatest worldwide witness and one of the most dynamic unifying influences there has ever been, proclaiming the good news of Jesus, and declaring defeat to opposing principalities and powers.

My ever expanding family

I have already mentioned that I have three children, but one of the advantages of getting old is that I have now discovered that the children of Ishmael are in the tens of thousands. My aim for my wider family is the same as that for my personal family, and that is to see them transformed into the children of God, to be taught their significance, to be given their rightful place as church and to be trained to be more than conquerors in a society that has rejected God.

2
Salvation

Babysitters

'Please, Mummy, don't make me go to that noisy children's meeting!' screams an insecure little nine-year-old, who is making as much fuss as a vegetarian forced to enter a steak house.

'But you must go to Ishmael's meeting. You'll be able to learn all about Jesus and how to become a Christian, and anyway Daddy and I have to go to our meeting, so you can't stay with us.'

This is quite a common occurrence, and of course some children are frightened on their first visit to a hall packed with hundreds of other excitable children whom they don't know. I'm sure I would be – wouldn't you? It doesn't help for the child to discover that another reason they must go and be with Ishmael is because the parents couldn't get another babysitter to look after them, and Ishmael is a good babysitter who also teaches stories from the Bible. But it goes further.

Do it all

There are so many times when I have found myself in a situation in which I just cannot win. 'I am sorry, Madam, but I cannot teach your child all about Jesus and salvation in the next hour. It will take your child that long to settle down and not feel scared, insecure and threatened, and it will take me that long to learn your child's name. But as I do preach on believing for the miraculous and achieving the impossible, I will do my best....'

Then come the 'divine' requests which, instead of being taken to the Lord, are brought to me. 'I believe that the Lord is going to use you tonight to save my child,' says one. 'I know mine will speak in tongues for the first time,' says another. 'God is going to anoint you to heal my son's deaf ear tonight,' pipes up a third, and from that moment on comes the flow of great expectations. It's all very flattering, but I know that if I allow that sort of pressure to get to me, I will end up praying for everything and seeing nothing happen. To try and get people to see that they must look to God and not to human beings seems almost as impossible as the miracle they are after.

Don't get me wrong: I love to see parents with great vision for their children. But I wish they could realize that I, like many others, am just a Spirit-filled Christian, and they have the same, or possibly more, access to the Holy Spirit, especially when their prayers involve their own children. So much more could be done in the home, if only they could believe and understand that.

Newborn babes

I am convinced that children can become believers at a very early age. I know that some critics would question exactly how much children can understand, but my argument is how much does anyone of any age really understand when they first become a believer?

I try to picture Mr Average, who almost certainly, if he lives in Britain, no longer comes from a Christian country. The chances are that except for the odd christening, wedding or funeral, he has never darkened the door of a building known to him as a church. As far as Christian teaching goes, all he remembers are a few well-diluted Bible verses delivered by an agnostic headmaster from his primary school assembly days. And his experience of worship is the odd Sunday evening in front of the telly, accidentally tuning into the wrong channel and ending up watching a few minutes of *Songs of Praise,* instead of the programme he was intending to see.

It is a similar process of learning and being re-educated for him as it is for a child. In fact, it will probably be easier for the child because he will not have lived as long on this planet and, although he has sinned, he has not had the time to be so tainted by the wickedness around him, or to develop the confusion and doubts that adults discover come quite naturally with age. Yes, children are much more open to being taught, as they, unlike many of their forebears, realize that they have not got all the answers to life's problems. All they have inherited are the unanswered questions.

It's easy to understand

I am thankful to the Lord that the great news of new birth and new life is simple. Some of our evangelists, however, would obviously disagree with me. Having heard some of their so-called simple expositions of 'salvation' I'd say that there was a lot more chance of a camel going sideways through the eye of a needle than of any normal pagan understanding a word of what was said.

Thankfully for the unsaved, the words of the Holy Spirit, whose voice they are really hearing, are a lot clearer, more direct, more precise and much easier to comprehend than most evangelists will ever be. I am sure that at almost any age people can understand what we call the 'ABC of salvation', and as in the Bible we are all called to share our faith with others, I am convinced that we do not need a degree in theology to tell people how to give their lives back to God.

It is a sad indictment on our church system that both adults and children are being taught how they ought to invite unbelievers along to a 'meeting', rather than being taught how to invite them to know the Lord Jesus. We need to teach both young and old how to pray with their friends and to see them 'saved', and show that this is not just the job of the church leader when he gives his Sunday evening appeal.

Although the Holy Spirit will lead individuals to pray in different ways, let me give you some guidelines on how I personally would pray for children, which may be of some help. Please bear with me as I run through a few details that I believe to be important for the children to have some knowledge of if they are to understand the basics of becoming a Christian. May I also add that it is not just the words that you say, but the sincerity and simplicity in the way you communicate this message that is going to help the children understand and respond. Obviously, the following is a more detailed guide for reference for the older reader. When passing it on to a child, one would need to use even simpler words and expressions. And remember that while we are doing the evangelizing, it is going to be the Holy Spirit who does the saving. Here we go then: imagine we are face to face with a child, or a crowd of children who are asking how they can become Christians.

'How do I become a Christian?'

First, I am a keen believer in teaching the theology of the Trinity. I believe that God, from the beginning of time till the end of time, exists in three persons: God the Father, God the Son and God the Holy Spirit. Although it is hard for our finite minds to understand, these three persons are not just three separate 'parts' of God – each of the persons is God.

Now, although the Father, Son and Holy Spirit do have different roles to play, they are all involved in bringing about the brand-new life of the born-again Christian. So right from the start I teach the person with whom I am sharing the good news just a little bit of how the three persons of the Trinity are involved. Although some may think this would sound confusing to children at such an early stage, I have found it to be a lot less confusing than children hearing people singing about and praying to various members of the Trinity without having a clue about what they are doing, or who they are speaking to.

Father God

I make it clear that the Bible teaches us we have all sinned (done things that have hurt God) and fallen short of Father God's glory (not been the kind of people that he created us to be). So that they don't suspect that I am making things up, I find it a good idea to show them Romans 3:23, so they can see this is what the Bible teaches. (Please make sure you use a modern translation, so they can understand it.)

I then explain that doing wrong comes naturally, and doing right demands effort. Even if no one has ever taught them to do wrong things, no one needed to; it was one of the few things that they were immediately good at. I remind them that it was not their mums and dads who taught them to do wrong; in fact, most mums and dads spend most of their time struggling to teach them to do right.

I tell them about my own children: when they were tiny I never had to teach them that if they did not like their food they could throw it all over the floor or the wall – they did it quite naturally. They did not need a demonstration from Dad. Then there was bedtime: I knew they were tired and needed sleep, but sometimes they thought they knew better. Who told them that parents were a soft touch, and that if they yelled at the tops of their voices, as if they were in total agony, for long enough then someone would come running up the stairs to obey their every wish?

How about those times when they were playing with their toys and refused to share them, or took their friend's toy and refused to give it back? I never taught them to behave like this, but somehow from a very young age they had learned to do wrong things without me having to influence them. I have never had to spend long convincing a child that he is not perfect. Nowadays I have more trouble trying to teach a child self-worth. Let me emphasize that no one has forced them to do wrong actions, have wrong thoughts and say wrong things; they have, in fact, consciously or subconsciously chosen to do these things for themselves.

I will ask if they realize how it breaks Father God's heart when we choose to do things that, deep down, we know upset him. I then ask the child to say sorry for the things that come to mind, and if they can think of only one specific thing they continually do that upsets Father God, I ask them to not only say sorry for this but also ask God to give them the strength to stop doing it. Although I may not use such a long word as repentance, that is what I know God wants to see: a complete change of mind, and an attitude that says they are going to stop living just to please themselves, and start living to please God.

The Lord Jesus, God's Son

If they believe in the Lord Jesus Christ they will be saved: scriptural references include Acts 16:31, and many more. I try not to take anything for granted, and knowing that some children have been taught nothing in their homes about the Lord Jesus, and taught wrong concepts and ideas in their schools, I try to explain in a few simple sentences who Jesus is.

I begin by saying that the world is in a mess. Satan (the devil) who is against God and all that is good, but nowhere near as powerful as God, fooled many into following him and his evil ways, just as he does today. But Father God so loved people that even though they were not being obedient to him he sent his only

SALVATION   39

Son, Jesus, down to earth to show them how good life could be if
we lived in a way that pleased him.

I make no apology in teaching children about Satan and sin, as
it is impossible to be saved from sin without understanding a bit
about what it is, but neither do I spend a lot of time discussing
with small children Satan and his works. I would rather spend
that time telling them about Jesus and his grace and love. I go
into quite a bit of detail about how the so-called religious people
of Jesus' time couldn't cope with the Lord Jesus because he
showed them up for the wicked people they really were. I also
explain that they fixed up a false trial, that they were happy to
watch Jesus being beaten up, and that even as he suffered excru-
ciating pain as he was nailed to a wooden cross, they still felt no
guilt or shame.

Then I ask the children, 'How would you feel if someone had
done that to you when you were innocent? I imagine you would
have been shouting things back at them, telling them how unfair
they were being. But the Lord Jesus didn't act like that. In fact,
he was just the opposite. He loved those who were killing him,
and he asked his Father to forgive them because they didn't
understand what they were doing.'

Then comes the hardest, yet most important, detail to explain.
In the Old Testament, animals were a substitute for man, and that
is why they were sacrificed to take away the wrong things that
man had done. But here on the cross Jesus was the perfect Lamb
of God, and as he was being sacrificed to deal with all man's
wickedness – past, present and future – even Father God couldn't
look at his Son as he carried in his body all mankind's sin. He
didn't deserve to die; we do. Jesus was our substitute, and he
paid the death penalty for our wrongdoing.

As Satan saw Jesus dying on the cross he must have been
thrilled because he thought that he had destroyed God's Son. But
it was then that, with his fading breath, Jesus shouted out, 'It is
finished', which was not a cry of defeat but a cry of victory. It

literally meant, 'My work is completed.' Satan, sin and death need no longer be man's destiny. Jesus, through his suffering, has unlocked the gates of heaven and offers life without end for those who believe in him.

Being physically dead, Jesus was buried in a tomb, like other men, but in those days it was more like a cave and had a big stone rolled over the entrance. After three days, an angel of God rolled away the big stone and when people looked inside there was no dead body to be found because Jesus had come back to life. For a short while afterwards, he showed himself to many, even telling them to touch him to prove that he was not a ghost but the real Jesus who had risen from the dead.

This is not a story or a fable: this is the truth. To become a Christian it is important to believe that these things really did happen.

And finally, this means little if we don't allow God to come into our lives and change us.

So where are they all now?

After just a few years into life on earth a child's mind is very questioning. A lot of questions have very obvious answers and can soon become tedious or embarrassing. 'Why are you doing that?' as you scratch your head. 'Why is that lady so fat?' as they point to the vicar's wife. 'Are we nearly there yet?' as you pull out of the driveway, ready to embark on a three hundred mile journey. But not all questions are quite so trivial or easy to answer. 'Where are Father God and the Lord Jesus now?'

Once you start explaining the different functions of the Trinity, this question is likely to arise and can often send a parent or children's leader into panic mode. I explain that according to the Lord's Prayer, Father God is in heaven. It's a good answer unless they follow it up by asking where heaven is, or you have just sung a song about heaven being in your heart. So where is the

Lord Jesus now? That is a bit harder to explain.

Most Sunday schools teach that when someone becomes a Christian, Jesus comes and lives in their hearts. The thinking child will find this hard to understand. They have learned that Jesus remained in his body after the Resurrection; at that time the disciples not only saw and touched the body of Jesus, they also saw him physically ascend into heaven and were told that they would see him return in the same way. If Jesus is still in his body, how can the big body of a man come and live in the small heart of a child?

Others teach that Jesus is walking in front of Christians, showing them the way that he wants them to go. The child then wonders how Jesus can be both in their heart and in front of them at the same time. Finally, we add that Jesus is in heaven, waiting to return again for those who love him. The child is now totally confused. They wonder how Jesus can be in them, in front of them and way up above them all at the same time.

To simplify this, I explain that Jesus did ascend into heaven and he is at this present time sitting next to Father God. He is waiting for Father God to tell him when to return to earth, but while he is waiting, he is watching over and praying for every boy, girl and grown-up all over the world that loves him and follows him. I tell the children that unlike most people on earth, he does not just see the wrong we do; he also sees all the good things that we do. He really wants us to stay close to him in our prayers so that he can give us the best life possible.

So have we had bad teaching over all these years? Is it wrong to tell children that Jesus lives in their hearts? Well, in my opinion it's not so much wrong as slightly confusing, because the Bible also teaches us that one name for the Holy Spirit is the Spirit of Jesus.

So to recap: every human explanation of the Trinity falls short, but I find the easiest way to explain it is to say that Father God is in heaven, Jesus is sitting next to Father God, and the Holy Spirit came down to earth in a very special way at Pentecost. I continue by saying that Jesus, being in human body like you and me, could only be in one place at one time, so Jesus said that he was going to go back and be with his Father until the time was right for him to come back and wind up man's time on earth for good.

He also said that he wouldn't leave us by ourselves: he would send his Holy Spirit, who, being Spirit, could be everywhere and in everyone at the same time, and that if we invited his Spirit to come and live in our lives, he would not only start changing us so that we could be more like the Lord Jesus, but he would also give us power to live out our lives on earth in a way that pleases God.

After this, it is important to have just a short time where the children can reflect upon what they have heard, pray and also be encouraged to speak out loud and thank God that he has not only heard their prayers but has also already begun to answer them. Teaching them to speak out loud is again a good starting point, because you want them in time to be unafraid to speak out and pray in public.

Although this may sound wordy and too simplistic in parts for the older Christian, I hope you get the point that I am making. Just as children and adults have varying degrees of intelligence, so their understanding will vary, but if we present the biblical way of salvation in a way that they can understand, the Holy Spirit will reveal the truth, whatever their mental or physical age.

I know nothing

When a little baby is born into this world it knows nothing and has nearly everything to learn. It is the same when someone is reborn into the family of God and becomes a Christian. They, too, begin a new life and have nearly everything to learn. The day our miraculous new life begins, we know that a change has taken place – to use a Bible quotation, 'We have passed from death to life' (1 John 3:14). But it is going to take a little while before we start to understand what exactly has happened. The Christian life is not a one-off experience, where we are filled with all knowledge and become instantly perfect; once born, we start to develop and grow, and it is as we mature that we start to realize what exactly has happened to us.

It infuriates me when parents see me a few hours later and say that they can see no change in their child, or worse still, when they confront the child after a slight misdemeanour and use such words as, 'Call yourself a Christian?' Internal change is instant, but habits of a lifetime, even of a short lifetime, may take a little while to die. That is the straightforward bit, which I share with either an individual or a crowd. This may give some clue to the parent who is not sure what to say to their seeking child and is hoping an itinerant children's evangelist will come along and do the work for them.

Time together

Expect to see your children become Christians at an early age, and also expect to be the ones who will be introducing them to Jesus and praying with them for their salvation. This will often happen quite naturally at bath times or bedtimes, as you are together. Allow times for questions to flow, especially during or after a bedtime Bible story, or while you're enjoying the relaxed atmosphere after your Sunday lunch. Remember that the actual moment a child decides to become a Christian, whether in the home or in a meeting, is so often a culmination of many little 'chats' that you have been having together. It is important to keep sowing.

Parents shouldn't feel they will be doing the children's workers out of a job if they help their children to become Christians. I often feel that I am doing parents out of a job. Ephesians 6:4 says, 'Fathers, do not exasperate your children; instead, bring them up in the training and instruction of the Lord.' OK, mums and dads, get on with it! Why leave all the blessings to children's ministry teams? You deserve a few blessings yourselves!

Lost in a crowd

Moving on from the individual to the larger group, I usually feel it right to give those to whom God is speaking a chance to respond to him in a public way. It's not that I want to embarrass them; it's just that once they have made a stand in front of their friends, declaring that they want to serve God, they do seem a lot stronger and it will not be so hard for them when they start to tell other friends what Jesus means to them. But any sort of appeal involving children has to be thought through.

We evangelists love to quote numbers. It looks very impressive in a newsletter when 'hundreds come to the front'. As well as giving us a sense of security, it also lets others know that we are doing our job well. Personally, numbers have never impressed me, and since working with children I have noticed just how inaccurate head-hunters or hand-counters can be.

A short while ago I was in a meeting with about 750 eight- to eleven-year-olds, and after some fun and worship I presented the good news of Jesus to them. While still in quite an emotional atmosphere, I appealed to all those who wanted to give their lives to Jesus for the very first time to stand up and come to the front. Before anyone moved I repeated two more times that it was only for those who had never done this before. The minute I finished speaking, about 350 squeezed their way up to the front, and as I stood on the stage and saw the enormous mass of little heads in front of me, the optimist would have thought that revival had broken out, while the pessimist would have thought that it was pure emotionalism.

The truth was that it was neither. As we took the children to one side to pray for them, we discovered that the words I had used in my appeal had changed by the time they had reached these young ears. 'I came forward to keep my friend company,' said one. 'I wanted Ishmael's autograph,' said another. One even commented that we had given him a little booklet the year before, but he feared that when he lost this, he may also have lost his salvation, so he thought he had better come forward and get another one.

This is one of the reasons why we sometimes put up a prayer rainbow and ask the children to write down on a piece of paper a prayer of thanks to God for what he has done in their lives. We then stick it to the rainbow. It's then, and only then, as we read the notes, that we start to get a realistic idea of what has actually been happening. On this evening, out of the 350 initial respon- ders, about 100 children genuinely became Christians for the first time. This was confirmed by the number of parents I have seen subsequently, who have told me of a dramatic change in their children's lives since that evening. That is exciting. As for the rest of the children who responded, I praise God for them too, for a couple of reasons.

The first reason is that we had a chance to pray for them and it's always a great privilege to pray into these little ones' lives. Secondly, it's great that they are not frightened to stand up and let those around them know what they have done. Church will be much healthier if, when these young ones reach adulthood, they are still as open to respond. I believe that a lot of adults (particu- larly in the UK) miss out because they are too embarrassed to respond openly when God speaks to them.

There are, of course, many other ways of finding out those who genuinely would like to be prayed with or who wish to know more. The most common is the 'hands up, stay where you are' appeal. The only trouble I've personally found with this is that while the Spirit of God is moving in their lives we encour- age those who are already Christians to praise the Lord, and of course for many of them nowadays their most natural expression of praise involves raising their hands. It looks great from the front, but unless you are good with your words of knowledge, it is going to be a bit of a job to sort out the sheep from the would-be sheep.

I suppose the most accurate means I have found for discovering those who want to become Christians involves taking into account two things:

1. Everlasting life ... and other rewards

In my earlier thinking I was dogmatically against offering bait or rewards when allowing for response: for instance, telling children that if they respond we will give them a free booklet. Why? Because I know that most kids will rush in the direction of a free gift.

Nowadays I try to remain open on this issue. There are times when I would invite the children to respond, with no mention of anything except that if they do they will be prayed for. But there are other times when, after leading a prayer for salvation from the front, I would openly say that all those who prayed that prayer should go and collect a salvation booklet from one of the leaders, as these booklets explain in more detail about what God has begun to do in their lives.

Yes, of course masses of children will surge upon the leaders to get their free gift, but I have discovered that some who did not want to become Christians at the meeting actually read the booklet when they got home and gave their lives to the Lord Jesus. I have also discovered that the little booklet left lying around a house can be picked up and read by many other people as well.

On my first visits to America I was shocked when I saw that many children's meetings seemed to be hinged around bribery and rewards. If you sit still for an hour you will get a free hot dog. If you answer this question correctly you will get a free plastic doll. But then I remember years ago when I went to Sunday school, if I attended I would get a free sticker. If I filled up my sticker book, I would get a free Bible. The difference is that nowadays the prizes seem less educational, and more expensive or unhealthy.

It's also amazing how children's leaders use puppets and muppets. In the UK, puppets usually provide the fun and a human does the 'serious talk'. However, I was in one country where the humans did all the messing around while the puppet did the preaching and also did what they called the altar call. As I have travelled around the world, watching many cultures with their children, I have learned that although it's good to have an opinion, it's not for me to judge whether one method of encouraging children to decide to become Jesus' followers is right and another method is wrong. My prayer is that we all stay in tune with God and do things in the way that he wants them done, wherever we are.

Another way is, when you have finished sharing the good news with them, just say, 'For those who want to give their lives to Jesus, see me at the end of the meeting.' You only need to say this once. Then do something quite opposite, like a bouncy action song, to completely break the emotional atmosphere you have built up. I do believe that if the Spirit of God is really moving in a child's life, amid everything that may follow they will remember to come and see you after the meeting. In my experience, this has proved to be true. This is ideal for the smaller children's meeting that is held at regular intervals, where you have already built up a good relationship with your children, but weekly appeals become repetitious.

2. Emotions

It could be a song like 'Just as I am' playing on the organ, the tone of the subdued speaker's voice or even silence – all of these have been used after a talk has been given to encourage people to respond. Of course there is nothing unbiblical with playing to people's emotions – after all, God made human beings to have emotions. But we do need to be quite careful with children, because I have found they can easily get caught up in the excitement of a powerful talk but the following day they deny everything that happened the night before. Jesus does not just save our feelings, he saves our whole person.

I remember our band once stopped playing at a venue in London, to allow the preacher to come on and do his bit. The curtains on the stage closed to hide our musical equipment, so there would be no distraction. As he finished his talk you could have heard a pin drop as hundreds of teenagers reflected on what he had shared. At this point in the silence, he told everyone to close their eyes while he came behind the curtains to tell us which song to play next. Unfortunately, the stage lights had been turned off and the silence was shattered by the speaker falling headlong over the drum kit, sending the cymbals flying in all directions. It was very funny, and we fell about laughing. The audience opened their eyes and went into hysterics. It totally killed the emotional build-up, but still many genuinely became Christians. But I could just about detect a glimmer of a smile on their faces, as they could not forget what they had just observed.

Harvesting hints

Finally, a few hints for when you are leading an evangelistic meeting:

1. For those who have responded, it is good to get them to pray a prayer after you. It is important that you keep it short and speak slowly. I remember the first time I did this I spoke so quickly, and with such long sentences, that the children could not keep up with me, nor could they remember the sentence that I told them to repeat. Worse than that, neither could I.

2. Never, under any circumstances, take children out to another

room to pray for them. Non-Christian parents are very suspicious of Christians nowadays – understandably so, because of all the adverse press that we have been given. Be open, let people see what you are doing, and if they are nearby, invite them to join you as you pray.

3. When a child from a non-Christian background gives their life to Christ, someone needs to go and talk it through with the parents. Don't just leave it to the child to explain, as they may accidentally say all sorts of things that will horrify the parents. Send round your best evangelist – a great opportunity!

4. Don't forget to teach the children that they need to share what they have received. Also, teach them how to share it. They will be better than any schools workers as they get alongside friends of their own age. Oversee them, but don't feel that you have to be forever walking behind them, to see if they are saying the right words and doing it the way you would do it; they probably won't be. They are children and it is quite normal for them to say things in a childish way. If we have trained them well they will portray God's heart, if not our words, and there will not only be a lot more labourers going into the harvest field, but there will also be a lot more crops coming into the barn. Yes, God has put no age limit on his workers and neither should we.

3

Holy Spirit

Fight the bad fight

Ladies and gentlemen, in the right-hand corner we have the Reformed, conservative evangelical, who has grave doubts about such things as baptism in the Holy Spirit and the gifts of the Holy Spirit, especially speaking in other tongues. He says that he is solid, mature and not made up of froth and bubble, and agrees with the apostle Paul who once said that tongues will pass away. He believes that the greatest gift is love, especially for those who think the same way he does. In his mind, not only is he convinced that certain supernatural gifts did pass away a couple of thousand years ago, but he would have been highly delighted if those who differ from his opinion had passed away at the same time.

And in the left-hand corner, ladies and gentlemen, is his opponent: the renewed, revived and restored charismatic. He is not only Spirit-filled, but believes that the church should be known for its supernatural signs and wonders. He, too, agrees with the apostle Paul, who once said, 'I would like every one of you to speak in tongues' (1 Corinthians 14:5). He believes that love is not a gift, but the greatest fruit of the Spirit, and in practice he loves his gifts more than the people he is offending. He is convinced that the Reformed conservative evangelical won't put up much of a fight, because not only does he lack power, but he also lacks life, as he comes from what he would describe as a 'dead' church.

This is the so-called classic confrontation, to my mind probably the biggest time-waster and red herring of the last century. Personally, I believe in being baptized in the Spirit. I feel honoured that God should choose to share his supernatural gifts with me, and of course I teach people how the gifts can be of benefit to them and the kingdom. I also, however, have a lot of good friends who don't share my views, and I respect them as being very close to God. I know it breaks God's heart when we lose love for each other and just get involved in endless hours of swapping scriptures and argument.

Often people come up to me, saying that they don't particularly like the way I do things, and they often disagree with some of the things I say, but they praise God for me and for the way he is using me to help change others' lives. Now that is what I call an honest compliment.

It's healthy to have our own thoughts and ideas which are founded on our backgrounds, our interpretation of Scripture, and even our personalities. The biggest danger to the church is people not being allowed to think for themselves and hold their own opinions. They end up just becoming little clones of their leadership team or denomination. Thank God for our diversity. It is God's intention that being part of the same family we can still have a real love for each other that is stronger than any of our disagreements. And the term 'dead church' is a contradiction in terms, as the real church of our Lord Jesus Christ will never die.

Holy Spirit ... hot subject

But sadly, even after saying all that, the issue of the baptism in the Holy Spirit and his gifts is still an emotive one and one which causes many to separate and split from even their closest friends.

'Charismatic' and 'Reformed' are words which mean little – it is the life that speaks so much louder than the words. I know so many folk who would not claim to be charismatic but who are wonderfully used by God, and many that claim to be charismatic who are not only an embarrassment but will be judged for turning people's hearts away from God. I belong to an army, and I am not just an individual soldier seeking recognition. I may use different tactics and weapons from others, but I'm proud of being associated with any who are living their lives with one aim: to please their Commander. Not everyone, though, is quite so pleased about being associated with me!

My personal experience is that some are filled to overflowing with the Holy Spirit when they become Christians, and as I pray for people nowadays, I would expect that to be the norm. But others, including myself, have for many reasons (ignorance being the greatest) experienced a baptism of power at a later stage.

Expressions

Some people seem to get offended by the words we use to describe the Acts 2 experience. Does it really matter if we call it 'baptism in the Holy Spirit', being renewed, being refreshed or even being filled? Let's not get into a debate over terminology; let's just pray that people receive so much Holy Spirit power in their lives that they can be more than conquerors in this sinful world. Surely no Christian can object to that.

There are three main reasons why we need the Holy Spirit to fill us to overflowing:

1. He will help us to praise Jesus.
2. He will fill us with power to witness to the lost world around us.
3. He will give us supernatural gifts to prove to the unbelievers

around us that God is still alive and well, and able to do impossible things.

One of these impossible gifts is speaking in a language that we have never learned.

New power – new language

Praising God in new, unlearned languages seemed so often to be part of being drenched in the Holy Spirit in the New Testament, and again I believe that those who are overflowing with the Spirit of God have been given the ability to do just this. But because God would never force us to use any of his gifts, we need to ask him for them and also to understand that receiving them will require some participation from us, even if it is just opening our mouths and speaking out in faith.

Helpful hints on how to speak in God's language

Just a few words of advice here for those who may be seeking this wonderful experience. First, don't look at the gift, look at the giver; don't think about speaking in tongues, think about praising Jesus.

Second, don't be in fear that what you receive may come from the evil one or even be of your own making. Believe Matthew 7 when Jesus says how his Father in heaven will give good gifts to those who ask him. Remember, our heavenly Father is much more powerful than the evil one and you and me, and he wants us to have the best.

Third, don't panic if you don't feel much different, or nothing seems to happen while you are being prayed for. You have asked in faith, and it has been given. You will notice the new power in your life once you start witnessing to others, and you will probably start praising in tongues when you are relaxed and by yourself.

Fourth, the more you praise in new tongues, the more fluent the language or languages seem to become, so without making an exhibition of yourself, keep praising God at every opportunity.

The day of 'heavy-handed' people putting their hands on your head and shaking it until you speak in tongues is thankfully disappearing. Those who pray for others must realize it is wrong to try and force one of God's gifts on to someone. It is, as the word says, 'a gift from God', and only he can give it.

Finally, you must always bear in mind that God won't use your gift for you; he gave it to you for you to use, so use it whenever he leads you to, and use it wisely.

Now I've mentioned tongues first, not so much because it is the initial evidence, although it is certainly the evidence that most people experience first. Paul says in 1 Corinthians 14:4 that speaking in tongues edifies us; in other words, as we praise God with this gift, we actually get built up. We will also realize that we have been filled with power from on high so that we can go and give out more to others. Giving will, in time, drain us, so it makes sense that time needs to be spent praising in tongues so that we can re-stoke our boilers, or get plugged back into the power source for a recharge. We may only get baptized in the Holy Spirit once, but we do need constant refilling with the Holy Spirit.

My turn

My own personal testimony is that although I had been prayed with to be baptized in the Holy Spirit, and felt supernatural power fill me, I was not released in praising in new tongues until some time later. On reflection, the biggest disappointment for me was some of the unhelpful advice I was given by some of the leading Pentecostals of the day. As I questioned them about this gift, and told them I would love to use it to glorify God, they would just tell me not to worry about it and that God would give

it to me in his time. The truth was that they could not be bothered, or they were far too busy dealing with important problems,
to spare time for my burning questions and confusion.

One rainy night on the Sussex coast, I had just returned from a
meeting where it seemed that everyone, including Irene my wife,
was using this gift and consequently they all seemed to be on a
different level of praise than me. I was still struggling with the
good old English language, incessantly repeating such expressive
but earthly words as 'Hallelujah', 'Praise the Lord' and, of
course, a few 'Glory's', while everyone else around me seemed
to be taken up to the heavenlies, shouting out God-given phrases.
Now I know that the words are not all-important – it's what your
heart is feeling that matters to God – but I'm afraid that at that
moment this was no consolation to me. I just felt the odd one
out, rather like a cabbage in a Christmas tree plantation.

Maybe you have also felt this way. It's weird how in such a
large meeting, with so many brothers and sisters who love you, it
is possible to feel so alone and inadequate. That night, as we
approached the front door of our flat, I told Irene that I wasn't
coming home until God gave me this gift. Thankfully, she could
see my desperation and said that she would be waiting up and
praying for me till I received it.

Marching up and down the promenade, I was shouting to God
and asking him why he was withholding this gift from me. I paid
no attention to the nocturnal dog walkers, who passed by on the
other side and understandably considered me to be some sort of
nutcase. Even the rain, which had by now managed to soak
through to my underwear, was no distraction. In fact, I paid no
attention to anything, not even to God. I guess he knew that I
needed to let off steam and he allowed me to do just that. After a
long time, I was still shouting, but not in English any more. I am
guessing, but I think that I must have been shouting in tongues
for 15 minutes without realizing it.

Boy, did I feel good when I eventually started listening to

what I was saying. I still feel good as I reflect on that time. A wonderful warmth covered me all over on that cold, wet night, and I spent ages just dancing around, praising God for this wonderful gift that he had given me.

Please don't get me wrong: I am not recommending this as the normal way to be released in tongues (though I can guess that no one has ever described me as normal). But maybe you can see now why I sometimes feel annoyed when Christians look down on this gift by saying it is the least of the gifts, insinuating that it is of little use and that while seeking the 'higher' gifts, this one can be ignored. I believe that every gift from God is priceless and so valuable to you and me that it is close to blasphemy for us to downgrade any of them.

Perhaps this shows you a little of why releasing my praise while speaking in tongues is very precious to me. Nowadays it is invaluable, after having been criticized, hurt, or drained after ministry, just to fix my mind on Jesus and worship him in this way. It is indescribable – well, in English anyway.

What's your problem?

So what is the big controversy? Well, we don't need to make it one. When folk come up to me and say that speaking in tongues isn't for them – fine, I must respect their viewpoint. But on the other hand, if I say to them that it is for me, they must also respect mine. Nowadays I refuse to argue about it; as I mentioned earlier, it is more important for me to stay in good fellowship with people than to win a theological argument. After all, at the end of the day it is going to be the Holy Spirit who will change people's minds on issues like these, not me.

Children are the problem

So that is that – everybody's happy. Well no, not really! Most would find this highly acceptable for adults, but once children are mentioned, nearly everyone's viewpoint changes.

Biblically, I don't see why it should. I can find no reference to the above being for adults only, and surely if we are talking about this being a supernatural gift from God, God would not allow children to have it if it was bad for them, or even if there was the remotest chance of there being any adverse effect. The main problem that Christians have with this concept is that it has never really been part of their thinking. With all the talk of renewal that is spreading throughout the world, it seems that the main area of our church that still has very limited anointing is our children's work (with a few notable exceptions). We are still telling the same, sometimes unbiblical, stories in the same way, and singing the same old songs, with the same expectations as our great-great-great- (ad infinitum) grandparents had. The only difference today is we are using more modern communication methods, but the results, sadly, still leave us with small groups of powerless children.

I knew that God had something new and refreshing for our children, as well as for the rest of the church, and I was convinced that part of this was to introduce them to God the Holy Spirit. In most churches, all they had known was the Father, the Son and their own version of Holy Scripture.

All ages welcome

Again I repeat, scripturally we are given no age limits for most of the things we as Christians need to learn and experience. The prophet Joel prophesies that God will pour out his Spirit on 'all' people, and surely that 'all' must include children. I also find from Scripture that the Lord Jesus delivered a little girl who had an evil spirit. If a child is capable of being demon-possessed, this shows me that children are involved in spiritual warfare.

That is why I not only desire to see that my children are Spirit-filled, but I want them to have everything that Jesus has provided for them, both for their defence and to help them attack the evil one. I'm convinced that if the church equipped and trained children for battle, we could save a lot of their suffering and falling away – which I definitely do not see as the normal 'phase' through which they must pass as they move into adolescence. If we choose to place them in secular schools, we owe it to them to prepare them for the onslaughts and temptations that they are going to face. More important than this, we are shown in the Bible that there are things which are harmful, and we should shelter, protect and guard our children from them. How can any genuine Christian put the Holy Spirit in this category?

We must also realize that we are talking about a supernatural gift. Our finite minds, whether adult or child, will not be able to comprehend it fully. But books like 1 Corinthians give all sorts of instructions to help us, and these are so simple that, dare I say, even a child can understand them. It is certainly a lot more straightforward than teaching the meaning of water baptism, or what happens when we take communion, or the principles behind tithing and giving, which most of us would see as a priority in our children's education.

The power and the Glories

For the reader who knows little about me, I ought to explain that as well as preaching, my main means of communication is through music. Twenty years ago, I decided to make a record all about this subject, which hopefully children could relate to. It was a story album about some little characters called Glories, and in very simple terms it looked at the Holy Spirit and his gifts or presents in a way that most ages could understand.

I had decided to use both my sister's children and my children on the album, but really wanted the children to experience what they were singing about before they went into the studio. I told the Lord that I really did not want to pray for them myself, as these children would do anything for me, but sadly at this time people travelling around willing to pray for children to be filled with the Holy Spirit were not only very few, but also very far between. And I did not know any of them. The Lord seemed to understand my predicament and gave me peace of mind, telling me that the next time we met for a rehearsal I was to inform the children that they were going to receive what they had been singing about.

I'll never forget that evening in the front room of our small semi-detached house. I stood looking at them, wondering whom I should pray for first – the oldest or the youngest. I decided in a very human fashion that the oldest might be the easiest. As I walked over to begin praying for her, they all individually and spontaneously were filled with the Holy Spirit and started praising God in other tongues. As I stood watching them, I was a bit disappointed, really. After all, I hadn't done anything. It was then that the Holy Spirit seemed to whisper in my ear and remind me that I had told him I wanted someone else to do it and not me.

I looked and saw one of my little nieces giggling and laughing. Now I was a good Pentecostal, and I believed a serious thing was happening here and that it would be right to have a gentle word in her ear about being flippant. As I started to walk toward her, the Lord said, 'Where are you going now?' Before I could explain, he told me to let her be. He reminded me that she was a little child who loved giggling, and that I should not expect my adult, intense, heavy way of doing things to be imitated or copied by children. Then, as I looked at this little girl again, it was like seeing her with a new set of eyes. Without instruction, she had raised her hands in the air, and I saw that she was totally absorbed in worshipping her Lord.

The children's praise went on for ages and seemed to grow louder and louder as they ignored me, forgot about their own inhibitions and concentrated on the Lord. I wondered what the neighbours thought. Since then I have been privileged to pray for thousands of children and see them become Christians and filled with the Holy Spirit.

OK, I'm not perfect

Yes, I made my mistakes. Sometimes I got a bit carried away in a meeting and encouraged the children to go further in gifts of the Holy Spirit than their leaders had gone. Quite rightly, I got my knuckles rapped. But just as the children were learning, so was I.

Once, I was at a major Christian holiday camp, and while the adults were enjoying their meetings, my team and I were given one week to help train up nearly 1,000 eight- to eleven-year-olds. The subject the adults were studying was the power and gifts of the Holy Spirit, and I saw this as a great opportunity to teach the children the same.

I assumed that adult speakers like me would start day one with salvation, continue on day two with being filled with the Holy Spirit, then cover tongues, interpretation and prophecy on day three, and perhaps we would even see the dead being raised by the end of the week! It seemed logical to me to do things in this order, so that is what we did – and it was fantastic. Without any pressure on day two, we asked all the children who wanted to be filled with the Holy Spirit to stand in lines across the room, and hundreds of them did. Having nowhere enough team members to pray for the children individually, I decided to pray for the first one on the end of each row and let God do the rest. It was like a line of dominoes – the Holy Spirit seemed to flow down the lines, resting on and filling each child as he did so in the most amazing way. Nearly all started spontaneously to praise God in different languages they had never learned and, I hasten to add, with no human element persuading them. They all went back to the various lodgings praising God.

A while later, I heard a banging on my door and opened it to find a long line of angry parents waiting to talk to me about the terrible thing I had done to their children. Soon afterwards, the organizers called me into an office, waving at me letters of complaint that had been given to them by irate parents. I discovered what had gone wrong. It was not so much that their children were speaking in tongues; it was more that they did not know what they were gabbling on about. I also discovered that the main adult speakers knew that tongues was going to be the hot potato for this group of people, so they had decided not to talk about it on day two but leave it till day seven, to save having to face the furore.

Since then, I have become just a fraction more sensitive. I would still say and do exactly the same thing if I thought that God wanted me to do it, but I would also check out my timing with the other leaders and speakers. It seems the older you get, the more there is to learn.

It's not *all* my fault

I don't take all the blame for upsetting people, however. I was in one church and had just finished preaching in the Family Service when a mother brought her nine-year-old daughter up to see me. She explained that God had been speaking to the little girl and she asked if I would pray with her to become a Christian. I told the mother that I would love to, and then invited her to stay with me while I prayed, but she felt that for one reason or another she would rather not and walked off to the back of the hall.

I explained a bit more about what becoming a Christian was to this little girl and then got her simply to repeat a short prayer after me, similar to the prayer I described in the last chapter. After she had done this, I told her to start thanking God in her own words for hearing and answering her prayers. This was when the trouble started. This church had not been encouraged to use the supernatural gifts, so I had been very careful not to overstep my brief and deliberately avoided mentioning them. Then this little girl, without any instruction from me, started praising God not in English but in tongues, and her little face was radiant.

I must admit that even I was surprised, but not half as surprised as her mum. She must have had good ears, because she came flying down from the back of the hall, shouting at me and asking me what I had been teaching her daughter. She continued, before whisking the poor little girl out, 'I only wanted her to become a Christian. I didn't want her to have this.'

I've had this happen several times, the most embarrassing time being when a whole Brownie pack started praising God in new languages and the Brown Owl, who was not quite as wise as her position might suggest, flew out of the hall, her feathers very ruffled.

On another occasion, a youth leader from a church that would not claim to be in any way charismatic invited me to speak at their youth weekend, which was to be held in a big, old house in the middle of nowhere. The youth leader was also a musician and was very excited because he was convinced that he was going to be filled with the Holy Spirit during this weekend. Sure enough, the Saturday night took off. God arrived and his power seemed to fall on everyone – except the youth leader. He looked so upset that I decided to let everyone else carry on and took him into another room. He felt so miserable because he had been expecting so much, yet personally felt he had received so little.

Trying to encourage him, I told him to think of Jesus, close his eyes and just open his mouth and God would give him the words to say. Nothing happened. I was now running out of ideas as to what to say, so I reassured him that the gift of tongues was not everything and told him that, before we went back to join the others, he should try and cheer up, take his eyes off himself, and just tell the Lord in English how much he loved him. It was then that he burst into tongues.

After that, he was so excited, he hardly stopped speaking in tongues for the rest of the weekend. Our last meeting was back home on the Sunday night, and we were going to take the whole evening service between us. Knowing the church, I advised him that it might not be wise to mention the tongues yet – perhaps we should just tell people about all the other great things that God did throughout our time away. He agreed.

Sunday night came and he got up in front of the whole church, trying to keep a serious face. But after a few sentences he could not contain his excitement any longer, and with a beaming smile right across his face, he told everyone he had been filled with the Holy Spirit and could now speak in tongues. He didn't receive a standing ovation and cheers, well not from the congregation any-way, but ever since that time the whole church has been open to things of the Holy Spirit.

At another camp, I invited anyone who wanted prayer for the Holy Spirit to join me in my room. A teenage lad walked in with a guitar. I prayed for him for ages, but nothing seemed to happen. I then told him to play his guitar and sing to the Lord, and imme-diately he started singing in new languages.

It's a learning process. The Holy Spirit rarely seems to do the same thing in the same way with any two people. He treats everyone as an individual. I have also learned that I cannot give the Holy Spirit restrictions. As Scripture says, 'The wind blows wherever it pleases. You hear its sound, but you cannot tell where it comes from or where it is going. So it is with everyone born of the Spirit' (John 3:8).

As long as it is the Holy Spirit doing the work and not Ishmael, I can't go wrong – well, in his eyes, anyway.

4

Tongues, Interpretation and Prophecy

Christmas is coming

I must confess, when I was a young child the main thing I looked forward to at Christmas was not the celebration of the birth of the Lord Jesus, nor was it the roast turkey, potatoes, sprouts, peas and cranberry sauce for Christmas dinner. I'm ashamed to say that it was not even the chance to give to others. No, it was the thought of receiving all those wonderful presents that was the highlight of my Christmas.

It is also honest to say that, although I was not a selfish child, when I received a gift that had my name on it, my initial thought was that it was just for me, and not to be shared with others. After all, they had received their own gifts, so why should I share mine with them? Within a week or two, though, my attitudes changed, and, as the gift had received my undivided attention for quite a while, it was now not only time to let other people enjoy sharing it, but it was also time to see what they had got and to begin to share their treasured possessions too.

A few years later, my priorities changed again. Celebrating Jesus' birth had, of course, gone to the top of my list, but the other major change was that I had now discovered it was as much fun hunting around and finding gifts I knew would light up other people's faces as it was opening up the ones that were given to me.

Even more years passed, and nowadays I know the Lord Jesus better than I ever did. Now I've learned not just to celebrate his birth at Christmas, but I am thankful for him all year round. More about Christmas in Chapter 14.

Instead of getting the exciting toys I used to get, all I receive now are the boringly useful and practical items: you know, socks, pants and handkerchiefs, and most of these tend to be the wrong size, or the wrong colour, or duplicates of a gift given by someone else. I know I sound totally ungrateful, and of course I am exaggerating to get over the point that nowadays I much prefer giving to receiving. I get more satisfaction seeing someone's face as they open their presents than I do opening mine. What has all this got to do with anything? Well, let me try and explain.

Tongues-tied

When children are first filled with the Holy Spirit and released in the gift of tongues, it becomes like a new toy to them. They are able to do the impossible and speak in a language they have never learned. They didn't have to spend many hours reciting and practising, as they may have done at school during their French and German lessons. In a powerful way, they have discovered that by knowing a supernatural God, they are now able to do supernatural things. Not only is this gift going to build them up, it will also be a great outlet for expressing their praise.

As with the child and the Christmas present, in the first few weeks the gift they have been given is likely to become the be-all-and-end-all. It will be all they talk about: tongues for breakfast, tongues for dinner and tongues for tea, and there will still be a few things to say about it at supper time. That is quite normal, because understandably it has been a very exciting and unusual discovery.

The Bible instructs us that tongues of praise can be used any time, and this is again why Paul gives us guidelines on how and when to use them in public, so that things can be done decently and in order. But our young enthusiast in those early days will not understand, or even particularly want to understand, Paul's wise advice. There will be times when they go way over the top, either by using this gift at inappropriate times or even by looking down on others who have yet to receive it. At this stage, our friends who are not sure about this gift and its relevance for today are usually completely put off, and regard it as a strange experience especially for weirdos or fanatics.

Now a child needs to be taught that this is only the first step along a very exciting road, but the problem comes when their leaders have failed to let God develop them in other areas, because then the whole church is stuck at a tongues dead end. Unless they move on, they will become self-indulgent and of little use, not only to the church universal but, even more importantly, to those who are not Christians. 'Since you are eager to have spiritual gifts, try to excel in gifts that build up the church' (1 Corinthians 14:12).

I cannot underline enough times the fact that the main reasons the disciples were filled with the Holy Spirit on the Day of Pentecost were that they could give glory to Jesus, and that they might have the power to go out and supernaturally influence people, revealing that not only is the Lord Jesus alive but he is also all-powerful. Here we see the second stage of my Christmas illustration: not only is it exciting to receive gifts, but it's also exciting to give them away.

I would like to share with you how I have taught children the importance of some of the other supernatural gifts, and how they can bless others as they use them. This does not belittle the wonderful gift of tongues which they have received; it just moves them on, to show them that there is life beyond tongues.

A missing gift?

The gift that is most closely related to tongues is interpretation, which I personally believe to be a gift that has somehow gone missing and ended up being completely mixed up with prophecy. In 1 Corinthians 14:2–3 we are told: 'For anyone who speaks in a tongue does not speak to men but to God. Indeed, no-one understands him; he utters mysteries with his spirit. But everyone who prophesies speaks to men for their strengthening, encouragement and comfort.' Further on, in verse 29, we are told that what has been shared as a prophecy should be carefully weighed up by others, but nowhere are we told to weigh up an interpretation of a tongue.

I know that, although the gifts do overlap, interpretation of tongues and prophecy are two distinctly different gifts, but what is the difference? I discovered the answer 'out of the mouths of children' the first time I decided to do a children's house party.

Off we go

Having never arranged anything like this before, I was greener than an under-ripe tomato. I decided to seek advice from a much more experienced children's organization. Understandably, they did seem rather anxious about what I was experiencing, especially as I explained to them how children were being touched supernaturally by God. The main advice they gave me for my weekend was to have plenty of games and recreation, as children love these. Now again it's confession time because, although I had spent numerous evenings with children doing what we called 'Praise Parties' which were all-age celebrations, I had never played any games. I had tried to make whatever I taught fun, and considered other activities to be unnecessary and time-wasting.

The big weekend arrived and about 35 children, aged between eight and eleven, accompanied us to a Christian centre that was rather scruffy and inexpensive – in other words, ideal for our needs. The trouble with a lot of Christian centres is that they are only interested in adults – hence they are beautifully decorated and extremely expensive. It would be lovely to take children to some of these places, but many of them cannot cope with children, and by keeping their prices high, they ensure that no children's groups try and hire their facility.

Anyway, having listened and adhered to the advice given to me by my more experienced counterparts, I did arrange for a sports programme on the Saturday afternoon. As the weekend progressed, I was amazed by the insatiable appetite these children had for learning about Scripture. Apart from that Saturday afternoon, I had crammed the weekend with seminars on the Holy Spirit, which they soaked up like ink on blotting paper. It wasn't long before it was me who needed a break, and also a coffee, so I told them to go and get some fresh air. After a few minutes, though, I couldn't believe my eyes: they had all returned and were waiting eagerly for more, and I'd only had one mouthful of my coffee and half a biscuit. They exhausted me; they were draining every bit of information from me and they were excitedly coming back for more.

Not normal, you may say. I tend to agree with you. When I was younger and went to some of these weekends, the only reason I was able to survive the teaching sessions was because I knew that in an hour or so it would all be over and then I would have the chance to either play football or acquaint myself with the members of the fairer sex. If I was lucky, it would be both. But was I normal, or just downright unspiritual, and would I have been different if I'd had the opportunity to hear about the exciting, relevant truths that these children were learning about now?

Please do not misunderstand what I am trying to say here. John Wesley had no time for games and sports in his schools, as he saw these as a distraction and a waste of time. I love games and sports, and enjoying entertainment is an important part of the Christian life, but there are occasions when I believe we spend too much time on games, thinking that this is the height of excitement for children. This is illustrated by looking at some of our lads who seem to just live for football. But there are even more exciting experiences ahead, even for our football fanatics, and that is why we need to allow the Holy Spirit time to come and show them just how exciting and powerful the Christian life can be.

Learning from little ones

At one of these sessions, I was teaching what the Bible says about the gift of interpretation of tongues. I have always been of the opinion that not only tongues spoken in public, but also tongues spoken in private, can be interpreted, as I had done this myself many times and found it beneficial. I could never understand why people would say that praise tongues didn't warrant interpretation. Why on earth not?

Anyway, after the theory had been taught, then came the practical. We started to pray, and the children started praying in tongues. It was then that others spoke out and gave the interpretations. It was lovely to hear the ones who had given the tongues comment on how amazing it was that someone else had been able to put into English exactly what they were feeling, and also to see how the interpretation was so much more of a blessing to all of us than the tongues had been. Well, it's common sense really, because now of course we understood what was being said. But then came the most interesting revelation.

I had not taught these young ones how to interpret tongues; I simply told them to ask the Holy Spirit if he had something that he wanted to say through them, and if the answer was yes then to get on and speak it. The scripture I shared with you earlier stated that when we speak in tongues we speak to God, not to men, and these unconditioned children's interpretations were to God, not to men.

Suddenly it all made sense; the missing gift had been found. If tongues is Godward and an interpretation is translating that tongue into English so we can all understand it, it goes without saying that an interpretation is Godward as well. If a tongue is speaking to God, how can the interpretation be speaking to men? If a tongue is speaking to our Father, how can an interpretation start with the words 'my children' or 'the Lord would say'? For years I believe that many of us have followed a tongue with a prophecy and not waited to hear the interpretation.

If you are still a bit confused, let me give you an example. Imagine that I am speaking in tongues and my tongue is asking God the question, 'Lord, where do I go from here?' The interpretation in English will not be: 'go into all the world'; it will be the question that I asked, 'Lord, where do I go from here?' – the same as the tongue, but in a language that we can all now understand. Then comes the prophecy, and God says, 'Go into all the world.'

How much easier it is to understand now why Scripture teaches these as two separate gifts. A prophecy must be weighed up and judged, to make sure that it really is God speaking to man, but an interpretation does not need to pass through the same scrutiny, as it is man using a supernatural gift to pray to God.

Let me explain how varied these children's interpretations were. Some, as in Acts 1, were simply praising God, but it was as though their English language had been expanded to the nth degree. They were praising, using poetic phrases that were laced with the majesty of the Psalms of old. These were not just prayers of praise; these were anointed words of thanksgiving that none of the children could have possibly given without the supernatural input of the Holy Spirit.

But not all were praise; some were crying out to the Lord for help, and again you could hear that both tongue and interpretation were not joyful and ecstatic, but were sombre and serious, unquestionably Spirit-inspired, as these children would not have known how to pray with such depth and feeling.

So can the church be built up by an interpretation as much as by a prophecy? You'd better believe it! After the tongue, to hear someone sharing with God their feelings under supernatural anointing not only has a great influence on those around, but it also often paves the way for God to respond and speak to us through the prophetic word.

So to sum up, I am not saying that it's impossible to have an interpretation where God speaks to man, and that the church has been misguided for all these years. No, it would be wrong to be so categorical, but what I would say is that we need to define these two gifts of interpretation and prophecy, even if it is only for the sake of teaching our children. As the Bible defines prophecy as God speaking to man, maybe a few words about children and this gift would be appropriate.

Can we be God's mouthpiece?

A few common sense facts first. We all know that not everyone who is used in prophecy is automatically a prophet, just as not everyone who has witnessed to people is necessarily an evangelist. Some prophecies are predictive, but to be genuine God-given prophecies they must, of course, come true. The majority of today's prophecies are summed up in Corinthians, when Paul says that everyone who prophesies speaks to men for their strengthening, encouragement and comfort. It is worth remembering that they don't hack down and destroy.

I expect we have all heard some wild prophecies, and maybe in our less experienced years we have even given some. It is important that we don't become lone rangers but always have godly men and women around us either to confirm what we are saying or to tell us honestly when we are 'up the creek'. It is silly, if not untruthful, to prefix a prayer with 'Thus saith the Lord' or 'God says' for a few reasons, but before I give them to you, let me tell you some funny yet embarrassing stories about people who have used this prefix to their so-called prophecy.

One said, 'Thus saith the Lord, as I said to my servant Moses – or was it Abraham . . . ?' Another laid hands on an individual and began, 'Thus saith the Lord – oh dear, I have forgotten thy name.' And a final one that was given the day after a church had held a barn dance: 'Thus saith the Lord, I was with you at your barn dance last night. Verily I enjoyed being with you; in fact, I haven't enjoyed myself so much since I parted the Red Sea . . . .'

Clangers? I'd say! Once you've had one of those spoken to you, or over you, it is quite understandable why this sort of prophet would not be accepted in his own town, or in anyone else's.

Thus saith me

Here are a few reasons why it is unhelpful to prefix what God wants to say through you with the words 'Thus saith the Lord'. First, in any prophetic statement, very rarely is it 100 per cent God speaking. Parts of it may be, but so often the human influence is very detectable, especially when it seems to go on for a long while and it has that nice refined, well-rehearsed ending. No wonder the preacher in Ecclesiastes tells us to let our words be few. Most prophecies do seem to start off with the human preamble and finish with a thought-out ending. I often think it is like a sandwich, with a thick slice of bread on top, another thick slice of bread underneath and a thin layer of meat in the middle. But we must still keep our ears wide open for the meat in the middle.

Second, it is unnecessary to tag these phrases on. Some may consider that it adds clout to what is being said, or wakes people up to the fact that a prophecy is on the way, but if it is a supernaturally anointed word, people will sense God's authority as it is spoken.

Third, if it turns out that it was not a prophecy that was shared, but some human feeling that was sincerely imparted, not only will the prophecy be false, but its proclaimer could be judged as a liar as well.

Children need to be taught these facts, and as they are learning to hear and know the voice of God, be prepared for a few human errors. Mistakes will be made, but remember not all mistakes are sin, and we do learn by them. Sin is when God tells us to say something and we don't say it – it is disobedience – not when we say something with pure motives but get it wrong. Don't be too hard; just lovingly train up and educate them in a way that they can understand. Remember, if you are too harsh on them, or leave them in any way looking silly, you can guarantee it will take them years before they are willing to speak out again, if ever.

Little voices

Let me share with you two visions that Jonathan, a young boy of five, had. He saw two rabbits in a hutch, a mother and a baby. The mother was glossy and well-fed, but the baby was thin and scraggy. The humans had been feeding the mother but not the baby, and at night it would try to escape, to look for food.

After weighing this up, the parents took this as a word to themselves and the church. They had been feeding the adults spiritually but neglecting the children, and so the children would look elsewhere for what they needed.

He also described two men: a man who loved and a man who hated. The man who hated built a wall between them. The man who loved planted seeds and plants on his side, but the other man would sneak around at night, steal them and plant them on his side.

They shared this vision with their church, as they felt it applied to the evangelism they had just begun, and warned them the enemy would use people in the town to steal the seeds they had planted in people's lives.

Jonathan's older brother, Simon, had a vision at one of our weekends away. He saw a rugby team playing a match. One of the team had the ball, but would not pass it on to the rest of the team and held on to it himself. His father shared this vision at a leaders' conference, along with other words and visions. It was a simple matter to apply it to a leader who was organizing a major project against all advice and was holding it to himself, instead of being part of a team.

At one of my meetings I got all the leaders to kneel on the floor, and told the children that if God had given them anything to say into our lives to come and share it with us. Out they came, one at a time, and spoke with the accuracy of an arrow hitting the bull's eye. I remember at one time I was struggling with a personal problem in my life that I did not want anyone, including God, to know about. I invited the children to come and pray over us leaders and not to be afraid to speak out anything that they believed God wanted to say to us. We in turn knelt down, so we were roughly the same height as they were. It was then that a little boy put his hand on my shoulder and started, under the anointing of the Holy Spirit, to explain what I was trying to hide in my life. It was so embarrassing. I remember saying shhh, hoping that he would lower his voice, but for some reason it was at that point that not only did his voice increase in volume, but also everyone else seemed to stop praying, to listen to what was being said to me.

After that day I have tried not to keep any secrets, especially from God, because I know that if I do, some little child is likely to appear – and shout them from the rooftops.

Unlike adults, children don't waffle or wrap up what they have to say in nice, polite sentences; they simply say it as it is, short and sweet and straight to the point. I do not recommend this exercise for the faint of heart, or for those who are not prepared to hear the truth about themselves!

5

Gifts of Healing

Tobie's tale

Dear Ishmael,
We want to tell you what happened when you visited our town last year – what the Lord has done for our eldest son, Tobie – and to thank you for your ministry.

Tobie had been having fits very regularly, often daily, for the previous year-and-a-half. At his worst he had eleven in one day and he could be unconscious for up to three-quarters of an hour, and was usually quite unaware of what he had been doing for many minutes before each fit. He was beginning to lose great chunks of his life. Of course, we, his family, friends and church, were worried. He underwent many tests, was regularly hospitalized, passed from consultant to consultant and still no cause was confirmed.

My husband and I had been sure at the beginning that God would heal Tobie, probably by using the medical profession. Many people prayed regularly for him, but over the months our family prayers became less hopeful, less trusting. After all, if God was going to heal him, why was he continuing to have fits? Knowing that God's time span and ours are very different was no comfort. Sometimes I felt Jesus to be very far away. He was letting me down. I was building worldly barriers between us.

Tobie had been a thoughtful child, and he had often spoken of the

76

difference that occurred in the family when my husband and I had asked Jesus into our hearts a few years earlier. Following a week with friends at a Christian holiday, where he continued to have fits, Tobie's own faith became very strong, very alive, and he was filled with the Holy Spirit. He ministered to others and he prayed in a way new to me – such an intimate way with the Lord, a sure way, knowing he was being heard, that the Lord was a loving Father who was listening to this 13-year-old, and would answer his prayer.

I think that Tobie prayed for others at this time, rather than himself. Seeing him reassured me in my faith, but we still found it hard to pray for his healing with any conviction.

Then you came to our town. The Lord used you that day to minister to Tobie. Tobie asked the Lord whether he was going to heal him or not, and as he closed his eyes a massive yellow 'YES' was all he could see. His father and an older friend stood and prayed with him, and Tobie knew he was healed. He told us, and although we rejoiced and thanked the Lord, we continued to have our doubts. But what worldly-wise, God-ignorant children we are. Of course Tobie was healed, and has come on this past year in strength and grace, continuing a wonderful relationship with the Lord. He had one final fit, and was able to tell the consultant that he would not need the hospital any more.

Not everyone gets healed

This is just one of the many exciting letters I have received, but sadly my success rate in healing is far from 100 per cent. Once I was in a large room with hundreds of children from every conceivable background sitting in front of me. My subject was 'God still heals those who are ill today'. I wanted to find out what the children already knew about the subject, so I asked them to put their hands up if they had ever seen people who were sick being prayed for. A blanket of hands went up.

I then asked if any of them had ever prayed for a sick person and, through their prayers, had seen people healed. Understandably, the response was nowhere near as large, but there were still quite a few who responded.

I then asked if any of them would like to come out to the front and tell us all how God had used them in this area, so together we could praise God for what he had done through them, and I chose a couple to come and join me. One of these was a young lad who looked very serious, so I brought him over to the microphone and asked him who he had prayed for, to which he quickly replied, 'My dad.' I then asked what had been the matter with his father, expecting maybe to be told that he had had flu, or back trouble, or something similar. However, the little boy said that it was cancer. There was a visible gasp around the hall, as I could sense the children getting very excited at what was about to be said. I certainly was very excited. I then said to the little chap, 'And how is your dad now?', waiting with baited breath and convinced that I knew what his reply would be. After a short pause, the little boy answered, 'He is dead.'

Silence fell all around the hall. Even yours truly couldn't think of anything to follow that. I did find it interesting to note, however, that the child was not sad. He had obviously seen his dad suffering so much that the greatest healing he could in fact receive, and presumably the best answer to his prayer, was for his dad to go and be with the Lord Jesus.

My dad

I have always been brought up to believe that we worship a God who heals. My own father had a piece of shrapnel lodged so close to his brain that surgeons could not operate on it and predicted, at best, terrible regular headaches and, at worst, I dread to think. But Dad rejected their human wisdom and obeyed James chapter 5 by calling together some of the leaders of the church to pray over him and to anoint his head with oil. It must be noted, though, that some of these leaders knew nothing about healing and had never dreamed of being involved in this sort of thing.

After that prayer, God saw to it that the shrapnel would no longer cause any pain.

Years later, at a large Christian camp, my parents were enjoying the adult meetings, while I was overseeing the children's work. Halfway through the week, Dad was rushed into the local hospital, having suffered a heart attack. As my family and I prayed for his healing, I was told that the children were also praying. In a relatively short period of time, Dad was back on his feet again, digging his garden.

A few years later, he was diagnosed as having cancer and my heart was broken seeing him lying, deteriorating rapidly, in agony in a hospice. I prayed every healing prayer I knew, but God did not seem to answer me, and a while later Dad died. For a while, my faith level was shattered. Could I ever pray for healing for another person when God had not answered my prayers in the way I wanted him to with my Dad? Years later, I still have questions, and on self-examination I wonder if my faith level will ever be what it was, but I do believe that God is God and what he does and does not do must be part of his perfect plan. I also know that Dad's exit from earth had nothing to do with the metal in his head or his earlier heart problems. I realize death has no sting for Christians, but the sting for me is that I still can't understand why my prayers did not seem to relieve his suffering.

Please understand what I am saying. In no way do I blame God, and I will continue to pray for the sick. I know the problem must lie with me. Maybe it only takes faith the size of a mustard seed to move an inanimate mountain, but a larger portion may be needed to move a living person's pain. Lord, give me more faith.

Oh me of little faith

Having in later years also been involved in traditional Pentecostalism, I had learned good and not so good things about healing. As a pastor, it was always my duty to pray for those who needed prayer, but in all honesty it was a miracle that anyone got healed (please excuse the pun). I really didn't have a clue as to how to pray over people, and my faith was not even hope. Many times, as I prayed, my mind was either a blank or thinking about what song I would follow this part of the service with.

I was never disappointed, though, because I never really expected anything to happen. Most of the old folk would mutter something after I had prayed for them, like, 'Thank you, Pastor. I think I feel a bit better now,' and as for those who were obviously no better, I would advise them to just keep looking to the Lord.

It was a few years later that I had the tremendous privilege and opportunity to meet and become good friends with such great men of faith as Colin Urquhart, Ian Andrews, Roger Forster and the late Roger Price, and I spent many hours not only listening to what they had to say on the subject, but also watching how they went about praying for people.

At first, I tried to copy their methods, but this turned out to be disastrous, as they were all unique and none of them did things in the same way. Then I started to glean a bit from each of them which seemed to be appropriate for me, and at the same time as doing this, I started spending more time with the Lord to find out how he wanted to use me in this area.

As well as learning from these and other great men and women, I also had a lot to learn about healing from children.

The Bible on healing

At another of my weekends away, again with about 35 children, I started sharing with them about healing. I wanted to show them how important this gift was, because about one-third of the material in the four Gospels gives accounts of healing miracles. I went on to explain that although Jesus was the greatest preacher the world will ever know, he knew what people were like and that, as well as hearing words, they needed to see supernatural signs and wonders. I pointed out that Jesus didn't just heal people to get a crowd around to hear him preach. No, he healed people because he wanted to see them made well.

I told them how Jesus had no set routine. In Matthew 8 he touched Peter's mother-in-law. Another time he used spittle for the blind man. In Matthew 12 he spoke to the man with the withered hand. In John 9 he prepared a plaster for the blind beggar, and the woman with the haemorrhage touched him in Matthew 9. Jesus never wanted us to copy a method.

I also made it clear that we could not heal anybody; it was God who was going to do the healing, but faith is required. Faith, I discovered, was a word that all of the children had heard before, but none were quite sure what it meant. I found the best way to describe faith in simple terms was to quote and try to explain Hebrews 11, 'Now faith is being sure of what we hope for and certain of what we do not see' (Hebrews 11:1).

I do make it very clear, though, that faith is not just believing that something impossible will happen. I have met a lot of people who are believing God for something, but it's something that God doesn't want them to have, so they won't get it. We must understand that faith comes from hearing the voice of God, and when God tells you that something is going to happen, you not only believe it but it is as though you actually see it take place and start thanking him for it before it actually occurs.

In healing, I encourage the children, before they pray, to ask God if he wants to heal that person, or if there is something stopping them from getting healed which may need to be dealt with first. We may be able to bluff our way through with adults, but you can't fool children. If we teach that all who are prayed for are instantly healed, the child will believe us. But should they pray for someone and healing doesn't take place, they immediately become shattered and disillusioned and may even wonder if Jesus has let them down. Their belief and faith take a nosedive. That is why we must be honest in our teaching.

It may come as a surprise to you that although I have seen thousands of children healed, I have also seen many who have not been healed. Sometimes we really don't know the answer and have to trust God. Sometimes there are reasons we can comprehend.

Why people don't get healed

John 5 tells us about a paralysed man who was healed, but he was warned to go away and sin no more so that something worse would not happen to him. Deliberate sin is one reason why people don't get healed; unbelief is another reason. Matthew 13 tells us that Jesus could not do many miracles, because of the people's lack of faith. The passage 2 Corinthians 12:7–10 talks about Paul's thorn in the flesh, which some say was his wife. I personally believe it was some kind of physical or mental ailment, which remained with him to keep him humble.

Another relevant part of Scripture is 1 Corinthians 11:29–34. Talking about breaking of bread, it says, 'For anyone who eats and drinks without recognising the body of the Lord eats and drinks judgment on himself. That is why many among you are weak and sick, and a number of you have fallen asleep' (1 Corinthians 11:29–30). And then there is good old Job, whom God allowed to go through all sorts of physical horrors, to test his faith.

Overcoming fears

There are many more reasons why we sometimes need to discover the root cause of the problem. Fear could be the cause. I remember for some time Irene's arm was aching badly, and she asked me to pray for it. I asked the Lord what was causing this discomfort and he showed me that she had a certain fear in her life that was the problem. As I prayed against this fear she felt a sensation like water draining down her arm and out through her fingertips. That trouble has never recurred to this day.

A little girl had warts and scars on her hand that she wanted God to heal. As she asked God why they were there, he told her that she had a strong fear of catching any contagious illness that happened to be around. Through this immense fear, she usually caught it. As she prayed to God and asked him to take that fear away, not only did she know that the fear had gone, but she also saw the warts and scars immediately disappear from her hand. I'll never forget seeing her overjoyed mother afterwards, who just could not believe what she was seeing.

We must also realize that, unless we are around when the Lord Jesus returns, we all have a time to die. Bodies do grow old and deteriorate. It does not seem so long ago that my eyes could read anything, and I could leap around on a stage for hours and still be full of energy. Nowadays, I need spectacles even to read a restaurant menu, and after just an hour of jumping around, my muscles and limbs are screaming out at me to remember my age and to give them a break. Some do choose to over-indulge and eat and drink in excess, or maybe smoke, which helps speed up the process. Some literally take no thought for their bodies and give them no exercise, which again could give us a shorter term on this planet. Whatever the facts are, one day our limited time down here will be up.

I seriously believe that we sometimes do not see people healed because we are praying that they should stay down here, but the Lord has planned it that it is their time to join him. Please don't get me wrong. I would still pray that they can be released from pain, but when false prophecies are given about somebody living who then dies, this is not only devastating for their loved ones, but it is in no way glorifying to God. The point I am making is this: before we pray wild prayers of hope, someone needs to have a talk with Father. The disciples asked the Lord Jesus to teach them about prayer.

How to pray for others

A young girl went to pray for an older lady in a family service that I was attending. The lady had nasal trouble and the medical profession had not been able to provide any cure for her. I told this girl to pray with a voice of authority, a bit like a sergeant major, as she was on the King's business. I told her in the meeting simply to speak to the ailment and tell it that it did not belong in this lady's life and therefore in the name of Jesus it must go and leave her alone. She then should pray that the healing power of Jesus would come upon this lady. Well, this she did and with such a loud voice that everyone nearly jumped out of their skin and turned around in amazement. She didn't wait to find out if the lady was healed; the possibility of anything but that happening never occurred to her.

It took a few minutes before the lady leapt to her feet and with a smile that beamed, shouted out that for the first time for ages she could breathe normally. I saw the leaders of that church about six months after that and they confirmed to me that the lady had had no trouble since that evening.

However, as important as praying for others will always be, I was also learning how important it was to teach the children how to pray for themselves.

How to pray for ourselves

This seems to be a much harder thing to do. I was a classic migraine sufferer and I knew that because I allowed myself to get anxious and tense, I often brought it upon myself. I went to Roger Price to pray for my healing, but before he prayed for me he spoke to the Lord and said that the Lord wanted me to be part of my own healing. He told me that I would be given a warning when the attack was about to start and then I should go somewhere quietly and pray to God that the pain would go.

That was not really what I wanted to hear. I thought that Roger would pray over me and I would be instantly healed, as I had seen happen to other people earlier that evening. But I listened to what he said and thought I would try it and see what happened.

It was fantastic. The first time it took me a few hours of prayer to get rid of the pain, but that was better than the 24 hours that it normally took, and this was without using the powerful painkilling drugs that I had got used to. The next attack it took less time, and the next even less, and even the attacks became weaker and weaker, until nowadays even when I do feel stress, the attacks are so short and mild that I hardly notice them. My faith was being built up.

Keep faith rising

The level of faith, both in the individual and the local fellowship, needs to be rising continually. Remember, low levels of faith can seriously inhibit healing, just as it did for Jesus in Nazareth.

I was amazed when I heard about the faith of two little girls in one of our meetings a short while ago. The children had separated off into pairs to pray for various things to be healed when one of my workers noticed one of these little girls taking her sock and shoe off. When my worker asked her what she was doing, she replied that she wanted to see her bare foot so that they could both watch her verrucas disappear as they prayed. My leader backed off a bit, but continued to watch them, and sure enough, with comparatively little surprise showing on their faces, they saw every verruca instantly vanish. It proved to be no big deal for them; it would have been more of a miracle if Jesus didn't heal them than if he did, as they knew that this was what he wanted to do.

I must add that I am not into the name it, claim it, everything on demand syndrome. Deep down, I am a realist. I teach the children that we do not have the right to tell God that we want something done and we want it now or else. He does not want spoilt brats; he wants loving children. I do, however, make it very clear that once God has said he is going to heal, he definitely will do it, but he will also do it in his time. Don't panic if it's not in your time, and don't give up believing that God will do it; God is as good as his word.

As part of their worship, I often get the children to reach out to the Lord and receive healing for themselves, and they do. This doesn't stop them praying for others, but it does build up their faith and strengthen them, and it gets them used to hearing and knowing the voice of God.

God uses doctors as well

Don't teach children to despise or belittle other types of healing, such as through doctors and medics. In the case of my father's heart attack mentioned earlier, God provided both the medical staff and the drugs to *assist* the healing. But doctors and drugs cannot actually *heal* anyone – that's God's domain. Medical expertise does have its place, but I personally believe that we should never teach our children to rely upon it at the expense of God the healer. Encourage them to take their pains to God first – prayer practice before medical practice.

I remember I was singing at a children's camp on the Isle of Wight when one morning I awoke in terrible pain in my lower abdomen. After prayer, I was rushed to the accident and emergency unit at the local hospital and soon told to lie down on a bed behind some drawn curtains. I could not lie down. I just kept walking around the bed, praying in tongues. It was strange because an Indian doctor kept poking his head around the curtains and I wondered if I was speaking in some language that he understood, and he thought I was talking to him. Eventually I was told I had a blocked kidney and stones and was given some heavy-duty painkillers, which I was very thankful for, then given a catheter and taken by ambulance to another hospital, which was not the most comfortable journey I've ever had. After two days in bed, and I hate lying in bed wasting time, I was still in pain but I decided to discharge myself from hospital, as I had a lot of work to do at home.

Once back with the family, they all prayed for me, especially my children, and within a few days the stones were rolled away and I was back rocking and rolling again on the road, having not had to miss an engagement.

A few weeks ago I was on stage in Devon when suddenly my knee was in shocking pain and I could not walk on my left leg. The doctor said it was my cartilage and I needed to go to physio-therapy, then maybe surgery. I didn't care what had to be done. I just wanted it done quickly, so I could get on and comfortably fulfil what I had been called to do.

The next week I was on a stage in an open-air festival at Glastonbury, with a large, white support bandage around my knee, while acting out a song that required marching around. Suddenly it gave out again and I started limping. It was very funny looking down at the audience of about one thousand people and seeing many of them start to limp as well. I guess they assumed that these were all part of the actions for the song.

I then went on holiday and, while away, celebrated yet another birthday. On the big day I said to the Lord that I did not want money or new golf clubs this year, but if he would like to give me a gift, I would like full use of my left leg back. This he did for the rest of the holiday and there was no more pain – it was back to normal. But on our return it was suddenly worse than it had ever been and the hospital gave me crutches to use. This was ridiculous. How could the Lord expect me to leap around at a celebration while leaning on two metal poles?

Then came all of the Job's comforters with their well-meaning advice. Perhaps it's the Lord telling you that you are getting too old for this sort of ministry. Perhaps you need to retire. Nobody else does this sort of thing at your age. Maybe you should just sit down for the rest of your days and write books.

Wonderful – that's all I needed to hear. They might as well have read me the last rites.

After that, a lot more prayer followed. At one Kids Club, children gathered around me, asking God to heal me. I also visited the physiotherapist and did my daily exercises like a good boy. I praise God that it seems the children's faith and the doctor's work has been very compatible, for now the knee feels great and I have not had to cancel one praise party.

Oh, and as for retiring, that will only happen when my heart gives out – not my knee.

But other times he chooses not to use doctors at all

At our large, week-long events, working with large numbers of children, we like to have a nurse or first-aid person in the team. A short while ago a ten-year-old was playing a ball game outdoors on the concrete when she fell and severely cut her leg. Our nurse saw that the cut would need stitches, and the little girl was crying so much and obviously in great pain. The first thing our nurse did was cover the wound with a piece of lint, and then, along with several others, she prayed. After a short while the blood-soaked cloth was lifted up, and there underneath was – nothing.

God had squeezed the skin back together again without leaving a scar, or the slightest mark. The little girl jumped up, said, 'Thank you, God,' and then ran back to carry on with her game. The only evidence of any sort of accident was a blood-soaked lint.

Beware the counterfeit

Don't forget to teach children the difference between God's

supernatural healing and the evil deceptions of the confusingly named 'Christian Spiritualist healings' which they may hear about at school. The evil one tries his best to imitate God, but the best he can offer anyone through his counterfeit healings is sadness and confusion.

Never let the counterfeit put you off teaching the real truth. Remember, if children are given good, honest instruction on the gifts of healing – not just about successes, but also our failures – because of their simple faith and their wonderful ability to hear God's voice clearly, many miraculous signs and wonders will take place through them.

6

Suffering and Discipline

It's a tough world

Do you remember the days when children used to be little bundles of fun and energy? When you walked past a playground the noise was deafening as you tried to dodge past the flying footballs, tennis balls, the pretend mummies with their dollies, little chaps with cars, trains, aeroplanes and little soldiers, cowboys and Indians, all rushing around everywhere. Children were action-packed and so often self-entertaining. They were effervescent, bubbly personalities who would never stand if they could jump, would never walk if they could skip, and would never talk if they could sing or shout.

But the pressures of our time and generation are gradually squeezing out childhood and replacing it with premature maturity brought about by unanswerable situations when young minds are forced to make adult decisions and try to cope with adult responsibilities. A primary school near our home recently had to send home two little girls who were genuinely suffering from depression. When I was a child I didn't even know what the word meant, let alone what it was to suffer from such a terrible plight.

Another primary school not so many miles away is still living in shock, after having learned that one of their nine-year-old pupils returned home from his school in a severe state of depression and hanged himself from his bunk-bed. It's something that the head teacher and other staff will never really get over.

On a recent trip to the shanty towns of Costa Rica, it was hard to cope with seeing many children holding in their arms their own young children. They were child mums, who would never experience what we think of as normal adolescent years.

Follow my leader

Children are repeatedly told that they should grow up, but they are rarely given a Christian role model to follow. Some tell their children that they should be like Jesus, but as children learn about the Lord's love and perfection and see so few human beings around who even vaguely resemble what they read about in the Bible, it seems an impossible task – even though in the long term they do want to grow to be more like him.

Maybe they should copy their leaders. It's exciting to know that there are a great number of godly men and women who are sold out for Jesus, but it would be no exaggeration to say that there are very few whom the children would find approachable and be able to call their friend, unless of course the leader happened to be some relative.

To a child, leaders can be like 'the management' who are above everyone else, and the only time these people in high places would actually take any notice of them would be if they were visiting their homes. Then, along with the dog, they may get the customary pat on the head, or if they had done something wrong in the church they would get a verbal ticking off.

It is also worth mentioning that in my experience, as I have observed the leader/flock relationship, few leaders find they are able to form a close mutual friendship with the non-leaders and their wives because position will not allow it, and certainly the non-leaders and wives find it hard to relax with them, so, realistically speaking, what hope have the children got?

Of course, it's obvious, a child should copy his parents. Yes, that is very true. But are we good examples? More on this in a moment.

Follow my hero

Therefore, what do they do? Well, the answer is painfully obvious: the same as the unbelieving child. They tend just to try and imitate their favourite hero of the time. Their walls are not covered with men and women of God. They are more often than not filled with pictures of people who at best could be described as idols who worship themselves – living for fame, money and things to excite their bodies – in fact, all the things we hope our child will not get involved in.

Just a part of growing up, some say; all children have to go through this stage. I am sorry, but I am not convinced of that. However, I am convinced that we need more Christian heroes involved in every walk of life, so our children do have national and international names they can look up to: people we wouldn't mind them imitating – knowing that what they are imitating, at worst, is harmless and, at best, encourages them to display Christian values in their lives.

Let us take a look at some of the pressures that are affecting God's little soldiers.

The pressure of a multitude of meetings

The place where they will be most influenced in life is the home, and the major problem they are going to have to cope with is feeling unloved or rejected.

As a pastor, I used to have the idea that the more meetings you held, the more spiritual your congregation would be. Therefore I deliberately made sure that every night of the week was filled, and it did look good to see a church notice-board crammed with events. I was also under the impression that a sign of an individual's spiritual state was their loyalty and commitment to God, which was portrayed by their loyalty and commitment to church meetings. So it was only right to think that those who managed to get to every meeting were in fact my spiritual giants.

It was only when I visited their homes that I discovered that nothing could be further from the truth. With either Mum or Dad out each night of the week, there was no time for any relationships or friendships inside the family and all sorts of dissension and rows were taking place. But it was the child who seemed to be showing the most strain. It was easy to see that even the most placid of children were becoming either aggressive or moody, and always seemed to be seeking attention.

As a so-called full-time Christian worker, I had forgotten that Dad had probably left his house before the children were even up, and by the time he returned home either the children were well involved with their homework or Dad was too tired to talk to anybody. All he felt like doing was sitting by the fire with his dinner on his lap and cheering himself up by watching the news. Then he would have his shower and was off to the meeting.

Saturdays and Sundays were no better for the children, as on Saturdays parents would be working on the car, garden, house or, worse still, shopping, and of course Sundays had more hours spent in meetings than the rest of the week put together.

Leaders' homes

But leaders' children surely cannot feel rejected. After all, Dad is usually self-employed and as his hours are so flexible, he is able to choose how much time is spent with his family. Nothing could be further from the truth. It's because his time is flexible that a leader who usually enjoys his job cannot figure out what is work and what is pleasure. A leader often has an insecurity that unless ministered to, could easily take all the joy out of him. This insecurity tells him that his congregation are always watching him to see that he is not just sitting at home reading his Bible but he is actually earning the investment of tithes and offerings, however small, that they put into the collection plate each week.

I remember that during my pastoral stint one old chap made it very clear that, because he was putting a certain sum into the offering plate every week, he not only expected me to visit him each week, but also I should be available 24 hours a day to rush over to his house should he need anything. A leader can be a bit like a learner driver who is taking a driving test. Everything must be exaggerated. He not only has to be an overworked, busy man, but he has to go out of his way to make sure that everyone else sees that he is the most active man in the church. But at what cost?

So often his home shows this lifestyle. I have walked into numerous leaders' houses and found the most undisciplined children I have ever seen. More than once I have walked into a house where a little child, whom I have never met before, comes up and starts hitting and kicking me. Dad and Mum smile in embarrassment, saying what a lively little fellow their son is and how he loves to have his bit of fun. The only trouble is that when they try to drag him off me, the child pays absolutely no attention to them and continues taking his rejection out on me.

Don't get me wrong; I am not expecting children to just sit down and smile as if butter wouldn't melt in their mouths. But spoilt and naughty children need discipline, and hurting children need help, and we must be careful that we don't get these two mixed up.

Hurtful or hurting

I had just finished doing a service in one church when one of the children's workers came rushing up to me in a state of frenzy, saying, 'Quick, there is a child at the back of the hall who needs deliverance.' I told her to calm down and explain herself. Pointing at some poor bedraggled lady a few feet away she told me that this lady, though once a witch, had just become a Christian, but her husband was definitely not a Christian – he was a warlock. She continued again, building up steam: 'On the floor is their son, who is uncontrollable, possessed, and has just been swearing at me. Now could you please come with me and deliver him?' I glanced at the poor mum, who just stood there and hadn't got a clue what was going on.

I told the over-zealous children's worker to stay with the mum and I would go and see the boy. It wasn't hard to find him, as he was sitting by himself, looking very afraid. I sat down next to him and the minute I did so he looked at me, eyes blazing with a mixture of fear and anger, and shouted, 'You won't cast anything out of me.' I smiled and reassured him that I did not intend to cast anything out of him; I had just come over to be friendly and to find out if he had enjoyed the meeting we had just had.

Suddenly his defences went down. I put my hand on his shoulder and started to talk to him all about music, instruments and anything really that he wanted to share, and I saw that this was just a normal little boy with a lot of hurts, who needed a lot of love.

A short while ago, we were organizing a series of meetings and in the mornings we had various activities going on to teach the children how to be more creative. One of my helpers asked me to have a word with another young lad who was causing a lot of trouble and not wanting to get involved with anything. I saw him standing in the corner with an anorak over his head and, calling him by his name, I took him for a little walk and had a talk with him. I asked what was wrong, to which he replied that he hated drama. In fact, he hated everything. I spent a little while longer with him and then I asked him the question again: what was wrong? This time his answer was different. He told me that everyone kept saying the word 'father', and this week his mum and dad had separated and every time he heard the word 'father' he felt like crying. At this point he did start crying. And for the rest of the time we had the meetings, we were not only able to talk to the boy's mother, but also to understand why the little chap was behaving like he was. We were able to pray with him and explain about a heavenly Father who would never leave him or forsake him.

Rejected by the family

In order to deal with a problem, we need to find out the root cause of why the child is behaving like he is. Girls tend to react differently when they are suffering from rejection. They are either very shy and never open up, or more usually they are the ones who hang around you, cling onto you and won't let you go.

I must repeat again that this feeling of rejection is very common in Christian children. Scripture teaches that we must seek first God's kingdom and his righteousness, but then I believe comes our family, not meetings or even ministries. Our families are our first congregation and responsibility, and we have no right to be in any form of leadership if we cannot lead our own family. We are told in 1 Timothy 3:5: 'If anyone does not know how to manage his own family, how can he take care of God's church?' If that is not enough, we also hear in 1 Timothy 5:8, 'If anyone does not provide for his relatives, and especially for his immediate family, he has denied the faith and is worse than an unbeliever.'

Our children are on loan to us from God; we only have them in our immediate care for a very short time. That is why it must be one of our priorities to spend time with them, and although praying with them and teaching them from the Bible is vital, so is playing with them and really building a friendship with them which will last long after they have left home. They need to feel that they are special to you and not just something tagged onto the 'any other business' of the church agenda.

Home from home

Remember, they find a lot of security in your home so don't make it a hotel or a hospital. Most houses have a family room, where you may sit, talk, play games or watch the television together. When you arrange an evening in with the children, make them your priority. Children need to feel wanted. I must say not all feelings of rejection are brought about by neglectful parents. Sometimes, for various reasons, the child chooses to want to feel unloved. This is another story, which again I have seen the power of prayer change.

Children can feel rejection at a very young age, and if it is not dealt with it will not only lead to massive problems in later life, but also extremely serious consequences while they are still young. There was an article in *The Times* some while ago, entitled 'Life and Death of a Child in Despair'. It went as follows:

> One profoundly disturbing American study published in 1984 looked at sixteen pre-school children, aged two-and-a-half to five, referred to a psychiatric clinic for suicidal behaviour. Thirteen of them had made multiple attempts. Most of the children were abused, neglected or unwanted by their parents. The others had experienced loss of a parent through divorce or death. Child psychiatrists said they expressed combinations of profound feelings of abandonment, yearning for reunion, despair and hope of remedying their painful lot. It went on to say that most children who deliberately harm themselves don't want to die, but simply 'to make people aware how bad they are feeling'.

True, these may be from non-Christian homes, but every year I am meeting more and more children with horror stories who come from Christian homes and who have seen their mums and dads separate. Some have bruises on their bodies where they have been assaulted, and some have stories of how they have been sexually abused.

We are not called to be psychologists, but we do need to get answers and learn how to counsel these little ones. .

Hints to help

Just a few hints on how we deal with some of these problems.

First, in conjunction with our leaders, we must contact the parents or parent with custody. They need to know what we have discovered and give us permission to pray with their child. They usually agree, as they can see how difficult and unmanageable their child has become, and they want to see change. It also gives a chance for the leaders to counsel and pray for parents, who will be needy people too.

Second, we need trust and respect from the child. This may not take very long because, although he may have been hurt by those he trusts, he is so desperate to be loved that he will recognize genuine affection and concern.

Third, go into some detail about God the Father and tell the child that he loves him, cares for him and even understands how he feels. Explain that God does not want him to be hurt, and even though things have taken place in his life where no person can help, God can not only help but can also heal every situation.

Lastly, ask the child if you can pray for him. Tell him that the rejection he is feeling is not really part of him, as he belongs to God, and go on to say that when you pray for him you are going to tell these feelings to leave him alone. Then, with a gentle voice, take authority in Jesus' name, break the hold of rejection and pray into that life the love of Father God, asking Father to fill any gaps in the little one's life that may have occurred.

Yes, the child has to understand and receive this prayer, but in my experience the vast majority of them do. Some of my most exciting moments have been as I have prayed over children in this way and seen an unbearable burden lifted off the child, then seen a wonderful transformation of character take place as God has come in and done what only he can do.

The place of discipline

With all this talk about ministry, let me stress once again that many children do not require this. All children are sometimes a little rebellious – maybe to God, or maybe to their parents – and what may be required is correction and discipline, not just prayer. Let's just spend a little while looking at the area of discipline.

The big issue of the new millennium is whether punishment in the home should be under the legislation of parents or under the legislation of the government. If physical punishment of any kind was made illegal, how would we as Christians cope? In Bible times, the father was definitely head of the family; he was the priest in the home, with the power of a judge. A Roman father had the right to punish any member of his family by death, without reference to the State.

Discipline in schools was handed out by severe floggings, sometimes using a leather whip. This was an integral part of a boy's education. Quintilion, who was looked upon by many as a weird eccentric, went against the majority and was against flogging. He believed that praise, competition, and even play, were better incentives than fear to bring about good behaviour. So we are not looking at a new debate.

Although, like most of you, I am strictly against any physical abuse of children, I am not in the position to judge a loving parent who gives their child a corrective tap. But seeing the different physical strengths of the punisher, when does a tap become a smack and a smack become a beating? It is vital to behave in a rational way and not allow temper to take over.

My brother-in-law lived in an end-of-terrace house where the back gate led into a passageway that ran between his house and the next and led into a quiet cul-de-sac. As he was standing in his gateway, his two-year-old daughter wandered out and started walking towards the road. My brother-in-law had instructed her that she could play in the passageway but must go no further than the end, where it met the pavement. The little girl thoroughly understood the rules and proceeded to walk to the very end of the passageway, to the edge where the forbidden zone began. At this point she stopped, turned round, and looked at her dad with a 'Shall I? Shan't I?' sort of look, which only a little girl of this age knows how to give.

Dad called out again and reminded her that she must go no further. My little niece turned round, took another look at her dad and another look at the road, decided to make a dash for it, then off she set as fast as her little legs would carry her. Fortunately, my brother-in-law ran in hot pursuit and caught her up before she actually reached the road. Picking her up, he told her that he was going to take her into the house and give her a smack, explaining that the rules he had laid down were for her own safety and she had deliberately chosen not to obey them, putting herself in potential danger. It only took one little smack and the tearful child was sent upstairs to think about what she had done.

It wasn't long before she had calmed down and returned, apologizing to Dad. He explained to her again that she had to be punished, as it was the only way she was going to learn, and even though at this young age she would not have understood it, he had to punish her because he loved her. (Great sermon illustration here.) My brother-in-law never had this sort of rebellion in his daughter from that day to this.

As all children are different, some may not learn so quickly, and a parent has to be prepared to persevere. Discipline of this nature will need to be repeated until the child learns.

Home truths

With my own children, I have never found that screaming at them has any positive effect, although like most parents it's an old habit that is very hard to break, especially if you are blessed with a very loud voice like mine. The worst punishment that I have ever needed to inflict on the boys as they grew older, and were experimenting with how far they could push me, was the threat of a wallop with my slipper. I think it was only twice that I gave their backsides a tap with it – it never needed to be any harder, as they were already in tears the minute I told them to bend over and touch their toes. That was about 18 years ago. Would I use the same punishment today, knowing what I know now? Probably not.

The one time I punished the boys that I will never forget and will always regret was one year when we were on holiday in the Isle of Wight. I had just bought them each a water pistol, but set the rules that they were not to squirt them in the house. They disobeyed me and I went mad. I grabbed both pistols and threw them out of the window, and they smashed on the concrete below. Even as I reflect on this incident, tears come to my eyes. I should never try and discipline my children if I have lost control of my own temper. I learned my lesson. I don't think it ever happened again – but I still feel bad about doing it.

I would never physically smack my daughter; one of the reasons being that I am an ex-farmer and sometimes don't know my own strength. The other is I could never hit a woman. Stern words, cut-off privileges and grounding have always been sufficient to get the message home to her.

Spare the rod, and check your Bible

I cannot understand anyone who thinks they are in the will of God by beating their child with a stick. Let me explain.

We have just three biblical references to the rod and children and all are found in Proverbs. Solomon, who wrote these down, came from one of the most undisciplined families in the Bible – David's. Just read about his children and you will see what I mean. Solomon tried to bring discipline into his family, although one wonders how many children he would have to discipline, bearing in mind he was sleeping with one thousand women!

Did it work? Judging by Rehoboam – who was arrogant, lived for himself, and refused to listen to older, wiser advice – I think not. We must not just grab three verses out of the Old Testament and say they are for today. Otherwise, what is to stop parents putting into action Deuteronomy 21:18–20, which says that a rebellious son who does not obey his parents should be dragged before the elders and then be stoned to death?

Nowhere do I find Jesus confirming Solomon's words and bringing them into the age of grace. Nowhere do I find the New Testament writers encouraging or endorsing Solomon's actions. But I do find 1 Thessalonians 2:11 saying: 'For you know that we dealt with each of you as a father deals with his own children, encouraging, comforting and urging you to live lives worthy of God.' Perhaps Quintilion was not so eccentric after all.

Instruction, correction and discipline are vital in parenting. Discipline is an act of love, not anger; but it's how we choose to discipline our children that is important. Parents: this is between you and God.

Love and respect

I've discovered that so often a child's response to discipline depends on how much or little he loves and respects his parents. If the parents have not earned that love and respect, they will never be able to shout it or beat it into their child. The child will just get rapidly worse, suffering from rebellion, rejection, fear and hatred.

Here are just some of the prayers and comments that children have written that will show children's workers some of the areas of hurt in children, and how they are going to need to pray for God's wisdom in dealing with them. As the family unit continues to disintegrate, and as divorce is escalating among Christian and non-Christian parents, tragically these 'horrors' are going to become more commonplace. Obviously, I have left out the names of the children.

- We prayed that my dad would love me.
- Thank you, Lord, that I don't hate my dad any more.
- Thank you, Jesus, for freeing me from the hatred that was buried in my heart against my mother and my father.
- I was prayed for that God would take away my fear of getting divorced, because my mum has been twice.
- I prayed that I will have a love towards my stepfather, even though I find it difficult. And that the Lord will help me to be with him like I would my real father.
- I am not frightened of dying of leukaemia or heart problems now. I was frightened because my dad died of leukaemia.
- Dear God, I am not going to be afraid of car crashes and my mum and dad fighting.
- I was healed from hurt from when my dad left seven years ago.
- God has helped me to understand why my mum killed herself. She did it because she was depressed and she loved me.
- I am frightened because my dad might come and spoil our family 'cos Mum and Dad are not married.
- Lord, help me to stop crying over my mum and dad's divorce.
- Jesus, I am sorry that I ran out in front of a car and almost killed myself.
- I fear that my dad is going to get married to his girlfriend and care more about her children than me.
- Thank you, Lord, that I don't hate my brother any more, and

please bring my family back together.

- Lord, I am not frightened of my mum any more, and I am not frightened of anything horrid on telly because I have faith in you and I know you're always there beside me.
- Dear Lord, please help my dad not to take it out on me and my brothers when he is cross, and help him not to smack us, because I fear him very much.
- [Saying no to the voice of the evil one] I said no to hitting my sister when she was cuddling me. [From a little girl.]
- Tonight God made me sure that my daddy loves me, even though he doesn't live with us, and I didn't think he did.
- Thank you so much. I came here feeling so depressed. I'm fifteen and I've just tried to commit suicide. I've been living by myself and I don't get on with my mum. My parents are divorced, but tonight when we prayed I physically felt my head and body get lighter. I feel everything will now open up. I can now stop smoking and drinking.
- Dear Lord Jesus, I pray that my mum will come and see me more often because you know how much I miss her, and that she will come and see me and my sisters.
- I wanted to be prayed for because I do not like my brother, and also my dad has died and I had put that hatred on my brother.
- I had sex with my boyfriend. I am a Christian; he isn't. My conscience was pricked, but God is healing me. [From a very young girl.]
- A little voice said in my mind to laugh when Mum and Dad had a row and Mum cried. But I said no to that voice.

7

Fears

Don't be afraid

In the Bible there is the story of Elisha and his servant, who discover that their house is surrounded by an Aramean army who have come to capture them. A very human, petrified servant shouts in panic to his master, 'Oh my lord, what shall we do?' Elisha, being the mature prophet of God that he is, seems amazingly cool, calm and collected about the whole situation. In fact the only answer he gives is, 'Don't be afraid. . . . Those who are with us are more than those who are with them' (2 Kings 6:16).

I picture this poor young servant scratching his head, and although he may not have been the most mathematically intelligent servant in the world, every time he counted himself and his master, there was no way he could get beyond the number two. Yet there facing him, peering up at his window, was a large army. Seeing his poor, confused servant and wanting to put his mind at rest, Elisha prayed to God and asked him to open his eyes so that he would be able to see. It was then that the servant's immense fear left him. He took his eyes off the human and physical dilemma and realized that he had nothing to be afraid of, because in the hills he saw God's army of horses and chariots of fire surrounding them, just in case protection was needed, which of course in this case it wasn't. God and Elisha had no trouble dealing with the situation.

Jesus reminds us in John 14:26–27:

> But the Counsellor, the Holy Spirit, whom the Father will send in my name, will teach you all things and will remind you of everything I have said to you. Peace I leave with you; my peace I give you. I do not give to you as the world gives. Do not let your hearts be troubled and do not be afraid.

Then Jesus talked about how the world would hate his disciples, but he also encouraged them by telling them about the work of the Holy Spirit and how the disciples' grief would turn to joy. He concluded by saying:

> I have told you these things so that in Me you may have perfect peace and confidence. In the world you have tribulation and trials and distress and frustration; but be of good cheer – take courage, be confident, certain, undaunted – for I have overcome the world. – I have deprived it of power to harm, have conquered it [for you]. (16:33, Amplified Bible)

If that does not encourage the most heavy-hearted, nothing will.

Fears are strange

Everyone has a fear of something, and while some learn to live with their fears, others feel they either need prayer for them or they need to conquer the fears themselves. I believe that so often fear is the opposite to trust, and the last thing that God wants is for his children to live under its domination and for it to rule their lives. It is one of the greatest means the evil one will use to convince us that we are cowards and wimps and far from being more than conquerors and the victorious Christians that, thanks to the Lord Jesus, we should be.

Maybe it would be good to have a look at a few types of fears.

Holy fear

The first fear is one that is definitely not wrong and not sent to distract us, and that is 'holy fear'. This fear comes from God and helps people not only to hold in reverence his authority and to obey his laws, but also encourages people to hate all forms of evil. It is taught so often in the Old Testament, and it never became outdated, because in the New Testament we find that the young Christians were taught to 'walk in the fear of the Lord'. To fear God did not mean to live in terror of him; we know the Bible gives great emphasis to God being both loving and forgiving.

Vine's Expository Dictionary (Thomas Nelson Publishers, 1995) tells us that the Greek word for fear of God signifies first caution, then reverence (godly fear). It continues by describing it as:

> that mingled fear and love which, combined, constitute the piety [devoutness] of man toward God; the Old Testament places its emphasis on the 'fear', the New Testament on the 'love', though there was love in the fear of God's saints in Old Testament times, as there must be fear in their love now.

Nice one, Mr V. I couldn't have put it better myself!

It is vitally important that children learn Jesus is their best friend, but it is also important they do not treat him in the casual way they treat their best friend. The old saying of 'familiarity breeds contempt' is still a good one. We must teach our children that our best friend Jesus is Almighty God, and they do need to be careful about what they say to him and about him. Christians are sometimes rightly accused of being irreverent, whereas non-Christians are the ones who are blasphemous. Is there really any difference between these two words? A child wouldn't think so.

Children need to be taught that reverence is part of their true love for God, and far from inhibiting or restricting their friendship, it will enhance it and lead them deeper into a real and true relationship with the One they have chosen to serve and to follow.

The next fear is also not a bad fear.

Caution

While we instruct children that they must fear nothing, there are things we want them to be sensible about. When I was a teenager, I did crazy things. I had no fear of getting hurt or dying; because I was young and reckless, these things never crossed my mind. I was convinced that my innings down on this earth were at least three score years and ten, and, with a bit of good fortune, hopefully a bit longer. The rock band called The Who wrote a cheerful little song called 'My Generation', and one of the lines went: 'I hope I die before I get old.' The drummer of the band, Keith Moon, was the only one who lived up to the lyrics and managed to die a relatively short while after the song became a smash hit. The songwriter and lead guitarist, Pete Townshend, however, is still well and truly alive, and, dare I say it, getting rather old.

Pete Townshend wrote this song when he was young, wild and reckless, for a generation that largely felt the same way. But Pete and his generation, as they creep into their 'golden years', are not only a lot more cautious and careful nowadays, but probably would advise any of their own offspring to be the same. Most have discovered that it wasn't quite so bad growing old, and are quite thankful that they are not dead.

Protection

We instil certain fears in our children because we want to protect them. We tell them that they must not talk to people they don't know, or get a lift in someone's car, however friendly they seem to be, because it is not safe.

We tell them not to touch plugs, cookers, certain dogs, fires, bleach, nettles, bees, wasps, slugs, paint, weedkiller, matches, fireworks, knives, razor blades, chisels, hammers, sewing-machines, kettles, the hot tap, ink bottles, shoe polish, worms, toilets, glass, china, plus millions of other items.

We instruct them that they must not: open the door to strangers, for fear of thieves; answer the phone, for fear of obscene phone calls; play with keys and locks in doors, for fear of being locked in or out; open the upstairs windows, for fear of falling out; have the bath too full of water, for fear of drowning; have the music too loud, for fear of going deaf; or play on the grass, for fear of what they might tread in. This is just a tip of the iceberg of the actual fears that we have, and that we want our children to share with us.

It is a fact that we do pass on these fears. Let me explain. I remember seeing a little girl knocked down by the car in front of me. From that time on, I had this mental picture of it being my child, and I was quite obsessive when teaching them road safety. Another time, on a Christian holiday, we were climbing up Snowdon in North Wales when one of the worst gales I had ever encountered hit us as we were halfway up the mountain. As ladies in the party were screaming and crying, I grabbed hold of my two boys, and although I tried to look brave, I don't mind admitting that I was scared stiff they might come to harm. I tried to put them off climbing after that.

Through a bad experience, my wife Irene had a fear of large dogs, and quite naturally she always taught Suzy to be wary of them. Both of them wouldn't mind if they never saw a dog again, and would think twice before accepting an invitation to go to tea with someone who had a basset-hound, let alone a lovely, cuddly, large Alsatian or Rottweiler.

Teaching children caution is vital in today's society, and passing on our fears to our children is inevitable.

Minor fears

Some minor fears will be grown out of, some will be humanly conquered, while others seem to make up our personality and make little or no difference to us. Small fears can be tolerated, but if the minor develops into the major, if what once sent a little shiver starts to get you shaking, if any fear starts to take a stronghold in a Christian's life, then this is another story. Read on.

Uncontrollable fear

An evil kind of fear is the one you are not in control of. It has gained control over you; it has made you its slave and is seriously in opposition with 'the great and mighty warrior' that God has called you to be. Christians should not, and do not have to, live with these, and either through their own prayers or somebody else praying for them, need to ask God to deliver them from these mantraps of the enemy.

These fears enter us through various ways and means, and sadly can have a devastating effect on children. Children cannot always be blamed for their fears. Some of the saddest cases have been when they have in fact been the victims and understandably have allowed certain fears to be part of them. A child who has been molested will often have a fear of adults, especially men, and many feel unclean and do not want any physical contact. A child who has been excessively beaten will cower if you just raise your hand while near him. There are many such tragic and extreme cases, and they are growing in numbers, even in Christian homes. As depressing as this might seem, the good news is that Jesus can and will perfectly heal and restore these little ones if they will allow him to. It has been so exciting to see this happen so many times when this evil fear has been commanded to leave in the name of Jesus.

Self-inflicted fears

Most fears in children are self-inflicted. A lot of fears seem to enter through the window of the soul: the eye. Films and videos can be wonderful tools of the enemy. It's expected that the 18 certificate films, when shown to young ones, will have a detrimental effect, and, of course, they usually do. Whether it's the bloody horror of the reality of war, or the fictitious horror of a fantasy hero who has to kill everybody in a brutal fashion to save the world, it's not long before children can see these figures lurking in every woodland and behind every tree, and in comes a fear of going out, especially on their own.

The original 'screamy' horror movies have progressed into the supernatural, and now children not only have a fear of big houses, ghosts and the dark, but they are also given the Hollywood interpretation of the devil, the occult, demon possession and the messy business of exorcism. It's interesting to note that the re-release of *The Exorcist* had little effect on today's generation. Unlike the original release, demonstrators were not parading outside the cinemas, warning people not to feast their eyes upon such evil. Neither were today's viewers fainting or running to the toilets to vomit. After watching years of progressive, gratuitous screenplay, eyes, minds and even bodily functions adapt to such excesses, so nowadays for a movie to bring fear to older audiences it must be even more horrific or more gratuitous than the last one.

Nasty films made fun

If adults want to fill their minds with this sort of rubbish and live with the consequences, I suppose that is up to them, but what really makes me mad is that some of these subjects have had a bit of humour added to them, or a good musical score, and are now being made specifically for our children to watch on television at peak family viewing time. I have prayed for hundreds of children who have innocently watched these sorts of films and found they can't forget certain gruesome sequences, or have recurring nightmares. So-called children's programmes can provide more fears in a child's life than many adult ones, so that is why the programmes our children watch need to be prayerfully and carefully selected.

A while ago we had a family staying with us who had three young children. While Mum was making the tea, I offered to take them into the lounge and put the television on for them. Thanks to satellite, we now have more channels than I have brain cells, but every children's channel I switched on to was showing cartoons that were either violent, scary or portraying some form of occult.

We must remember that every child will be susceptible to different fears; they are not all scared by the same things. I remember we had to pray for one little girl who had a real fear of water after watching the film *Jaws*. Yet I know many children who have watched that same film and suffered no adverse effects. Someone else saw *Mary Poppins* and, after seeing all those chimney-sweeps dancing on a roof and then coming down the chimney, had a real fear of people climbing down her chimney.

I do not mean to be a killjoy. I spend many happy hours watching television and videos, but it is a parent's responsibility to find out the vulnerable spots in their children, especially when they are very young, and do their best to keep them away from them.

I've mentioned television, but don't forget to keep your eyes on computer games, books, comics and magazines (especially computer magazines), and most definitely any role-playing games which encourage the mind to focus on the more sinister and dark side of life and give room for fear to start to dominate. More on screen entertainment in Chapter 15.

I must make it clear that with major fears, time is not the

healer; God is. If left and not dealt with, the fears will remain with that person right the way through their lives, and no doctor's prescription or psychiatric help will be able to cure them, although temporary relief may be found through nicotine or alcohol, tranquillizers and sleeping-tablets. However, no Christian in his right mind (excuse the pun) would ever see any of these as God's answer to fears.

To finish this chapter, let us have a look at how we can pray for these fears in our children and see them go once and for all.

How to pray against fears

As with healing, gentleness and simplicity in our ministering are the two important factors. It is unnecessary to lay big adult hands on small children's heads, and if you use a loud voice and shout as you pray, you are very likely to put more fear into that child than you are actually getting out.

For very young children, again as with physical healing, it is fine to pray over them while they are asleep. For older ones, confession is often needed. When children talk to Father and say sorry they watched this or read that, it helps them see that it was wrong, and also shows them that from that moment onwards they must try not to fall into the same trap again. Obviously where a child has been abused there may be nothing to confess, but if there is hatred towards a parent, this will need dealing with.

After confession, I break the hold of that fear in the child's life in the name of Jesus, and pray for the peace of God to fill the gap where the fear had been. Then I get the child to name that fear and tell it that because he belongs to the Lord Jesus it has no right to be part of him. Then I get the child in his own words to tell that fear to leave him. After this, we praise God together, and what a wonderful experience it is to see one of these young ones, who seconds ago looked so heavy, now fully released and shining with the joy that only God can give.

This is not pie-in-the-sky stuff; this is reality. I have seen hundreds, if not thousands, prayed for in this way, and have seen God move in and perform a miracle that no amount of autosuggestion or manipulation could achieve. And the proof that it was God was that it lasted, and the children really did lose those fears.

Real-life prayers

Here are just a few of the prayers and comments that the children wrote, some before their fears were dealt with, and some after. Remember, as you read them, that although some of these fears may seem trivial to you, they were not for the child who had them.

- Please, God, help me not to be frightened of AIDS. Now, God, take this fear out of me.
- I am no longer frightened of the hound of the Baskervilles.
- I'm not afraid of anyone noticing me because of my eczema.
- [A *Jaws* watcher.] I was afraid of sharks. I kept thinking that they were in the swimming-pool. Now I am not afraid.
- Lord, please help me not to be scared of being killed in the night.
- I'm not frightened, in the name of Jesus, of hearing footsteps in the bathroom and the water pipes clanking.
- I am not frightened of world wars, burglars and my teacher.
- I am no longer frightened of *Ghostbusters* and cracking my head open.
- I am not frightened of things on the floor and things that are on my dressing-table. I am frightened of things in the air, like clothes in my cupboard, as they look as if they are moving.
- I will stop having nightmares, and I will stop watching late night movies.

- I was prayed for over my fear of illness and now all the scabs on my fingers have all gone. Praise the Lord. [Yes I remember it well; it happened instantly.]
- Fear of dying of blindness.
- My brother has leukaemia and he is ill, and I think you know what I am scared of, and I do pray that the Lord Jesus will make him better.
- Lord, you know that I was scared of running fast because of my accident when I was young. Now it is no longer part of me.
- If someone is killed my age, I think that I'll die like that. When I was prayed for, my fear seemed to come down my body and out of my toes.
- I am afraid that my mum will have a fit when I am on my own with her.
- Thank you for taking away my fear about being killed in a car, aeroplane or boat.
- Fear of getting water inside my head and dying.
- I was scared when people talked about witches and things like that.
- I am afraid of the dark, but Father God loves me and cares for me so I have nothing to fear.
- I am full of fear when I walk to school on my own, and kid-nappers.
- I am afraid of people snatching me when I am in bed.

8

The Family Outing

And now for a short intermission, while I tell you a story. . . .

There are few events of more importance than that special day – sadly all too infrequent – when Mum and Dad put all the usual mundane Saturday chores to one side, to devote the whole day to their family. For many, the pressure of having such a day proves too much and they end up having to inform their children that unfortunately it has been indefinitely cancelled. The disillusioned children are promised they will have it another time, but once let down they soon realize there is more chance of getting Christmas presents in July.

Some parents fight off all else and prove to be as good as their word, but for others the saga begins on the Friday night prior to the big day.

Part 1. The evening of the night before

The big question under debate centres around where they should go and what they should do. Dad thinks they would enjoy a nice day fishing, because he would enjoy a nice day fishing. But Mum thinks they would enjoy a nice day looking around the shops. And with both of these rather biased ideas in mind, Mum and Dad get into quite a heated debate together, each accusing the other of being selfish and trying to convince the other that the opposing suggestion is the last thing that the children would like to do.

A truce follows a short while later, and they decide to put their suggestions to the children and let them choose which one is the best plan for the day. The children sit listening intently as Mum and Dad communicate their ideas with all the skills of a loft insulation agent working on commission, trying to sell his wares to the owner of a flat-roofed house. When their eloquent orations finish, however, instead of the expected standing ovation, all they get is a polite raspberry from all the children in unison. Neither of those ideas is on *their* agendas for tomorrow.

Dad then thinks he has a brainwave. He tells the children to write down some of their ideas, then they can all decide together. After a very short time, the children are standing in front of them, proudly holding up their sheets of paper, which seem to have more suggestions on them than an opinion poll on what is wrong with the world today.

As each piece of paper is carefully scrutinized, opinions vary from staying at home and watching television all day, to going to Disneyland on Concorde. But the thing that Mum and Dad find most amazing is that, with all these numerous suggestions, each of the children has written down something different.

After thanking the children, the parents, now suffering from exhaustion, decide it is the children's bedtime, explaining that they need an early night so that they will be wide awake for the excitement that tomorrow will bring. As the shouts of, 'But where are we going?' echo down the stairs, the confused adults shout back that it is going to be a surprise, but refrain from adding that it will also be a surprise for them.

With the children safely tucked in bed, fishing and shopping come back into the conversation.

Part 2. The night before

It is a restless night for Mum and Dad. They have laboriously read through all the 'What's On' columns in local papers, rung round to ask friends for suggestions, and even spent some time in prayer about it, but are still finding it hard to make a decision that everyone will be happy with. It proves to be a long night with little sleep, as two over-active adult minds refuse to rest up, give up, and relax.

But, however long the night may seem, the morning comes around far too soon.

Part 3. The big day is here

Weary and shattered, Mum and Dad have a rude awakening as their highly keyed-up, excited children bounce all over their bed, with loud voices still screaming out the same question they had been asking when they climbed those stairs four thousand ideas ago. The good news is that Dad has an idea, but it would be suicide to reveal it in case it got the thumbs down. He just repeats that it will remain a surprise, and adds that they are going on a mystery tour. Now this is inspired thinking, as it has the advantage that if he suddenly feels like a change of guidance while driving, he can always take the car in another direction without having to confess to the family that he has changed his mind.

In a very short time, breakfast is gulped down, and the car is packed full with every conceivable useless item which hopefully will cover all needs, whatever or wherever the destination turns out to be. What could be better than the open road, the sun shining in the windows, and the children singing along to an Ishmael tape playing at full blast on the cassette machine? Everyone is blissfully happy.

More accurately, everyone is happy for the first five miles, and it is at this point that one of the children feels sick, and another needs the loo, and Dad is getting rather annoyed, as Mum can't find where they are on the map. It is a bit premature, but they decide to pull in for a coffee break. After a short delay, the wheels start rolling again and off they all go, with the singing restarting. They are now even more determined that none of these little mishaps is going to be allowed to spoil their day.

Up until now, Dad has been tossing an imaginary coin in his mind for most of the journey, as to whether he should drive to the seaside or the countryside. The seaside has just won by an imaginary head, and he overtakes a yacht on a trailer that is obviously heading in that direction. Cleverly, he still manages to keep it a secret from the children, and inwardly he feels very pleased with himself when they arrive at Seatown and the children cheer as they get their first glimpse of the sea.

The seaside town is busy, and Dad is getting rather grumpy, both through not having had enough sleep, and also through not having taken Mum's advice to park in the multi-storey car park. He is sure that he will find somewhere nearer to the beach, but his assurance has been unfounded, and he humbly returns to the multi-storey, explaining how unusual it is that this extremely popular resort is so extremely popular.

But nobody minds; they load themselves up with every conceivable type of nautical apparatus and head for the golden sands. Excitement has now taken over as they run all the way, with Mum and Dad as emotionally aroused as the children, but they come to a sudden halt when they see that Dad's idea of coming to the beach is not unique. Millions of other dads have obviously had the same brainwave, and it is going to be like walking over a minefield, trying to avoid treading on some unsuspecting body.

Eventually, a few square feet of sand is located, which they make their own territory by laying out a couple of blankets and quickly sitting on them. Then comes the great unveiling. The children tear off their clothes as fast as they can, with no thought of modesty, and on goes the swimming gear. Dad takes a little while longer to get his swimming trunks on, while Mum takes an age, proving what a brilliant contortionist she is by putting on her bikini and still managing to keep her private parts from public viewing by using only one small towel. Others lying around them are a little less discreet, which of course the children soon notice.

The eldest one shouts out at the top of her voice: 'Mummy, why isn't that lady wearing a top?' Dad instinctively glances over, then, realizing what he is peering at, quickly gets out a Christian magazine and starts to try and read it. Red with embarrassment, not instant suntan, Mum notices that her child is pointing at a lady who has chosen to try for an almost-all-over, even tan. 'Shhh,' says Mum, 'just be quiet.' But she should have known that children will keep asking questions until they get an answer.

'Are you going to take your bra off too?' enquires the same voice, who has obviously only very recently learned what a bra is, and now likes using the word.

'No, I am not,' says Mum. 'Christians don't do that sort of thing.' She hopes that the lady in question cannot hear her, and that she isn't a liberated Christian. 'Now just be quiet.'

'But Adam and Eve didn't wear any clothes,' continues the eager little theological student. 'Does that mean that they weren't Christians?'

'I'm going swimming,' says Mum, and she rushes off towards the sea.

By midday, they have swum, played cricket and football, made sandcastles and tunnels, and even found time to bury Dad in the sand. But now stomachs are informing them that it is lunch time.

Dad has still not learned his lesson from the night before, and he tries to decide democratically what sort of food is the most desired. 'What does everyone feel like eating?' he asks. One wants beans on toast, one wants fish and chips, and the other really fancies a Chinese. Mum wants a salad. So up they all get, and to save any arguments, Dad pops into the first place they come to, which happens to be a burger bar. He buys everyone a hamburger, which is the only thing they unanimously don't want.

Walking along the promenade, they pass all the video game machines, and the children, relating the smell and the sound to that of a funfair, want to go in and see them. Dad and Mum say that they can, but tell them not to look at the machines, but to look at the expressions on the faces of the people playing them. They are only in the hall a few minutes, and once out in the fresh air again one of the children asks why the people look so serious and sad when they are playing a game. Dad explains that like cigarettes, these machines can become addictive, which means that although it starts off as a bit of fun it often ends up that you can't stop playing them. The people look sad because to some of them these machines have become such a major part of their lives, they have become like gods that they worship. Also, when they put their money into the machines, it is just like they are throwing their money away, which of course they could have spent on something that would have lasted or done them good.

Sensing that a bit of fun is needed, they find a crazy golf course. Having paid for their clubs and golf balls, off they go. Dad treats the game quite seriously and wants to prove to the children that he is a golfer that they can be proud of. Mum, however, sees it as a bit of fun, and just laughs as she pushes her ball nearer to the hole and kicks Dad's further away. The children just enjoy hitting the ball as hard as they can and watching people jump out of the way as it comes hurtling towards them.

Ice-cream time follows and Dad has at last learned his lesson. Instead of asking what everyone wants, he just orders cornets all round, for which everyone is thankful and delighted. After a return to the beach and another quick dip in the sea, which means a two-mile hike to find the water as it is now low tide, it is time to go home. The sun is going down and the car park ticket is expiring. The children are exhausted and fall asleep as soon as they get into the car.

As the hand brake is pulled on – with a loud clicking noise – outside their house, however, it is like an alarm bell. Everyone wakes up for tea, and ready for more fun in the evening.

Part 4. Good evening, mums and dads and boys and girls

While everyone is munching their sandwiches, Dad is trying to decide what they should do in the evening. He thinks of hiring a video film, but is a little bit disappointed that all the most exciting films seem to be full of profanities that he doesn't want to inflict on his children. He is also concerned that many children's television programmes seem to be based on witchcraft, sorcery and the occult. Each week he goes through the television magazines and suggests to his children what they may enjoy watching. Then, after explaining why, he instructs them about programmes that would not be good for Christian children.

But tonight the telly can stay cold; it is games night. It starts with real old-fashioned family games, like charades and other silly games, where no one actually wins and certainly no one loses. In fact, most of the games end with everyone rolling about on the floor in uncontrollable fits of laughter.

Then, when the youngest goes to bed, out come the board games, and attitudes become a little more serious. It is when they are about halfway through a game, right at the most exciting point, that the doorbell rings. Dad goes to the door and there is Mrs Dunnin. I failed to mention that Mum and Dad run a home group together and are responsible for the pastoral care of about a dozen folk, one of whom happens to be Mrs Dunnin.

There are always genuinely needy folk who need help, but Mrs Dunnin is not one of them. She always has a long, sad story to tell, always wants to be prayed for, and then always feels as bad, if not worse, after prayer than she did before. She is basically a lonely person who wants attention. Here on the doorstep Dad is faced with a problem: should he invite her in? The last thing he wants to be is inhospitable or rude, but would this spoil the day that he had specially set aside for his family, and, more to the point, would he ever finish his game?

Then he has an idea, 'Do come in, Mrs Dunnin,' he says, and he brings her into the room where the rest of the family are still sitting around the table looking at the board. The children get down from the table, expecting to hear the words they have heard so often, that they should go up to their rooms because Mum and Dad have to talk to someone. But no, this time it is different.

Dad explains to Mrs Dunnin that this is a special family day, and if she would like to sit in the chair, the family will pray over her – the children will start praying and then they will continue. Mrs Dunnin isn't given the opportunity of going through her long spiel, and even though it is unusual for the children to pray for her, she agrees to Dad's suggestion. After a few minutes of prayer, Mrs Dunnin is invited to join in the game, and it is then that the children see a different side to her; she is great fun and keeps making all sorts of jokes. Two hours later she leaves the house a much happier lady, not just because she has been welcomed as part of the family, but also because she has won the game.

At the end of the day the family thank God for each other, their health and wealth, and the fun that it is being part of his family.

9

Meetings and Ministries

Ye olde Sunday school

I just about remember going to Sunday school. While the second hymn was being sung, we would all file out down a corridor until we eventually arrived in a shabby little room, illuminated (if we were lucky) by a couple of ten-watt light-bulbs.

It was always a job to squeeze us all in, and that was not because the room was too small – it was quite a good size. It was more to do with the fact that we had to share this room with old projectors and screens, blackboard easels that must have been purchased during the Second World War, toys that a playgroup would use on weekday mornings, the minister's old waders that had been used for the odd baptismal service, and lots of other odd bits of old rubbish. It could be politely summed up by saying that we were in the church's junk room.

Our singing would be accompanied by an out-of-tune piano, and if we were not singing 'Deep and wide' or 'The wise man built his house upon the rock', we were forced to choose any of our favourite songs from a tattered CSSM chorus book that we held in our hands. The trouble was we had no favourites; in fact, we didn't like any of them, except

'Deep and wide' and 'The wise man built his house upon the rock', and we only liked them because they had action and movement.

After making noises, which some would call singing, we went through an exercise called 'sword drill'. This was really just a race to see who was the first person to find a verse in the Bible without tearing out too many pages. Once the verse had been found the competition continued by seeing who could get the most laughs out of making the long Old Testament names sound silly and funny.

When enough Bibles had been demolished, or we were out of control with laughter, we would sit down, and depending on our age and not our ability, we would either hear another exciting adventure from *Jungle Doctor*, or watch a flannel graph and count the bits as they fell on the floor. Failing this we'd get a long, boring sermon from someone who had been relegated from the main church service to the ladies' meeting because the church had found him boring, then further relegated from the ladies' meeting to us because even they found him too boring.

Ye olde teachers

I remember the teachers. I think many would have preferred to have been anywhere except with us. They only ended up in this position because there was no other function they could do in the church, or else it was the teenagers who took the job because it was the lesser of two evils – the greater being having to sit through the morning service.

Why did the children continue going? Well, it was for two reasons: first, because our parents made us, and second, because we wanted to fill up our sticker books and get our free Bible at the end of the year. The sticker collecting was not so much an incentive to us; it was more like a beginner's course in the art of deceit and gambling. If we were cunning, we could miss a morning, still get a sticker, and still get something for nothing at the end of the year. Maybe I was the odd one out, but I didn't like proper school from Monday to Friday anyway, even though it was run by trained professionals, so having to face another school on Sundays run by non-enthusiastic amateurs was pretty grim, to put it mildly.

Religious education for children has been around for longer than most encyclopaedias can remember. In fact, right from the beginning of time, children were taught by parents and others about the Lord God. Psalm 78 says:

> O my people, hear my teaching; listen to the words of my mouth. I will open my mouth in parables, I will utter hidden things, things from of old – what we have heard and known, what our fathers have told us. We will not hide them from their children; we will tell the next generation the praiseworthy deeds of the Lord, his power, and the wonders he has done. He decreed statutes for Jacob and established the law in Israel, which he commanded our forefathers to teach their children, so that the next generation would know them, even the children yet to be born, and they in turn would tell their children. Then they would put their trust in God and would not forget his deeds but would keep his commands. (Psalm 78:1–7)

Now this was all well and good, as long as those who were supposed to be passing on this vital information about God not only *did* pass it on but also *believed* in what they were passing on. But sadly, as time went by, and even though more and more nations had been taught about Christianity, it seemed that good biblical teaching was not reaching the ears of many children.

A hero arises

In 1736 a children's worker was not born, but a prison reformer was. His name was Robert Raikes and he was a newspaper publisher by trade. He noticed that many young children who spent their lives working in factories were getting involved with crime, and he had a feeling that a lot of this was due to the fact that they were uneducated.

Realizing that on six days did they labour, the only day left to give them any sort of instruction was, of course, on Sunday. It was in 1780 that his highly controversial Sunday school began, thanks to the support of an Anglican vicar and the dedication of many ordinary folk who opened up their homes to get the idea off the ground. So this was how the house church movement began!

Their teaching was not all about Christianity, however. They covered a variety of basic subjects they believed would be helpful to the children, hopefully keeping them out of trouble and ultimately out of prison. Many church leaders, however, could not cope with this revolutionary idea. One of their main arguments was that the teaching was interfering with the proper Sunday observance. Even in that day, Pharisees continued to make their presence felt by promoting the letter of the law and not understanding the spirit behind it.

Their other argument, which incenses me, was that they did not believe the poor children should be educated, as they may become too intelligent, disagree with the way the country was being run and cause a revolution. The good old church leaders of the day, as insecure as ever, were retaining the motto of 'keep the folk simple and nobody will be in a position to argue with our theological interpretations'. That's right: 'The less people know, the better off we will all be!'

Could there be a parallel today, as to why we leave certain scriptures out, like Acts 2 and 1 Corinthians 12 to name but two, when we are teaching the children? Could this be because we are not only frightened that we will not be able to answer all their questions, but also that they may cause a minor revolution if they discover that some of what we teach as essential we do not carry out? To do so would cause a major rethinking and even a restructuring of our meetings – more than a leader's job is worth.

Sunday school spreads

As you may have observed, though, Sunday schools did catch on, and they spread very quickly around the world. Before Raikes died it must have been a great encouragement to him that by 1803 a national Sunday school Union was founded. What he courageously pioneered had now become accepted as an institution.

Here we are, some 200 years later. Children in our society are not slaving in factories any more – many are lazing around the home, enjoying the luxury of the television and digital age. Very few are uneducated. In fact, many have started on the long educational road by the age of three, and because all subjects are taught in our state schools, the church now confines itself to teaching just Religious Education, with varying amounts of sincerity and commitment, depending on which church you attend.

So I am not being at all controversial when I make the statement: May Sunday schools rest in peace. You have had your day and done a grand job, but nowadays you are not relevant to the age we are living in. God has used you greatly in the past, but what does he want to use to affect our Christ-less generation today? I am a firm believer that although the fundamentals of what we believe and who we believe in never change – for Jesus Christ is the same, yesterday, today and for ever – the way in which we do things must be open to constant change and revision. The church should never be accused of being archaic, old-fashioned and outdated. We should not just wait for the unchurched to act and then react; we should be leading the way.

If we believe that Jesus provides life to the full – not the easiest life around, but certainly the most exciting and fulfilling – why aren't there more people who want to become Christians? One of the reasons is that we are caricatured as wimpy, weak-willed people – yesterday's people, who, unlike the Lord Jesus, have little relevance to today and no relevance to for ever. For most people, visiting a church is like visiting a museum, where they could find an interesting variety of old relics who portray how miserable life can be if you are a Christian.

Sunday school is yet another page out of the history books. Let us consider some major changes that may hopefully bring us more into the present.

Name change

First, the name Sunday school is, for unbelieving children, meaningless and a joke, and to our Christian children it is at best a total embarrassment. Can you put yourself in their position and, at the age of ten, expect them to witness to their friends and invite them to hear more about Jesus at Sunday school? They get enough persecution and intimidation without us adding to it by making them use a silly name.

Another reason for change is that a lot of children do not enjoy weekday school, especially as they grow older, and to have to tell their friends that they are going to school on Sundays as well is a big turn-off, both for Christians and also for the friends whom they are hoping to encourage along.

Junior church

Some have ceased to use the words Sunday school and replaced them with 'junior church'. I prefer 'children's church', so long as it really is a children's church, as outlined in another chapter.

It is very easy for adults to treat a junior church as inferior and to start believing that children are of less importance to Christ than they are. No one would dare tell you, but just a small indication can be found of how leaders view the junior church if you compare how much of the church's finances go towards adults, compared with that which is set aside for the children's work. Or answer me this one: if the junior church and the senior church both had overhead projectors, and the senior church's one failed to work, would they have a right to take and use the junior church's projector? Most would say yes, because they see the senior church as more important than the junior church.

Now I know that I am only talking about names, but in this day and age names are important. They do need to be thought out and prayed about. Each church may have a different name for its children's work which is suitable to its locality. When you have thought up a name, however, do remember to get it endorsed by the children, as they are going to be the ones who need to feel happy about using it as they make that personal invitation for their friends to join them.

What is the aim of our children's meetings? We need to have clear goals. Otherwise, if we try to do a bit of everything at every meeting, usually the children end up with a lot of nothing.

Food for growth

Let us begin with Bible teaching. We must remember that we

are teaching what the Bible actually says, and not what we would like it to say. There is a variety of teaching aids produced by various organizations, and they range from being very old-fashioned to very helpful. Before you decide to use one of these, do look around at all that is on offer – their emphasis can be quite different.

Now I have called these teaching 'aids', and that is all they are. They were never meant simply to be read out to the children, or to take the place of further research and preparation. Alongside these aids must come prayer and personal inspiration, otherwise the child will notice no difference between you and the teacher at school who so often just regurgitates a textbook. You are not only sharing divine truth, but truth that has affected your life; your teaching is not theoretical words alone, but a living experience.

Most important of all, you must communicate with the children. Truth, however important, needs to be delivered in a way that the listener will not only understand and be challenged by, but will also enjoy and remember. To do this, you either need to use visual aids or, if you are quite a colourful personality, you can be a visual aid yourself and hold children's attention that way.

Let me share with you one way that I often use. I believe that the days of the *Jungle Doctor* stories, or even the *Concrete Jungle Doctor* stories, are numbered as our main teaching emphasis. These may be great for a child to read and enjoy as bedtime stories, but our responsibility is to teach them the Bible.

Preparation

It may be of some help if I share with you how I would prepare a talk. I would start by using a story that was not so well known. Parts of the Old Testament are great action-packed stories and although they may at first seem to have little relevance to the New Testament, the more we study them, the more we realize how much God has to teach us through them.

I would read this story at least six to a dozen times from different translations, until it was firmly set in my memory. I would then go to Bible dictionaries and commentaries and follow up any cross-references, to find out even more about the passage. By this time I should have discovered the events before it, around it and after it, and have worked out its context.

Then, as I am not just going to read this story but live it out in front of the children and portray it in my own words in a way they will understand, I write down on a piece of card about 15 headings, so that if I do seize up with stage fright I can still glance down and hopefully continue. There may also be a Scripture verse in the middle of the story that I would like them to learn. I would write this down again, to make sure I get it right.

After all this, I would have some idea as to how the Lord wanted to apply certain things to the children's lives. I would underline these at the bottom of my card. While doing all this, I would spend a lot of time praying about it. Even though it may end up being the best and most polished talk I have ever given, without the anointing of the Holy Spirit on myself, the talk will do little to change lives.

If you are not a very visual person, you will need to help the children's memories with visual aids. Personally, I feel that the good old flannel graph (if you remember what that is!) should be returned to the soap bag because so many of the pictures are dated – but, in this retro era, who knows, it could be set for a comeback! I praise the Lord that he is raising up some very gifted artists who are using their talents with great inspiration and are not only equal to their modern-day non-Christian counterparts, but are even surpassing them.

I would sum up visual aids by saying that our children deserve the best, and the best is not always the most expensive, but usually it is. I find it exciting that new resources are regularly becoming available, but you will need to be a bit of a Sherlock Holmes to track them down.

Hearing God's voice

As well as teaching the children Bible stories, we need to teach them how to talk to and listen to God. In Chapter 5 I mentioned how to pray for others for healing, but children need to know first how God speaks and second how they can speak to God. Children need to learn that it is not common for God to speak to them from heaven in a loud voice that their ears can hear, just as it is not the norm that God will appear before their very eyes in person. Yes, these may have happened to some, but we don't want our children thinking that unless this happens to them they have no chance of communication with God.

God's voice is a gentle voice that can reach our hearts via our eyes and minds as we read the Bible. It can be a louder voice as it passes through our hearts via the mouth of the preacher, or it can be a flash that hits our conscience and then reaches our hearts. We can never tie God down to how he speaks – he even spoke through a donkey in the Bible. But we can be sure of a couple of things: the first is that what he says will never contradict the Bible, and the other is that when we are walking close to God his voice is unmistakable. Jesus said, 'My sheep hear my voice.'

When it comes to speaking to God, children must always remember that it is Almighty God to whom they are speaking. Through teaching that Jesus is our best friend, our prayers sometimes become so over-familiar that they are on the point of blasphemy. We must learn that real friendship demands real respect. We are living in a generation that believes in standing up for its rights and that the world and everyone in it owes it something. If not checked, this feeling can easily be transferred to God and people can live a life believing that instead of us being nothing and God being everything, God owes them and they deserve the best from him.

I do not teach name it and claim it, cash on demand, or trying to hold the Lord at ransom by saying, 'Do it now, or else.' I have no right to demand from God, but he is always available and has allowed me the privilege to talk to him and also to share with him my doubts, fears and questions. We must learn to come before God with a humble heart.

Concerning both how to listen and how to speak to God, I've found that sharing some personal experience of doing things the right way and wrong way has been a great help to the children. I have not covered songs and worship in this chapter because, again, they are covered elsewhere.

Children's leaders

I spend every week with children's leaders from every denomination and many countries. Often they look tired and exhausted; they feel neglected, vulnerable and unappreciated, and many feel that others see them as doing an inferior ministry to those who work with older age groups.

They feel this way for many reasons: the obvious one is that many local church leaders and members neglect to encourage them and often take them for granted, but I want to mention a couple of other reasons.

1. Christian parents

Some still have the idea that training up their child in the way of God is the church's responsibility, meaning the children's leaders – though they would never trust the leaders enough to hand their child over to them, like Hannah did with young Samuel. Others, of course, still feel that children's workers are just babysitting their children, to allow them to enjoy their meetings without their little ones causing distraction. Both of these attitudes by Christian parents add stress to the children's leader.

2. Children's ministry – no biblical role models

Callings and ministries can be found in the pages of our Bibles. We also find instruction and advice on how to fulfil our calling, and can learn from Bible characters who walked a similar path to the one we are walking.

But not with children's ministry. It is hard to find even a vague mention in Scripture of the work many of us are now doing with children. Children's and youth work really only began as a church function a few hundred years ago, and this being the case means we have no real biblical role models, and just general instructions that were normally given to parents on the work we feel called to do. We do learn from those who have gone before us in these latter years, but for most of us we learn by trial and error in our local situations.

The Bible mentions other ministries elsewhere (such as encouragement, hospitality etc.), but Ephesians 4 seems to name the big five which most churches readily accept as the major ministries: apostles, prophets, evangelists, pastors and teachers, although some would argue the latter two are usually found in the same person. In some churches, where the leader of leaders believes he or she is God's answer to the local church, one person tries to fulfil all these ministries themselves, while all inferior leaders stand around watching them. Of course, they fail dismally. Nowadays, most of us believe that leadership is made up of a team and different members of that team, alongside other members of the local church who together fulfil the above five ministries.

But not so with children's workers. We try and do what no other church leader in their right mind would even attempt to do. We not only try to do all five ministries, we try to do all five at every meeting in one hour. It's not surprising we are exhausted. Let me explain.

I can do everything?

We try to be apostles because we now understand that this is no longer a club; we are planting children's church. We try to be prophets as we speak God's messages to our little ones. We try to be evangelists as we give them a chance to become Christians. We try to be pastors as we care for the lambs. We try to be teachers as we attempt to expound the Bible to them. On top of all this, many of us work, and some even have other jobs in the local church, plus most of us try to run our families and homes at the same time. I get exhausted just thinking about it.

Specific ministry to children is hard to find in the pages of the Bible, but in today's culture we know that God has a place for it and even anoints people to work with boys and girls. However, the bigger question in my mind is should any ministry just be tied down to just one specific age group? This to me is to narrow down what God has gifted us to do.

Are there really such narrow callings?

Is there such a calling as a children's or youth evangelist? I don't think so, but I do believe in evangelists who have a special heart for children or young people. I am an evangelist, but as an evangelist I want to see all ages saved. Whoever I am with at the time, I want to share Jesus with them, but I do find something very special about introducing a child to Jesus.

Is there such a calling as a children's or youth pastor? I

don't think so. A pastor or shepherd cares for all sheep, not just lambs. If you have a pastor's heart, you will enjoy caring for people of all ages, but you may find something very special about caring for the little flock.

Likewise all the other named ministries – in the Bible, none of them seem to cover one age range. It's so often the case that it is we who feel confident in spending all our time with a particular age group, and this is usually the age group we find the most easy to relate to and communicate with.

The classic

The most extreme case of a narrow calling is the Bible teacher. Many say they cannot teach children, but, again, how can they justify from Scripture that they are anointed to teach just adults? Which Bible character's role are they imitating? Surely a real Bible teacher should be able to communicate Scripture to all ages – even Paul did this, and he would probably be the last person that you would invite to speak at your Sunday school anniversary. More about Bible teachers in a minute.

What is our calling?

Do you sometimes feel as though you are trying to be a jack of all trades: working with children and trying to be the master of everything, but never getting even close to being the master of one? Just as with the adult church, we need to find our calling and work as a team. Maybe you have not got an apostle in your group yet – I'm sure the Lord will provide one when you need one. This means that if we are not trying to do everything at once, we now have time to let God develop us in our one major ministry. He will take us deeper into our pastoring, prophetic gifting, evangelizing, etc., and I believe that this will not only give us a lot more satisfaction, but also provide a much greater strength to the whole church.

To sum up, God wants to use our ministry gifting with all ages, but this may include having a special desire to use it with young people or children.

Bible teachers continued

I believe this is the ministry that is most lacking, especially with our children. We do our best: we read our Bibles to children; we follow our curricula – both of which can be helpful, but if we are not Bible teachers, it does show and we do lack anointing and power.

Nowadays, I believe one of the reasons that many young people drift away from God is because they do not know their Bibles. We teach that the only way anyone can grow and become a strong Christian is by understanding and acting on God's word, yet most children get just a few minutes' teaching on a Sunday morning and maybe a few minutes with some very short Bible reading notes one or two days a week. Will this really give them the spiritual nutrition they need to help them to be more than conquerors in a hostile world? Please don't answer me by saying that the Holy Spirit will see them through because he is their teacher. Yes, of course he is their teacher, but how will even he bring truth into being if the truth from God's word has never been taught to them?

Looking back

Let's go back to go forward. The best Bible teachers the world has ever known did not just teach adults; they believed it was vital to share their gifting with children as well. That's why it is so strange to find hardly any of our local, national or international Bible teachers of great renown even dreaming of insisting that they must have time to teach the children.

Two thousand years ago, the greatest teacher of them all, Jesus, found time to bless and teach children. At that time the Jewish parents would teach the children until they were six, and then the boys from seven to eleven would be taught by the most qualified people of the day. (The rabbi had not spent just five years at theological college – his training took twenty-six years.)

In the early church days, we know that the church fathers taught the children. Great teachers like Tertullian, Origen and even Cyprian the Bishop of Carthage. The celtic missionaries were very practical in their teaching, and often took the young ones with them as they visited the local communities. In the Reformation, Martin Luther, John Knox and John Calvin were very involved in teaching children – some even spent time writing special doctrines for children. While in Geneva, Calvin set aside one hour each Sunday especially to teach children.

In the eighteenth century, John Wesley mentioned on many occasions how he taught hundreds of children in their newly formed Sabbath Schools. The Wesley brothers even wrote about 44 hymns just for children. Although George Whitefield may be labelled more of an evangelist than a teacher, it's wonderful to hear how his horse was often over-crowded with at least half a dozen children riding with him, as he took them to his meetings.

That brings us up to fairly recent times, and probably one of the most respected teachers of all, Charles Spurgeon. Read carefully the following words extracted from *Come Ye Children,* which was his training manual for parents and teachers:

> You who are teaching children are not dishonoured by that occu-
> pation; some may say you are only a Sunday school teacher, but

you are a noble personage holding an honourable office and having illustrious predecessors. We love to see persons of some standing in our society take an interest in Sabbath Schools.

But to convert children as children, and to regard them as being as much believers as their seniors, is regarded as absurd. To this supposed absurdity I cling with all my heart. I believe that of children is the kingdom of God, both on earth and in heaven. Was there ever a kingdom that had no children in it, how then could it grow?

One great fault in many of our churches is that the children are left for the young people to care for, the older members who have more wisdom, taking but very little notice of them, and very often the wealthier members of the church stand aside as if the teaching of the poor were not, as indeed it is, the business of the rich.

I hope for the day when the mighty men of Israel shall be found helping in this great warfare against the enemy.

In the United States we have heard of presidents, of judges, members of congress, and persons in the highest positions, not condescending, for I scorn such a term, but honouring themselves by teaching little children in Sabbath School. He who teaches in such a Sabbath School has earned a good degree. I would rather have the title of SST (Sabbath School Teacher) than MA BA or any other honour that was conferred by men.

What a shame that all the thousands of ministers who are great Spurgeon fans ignore this major part of his instruction and example. I have not mentioned any ladies, because very few of our godly ladies were Bible teachers in the same way that the men above were. But it's a bit like the chicken and the egg, because without such mothers as Susanna Wesley there would certainly be two names missing from the above list.

Challenge those in authority – in love

Now is the time to pass this over to your church leaders, who in turn will hopefully challenge your Bible teachers. I am not suggesting for one minute that your Bible teachers become part of your children's leadership team, unless of course they want to. Just invite them to join your meeting and share scriptures for five to ten minutes, and then afterwards children's leaders can continue by clarifying what has been said, if they need to. They don't need visual aids. (I cannot imagine John Calvin using a puppet, or Charles Spurgeon incorporating a gunge tank.) These people don't need the props that you or I may use in other parts of our meeting. They are Bible teachers and they just need God's anointing.

As I close, one last thought.

Where have all the old saints gone?

Church can be very ageist. Nowadays those who front our meetings need to be reasonably young, or, if older, we like them to look good. Image has crept in from the world outside and now plays a vital part with our preachers and teachers. It's not just what you hear, it's the appearance of the person so often performing that impresses the listeners and brings in the crowds.

I remember being invited to a church where 'revival' was taking place – but sadly it ended the week before I arrived. Mind you, it would have been worse if it had finished when I arrived! I discovered that the revival was a name given to meetings which took place most nights of the week, and a good-looking young preacher from a different city had been invited in to lead these meetings. The hall was packed every night. After a few weeks, however, the young preacher decided that he should return to his own city, and the meetings were put back under the leadership of the local team, comprising older church leaders. Instantly the revival finished, as people did not have the same desire to turn out each night to hear older people whom they saw every week anyway.

Sadly, some of the best teachers we ever had are now very old. They do not appear exciting and most would believe that they will never be acceptable to the young people. They have had a life of godly experience, but nowadays they neither look the part nor communicate in a way that is acceptable to most. After a lifelong walk with God they are now put out to graze, collecting dust until the Lord calls them home.

In Bible times, it appears to have been the opposite to this. The older and more experienced the person was, the higher position and respect they were given. These older people were really worth getting opinions from, and listening to. Unlike the biblical model, we show little of this respect to our real elders. Our missionaries, who have pioneered the way for many of our modern overseas initiatives at amazing cost, are humiliated. They arrive home after years of hardship to be greeted by people who often wonder why they ever bothered to return if they enjoyed their lives overseas so much. They have trouble fitting into local church, as all their qualifications in leadership are not seen as significant or valid in this country. On visits, they are not a priority, and the leaders allow them one hour on a miserable midweek night to tell of the adventures of the previous ten years. It turns out to be the worst attended meeting of the year, because neither old nor young have been encouraged to attend, and no leader would expect any young person to sit through an evening having to watch hundreds of low-tech photographic slides on a subject they consider will be of little interest to them.

When was the last time we heard from the pulpit a talk on tolerance and respect for the elderly? The reason many leaders could not do it is because they have not got it. In the end, just four or five elderly people turn up to the meeting, which has been transferred to the smallest room in the building, and they have only come because they are very close friends of the speaker, or maybe they have heard that tea with special biscuits will be available at the end!

Resurrection time

Maybe it's time to bring new life into our old saints and breathe new life into their old bones. If they are not trendy enough for your adult meetings, let the children benefit from their rich wisdom, knowledge and experience. Let the missionaries drop into the children's meeting as regular special guests and tell a story of their adventures. Let the children ask them questions.

Dust down the old Bible teachers, give them back some of the self-respect that the church has robbed them of, invite them to come and expound a story from the Bible, just for five to ten minutes. Their knowledge will strengthen the children. It may take quite a bit of encouragement to give them back their ministries and to get them back to the position they should be in, because their confidence will be very low. They will make all sorts of excuses why they can't teach any more and they will try to tell you they do not know how to speak to children. This is just fear. Watch the love and communication skills they have as they spend time with their grandchildren – is there any age group better at loving, communicating and holding young children's attention?

It's wake-up time

We need to start using all ages and skills that make up the church to teach our children. Many of us are crying out for more children's workers. Maybe it's not more personnel that's needed; maybe it's the people content to hide in the adult meeting who need to wake up to the fact that what they have been entrusted with was also given to them by God to pass on to the children. The children, of course, are the responsibility of their parents, but also of the whole body of the church. We should all be making it a priority to have input into these little ones. Wake up, church, and get alongside the children, for if they continue to drift away in their droves then we must all take the blame.

10
The Church

The church and the house of God

The church is made up of all persons who have, by the Holy Spirit, been reborn into God's family and have been made new creatures in the Lord Jesus. The Bible clearly tells us where God dwells: in his people. The church of God, therefore, never has been and never will be just a building or a meeting.

In Acts 17:24 Paul says, 'The God who made the world and everything in it is the Lord of heaven and earth and does not live in temples built by hands.' He then says in 1 Corinthians 3:16–17: 'Don't you know that you yourselves are God's temple and that God's Spirit lives in you? If anyone destroys God's temple, God will destroy him; for God's temple is sacred, and you are that temple.'

The holy building

Nowadays, does anyone consider the church to be a building? Some do, and many of those people tend to be the ones who never go inside it. Maybe they were taught that the church is a 'holy building', whether it's a thirteenth-century crumbling historical monument or a 1960s redbrick eyesore. It makes you wonder how we could ever imagine that four stone lifeless walls, with various shapes and colours of windows, could be what Jesus referred to as church.

People also refer to the church as God's house, the temple or the sanctuary: it's a shame these people did not manage to get past Malachi and start reading the New Testament. I still find it strange how nowadays some can find a building holy, even when there are no people inside it.

The dress code

A few years ago, I was invited to America, to lead a children's camp up in the mountains. It was brilliant. On the Sunday we had our final meeting at a gymnasium, which was where this church held their meetings, and a wonderful time was had of total freedom where all ages enjoyed the presence of God.

I was invited back the following year, and again the children's camp was wonderful. As we arrived back on the Sunday, the children's pastor started to tell me that since my last visit they had built a new sanctuary. The sound of the word sanctuary made me shiver a bit, but then I assumed the USA is a different culture, using a different word for what we call a church building. But sadly I was wrong, for along with the Old Testament name, came the Old Testament rules and restrictions.

As I was shown around the beautiful building, with its large stage, powerful sound system and its smell of fresh paint, I commented to the children's leader how much I was looking forward to ministering at the evening meeting. It was then that he paused and said, as though waiting for my disapproval, 'We do have one or two new rules that come with the new building – like male children and adults not being allowed to wear short trousers or caps.'

These sounded like the crazy, snobby rules that are insisted upon before entering my local golf club house, but even there you can wear what they have called tailored shorts. I assumed the caps rule was due to Paul's mention about head coverings in 1 Corinthians 11. We know the culture of Paul's day was that men did uncover their heads as a sign of respect and submission to God, just as 50 years ago men would touch their hats and caps, or even take them off, when approaching a lady. Is this the culture our children now live in?

Now please understand what I am saying. If you want to keep the cultural laws of Paul's day, that's fine. But it seems to me that in this church there was a great inconsistency. There were no rules about women keeping their heads covered and not cutting their hair. If you enforce the 'no hats for lads' rule, you also need to enforce the 'no haircuts for ladies' rule. In 1 Corinthians 11 Paul explains that every woman who prays should cover her head – the reason being that, in Paul's day, if a woman took off her head covering or shaved her head, it was a sign that she was either a disgraced rebel, a woman who refused to submit to her husband's authority, or a prostitute. I don't really think in today's culture that older ladies who regularly have their hair cut, or teenage girls who enjoy shaved heads, just do it out of rebellion, or because they enjoy sleeping around!

Many years ago I took my son Daniel to a venue with me. It was a time when he was struggling with the problems that early teenage years bring, so I was thrilled he wanted to be with his dad. It was a cold, wet night and the two of us carried all my equipment into the church building, while the organizers and leaders stood watching us. Daniel was wearing a cap.

It was while I was outside with the van, and Daniel was still helping to carry my gear in, that an older church leader came storming up to my son, demanding, in the most aggressive manner, that he take his hat off. Daniel was physically shaken by this reaction and verbal violence and obediently took it off. It's little wonder that our kids do not want to be part of such a group of people. I knew nothing about this till we got home, but things got worse.

Daniel played bass guitar for me that night and the church leader, recognizing whom he had verbally abused, came up to him and apologized, saying that he would not have dared say such a thing if he had known that Daniel was Ishmael's son. What difference does it make whose son he was? No kid deserves to be spoken to like that.

Anyway, enough of the hats – let's take a quick look at the short trousers in this modern American church. For this I could not find even a vague biblical confirmation, unless it tied up with King David leaping around, praising God in his underwear. Remember this is not the UK – men rarely get the chance to show off their legs in our uncertain climate! But in the US it was nearly one hundred degrees, and this seemed the most sensible and appropriate clothing to wear. Men and boys wearing short pants are rarely provocative or sensual, so I assumed these really go-ahead leaders had sadly decided to bow down to good old-time religion and added an eleventh commandment: God loves men but hates their short trousers.

I explained to the children's leader that I couldn't take a part in those rules. I had just taught of the wonderful freedom God gives and now I was going to go against everything I had said – it would be totally hypocritical. It was rather embarrassing, as these really nice people had paid for my airfare, and here was I refusing to preach in their new 'pride and joy' building. The children's leader was very understanding, and I am sure he knew it would only be a short matter of time before many of the children he led would be drifting off if these strange regulations stayed in place. I then had an idea. I discovered that the old gymnasium still existed, and suggested we hold the meeting back in there, so then people could come wearing what they liked. This was agreed, and sadly, rather than change the new church laws, all the PA and equipment was transported from the sanctuary to the gymnasium – a lot of hard work.

Everyone arrived at the meeting looking relaxed and thrilled to bits. Colourful baseball caps were worn, depicting their favourite sports teams (which, without instruction, were religiously taken off during any prayer times), and shorts were worn discreetly below the knee. What did I wear? If my memory serves me well, I think I wore a suit – I always did find it very hard to conform. I had far more important things to share than go down in history as a 'hat and short trousers reformer'. I was just the preacher. I had made my point and saw no reason to wear it out!

A waste of space

On another occasion, I was talking to the pastor of another beautiful new sanctuary. He assured me that this was just a building and they had no special rules. I asked him how often the building would be used, to which he replied, 'All day on Sunday.' I could not help but say, 'What a waste!', to which he looked shocked and asked what I meant. I explained that he had just spent a massive sum of money on four walls and a roof, which he was going to use only one day a week.

I pointed to the far end of the building. 'That would make a perfect indoor football pitch' – he could have this place buzzing with children and young people day and night. He covered his ears with his hands, as if I had just screamed out the worst profanity imaginable. 'You can't play football in God's house,' he wailed. I didn't answer. I did respect his opinion, and, after all, it was his building – and he was bigger than me. But I still failed to see how God would be more pleased to watch dust collect for six days than to see kids brought in off the streets and Christians donating a sports hall to the local community. You may feel you need a 'special' place reserved for quiet devotions in your building, but please don't think God is worried about children having fun there. Be honest and admit that any restriction is for your benefit, not God's.

Old buildings, young people

By now you will think I am a sacrilegious vandal, whose sole aim is to desecrate, or better still demolish, all religious buildings. That is not true. I have spent many happy hours walking around and admiring the craftsmanship and architecture of very ancient buildings, both in the UK and mainland Europe. I am fascinated by them and realize that they can teach us much about our heritage and church history. I am just of the opinion that these are not the best places nowadays for children to meet. They smell of the old and musty, and bodies in tombs surround the building that is supposed to be full of life. Some bishops seem to treat these buildings with more respect and reverence than they do God himself.

I was once invited to do a short musical tour of some of the English cathedrals, and hundreds of school children were invited to join us in a Songs of Praise time. I could not believe it when a man with a long face and a long robe to match informed us that we were not permitted to put up the overhead projector screen because 'it did not look right' in one of these buildings. That meant for the next hour the children had to try to sing along to new songs without being able to see any of the words.

My personal advice would be to move church out of some of these buildings, turn them into tourist attractions and make visitors pay to go in and enjoy the sightseeing. This would help with the upkeep to preserve their finery. Then move church to a modern, light, airy place that the kids can't destroy and where there are no tombs on display.

So, to sum up on church buildings, let me leave you with some wise words from the eighteenth-century revivalist George Whitefield. While in America, and having preached to thousands, the Americans wanted to build a huge building for his work. He told them that he never wanted to put the people in a 'church within walls'.

So what is church?

So if the church is not within walls, if it's not the building, then what is it? At this point everyone shouts, 'It's the people', which of course is the right answer, but it's not what we are teaching our children today. Today we have progressed from the church being the building, to the church being the Sunday meetings. One of the most confusing statements that we can say to our children is that we go to church. There is no such thing biblically as going to church. By this expression we are telling the children that they go to church on Sunday, but church has no relevance to any of the other six days of the week, unless of course they go to another meeting.

I teach children that although they may go to a meeting or gathering of the church on a Sunday, church is not something you go to, it's something you become part of and belong to when you become a Christian. So boys and girls are part of church – or in more adult terms, the body of Christ – when they are at school, when they are playing games, in fact whatever they are doing. All believers are part of church 24 hours a day, seven days a week.

In the beginning

Let's have a quick look at the first church. It was so simple: it was Jesus walking around with three or more of his friends. He would teach them, encourage them, pastor them, pray with them, equip them and then tell them to go to those who did not yet believe and put into practice what they had learned. After a while, they would come back tired and worn out, but with some amazing stories, so Jesus would once again teach them, encourage them, pastor them, pray with them, equip them and then send them out again. When Jesus ascended and Pentecost came, the church took to the road.

Notice that Jesus never planted any buildings. Although he began by speaking in the synagogues, he could never fix up regular meetings there, as some of his law-breaking followers – having been involved in violence or dodgy tax collecting jobs – would not have been allowed to enter, and Jesus himself, after a while, found he was unwelcome in such buildings.

So what Jesus began was a very flexible, forever changing and moving group of people, who were committed to him and to each other. Jesus never began a building campaign or initiated the weekly 10.30 a.m. and 6.30 p.m. Sunday meetings. Jesus also never tried to force people from different cultures to attend the same meeting. Never did he say to Nicodemus or Joseph of Arimathea, who were Pharisees, and in the top echelon of society, that to be a true believer they must join a cell group that has a new convert called Zacchaeus in it. The top Pharisees were not even allowed to talk to crooks like Zacchaeus – even if he was an ex-crook.

We may argue that Jesus' band of followers came from different culture groups and he encouraged them to stick together. And while Jesus was alive they did. We also know there was quite a bit of argument and debate among them, and we cannot be sure how close they really did become as friends, but we do know that after Pentecost many went in different directions. They never formed the 'Church of the Apostles'.

Jesus respected people for who they were. He wanted to plant church in all different cultures, not take people out of their cultures and form a new culture called church. We will look at that in more detail later.

Heavy duty

Over two thousand years have passed. Although our beliefs have hopefully remained true to Scripture, church bears little resemblance to what Jesus began. We have rigid buildings, rigid times and days of meeting, rigid orders of services and rigid freedom! I have met some evangelical and charismatic leaders who, in my opinion, are treading dangerously close to cult status. While they live in freedom, they have put bondage upon their people. Like the lord of the manor, with big houses and flash cars, they really believe they are superior to their congregations. Some even believe that the local Christian community should serve and obey them, and can bring great fear and guilt on their weaker or impressionable members who do not attend their meetings, cannot afford to pay their tithes, or even believe that they can find their own guidance for their own families.

Jesus died to set us all free, and we are all his servants.

It's go out – not come in

Jesus wants us to go out as church and collect people for the kingdom as we go, but nowadays our great aim is to try and entice the lost to a church meeting that often is irrelevant to where they are at. It's as though we have changed the parable of the sower so much that instead of us taking the seed from the barn to the field, we stand in the barn, waiting for the soil to make its way to the barn and grab its own seed.

If our church model is so different to what Jesus began, is it surprising that numbers of those attending meetings are falling so dramatically?

Joining up

Let me finish this chapter by talking about church membership.

Many consider that in the early church when a person was baptized, it was then that they were committing themselves to 'membership' of the body of Christ. Today, it's very different in most local churches. The qualifications usually are something like the following: you must be saved; you must be baptized; you must respect the leaders; you must abide by the local church rules and – you must be over 16 or 18. This is crazy. A child can become part of the kingdom when they are very young, but they cannot become part of the local church until they reach mid- to late-teens. Even in Old Testament days a boy became a son of the law at the age of twelve. It's not surprising many children do not stay on to become part of the adult church. Why should they? They never felt part of it when they were younger.

Christian children are keen to be discipled; they need to really know that they belong to a local family of God, especially because of some of the loveless home backgrounds they come from. They are our future. The football club knows that if its youth team feels a significant part of the club, they are going to have a loyalty like no other. Many of our children are more loyal to the local body and its leadership than many of the older members, yet their age stops them being accepted. Church meetings for members only, discussing future vision, mission work, new appointments, etc., is just the place where some of our young people should be if we really want them to get a heart for the local work. The things we are beginning today, our young ones should be bringing to harvest in the years to come – but it will not happen if they are no longer with us. What we are beginning now may end with us.

Some say that if a child's parents become members their children's names automatically go alongside them. But what about the poor child from the unsaved home? They feel even more alienated. Children are the church of today, and they should be made to know that they are part of that local church in every way and excluded from nothing. Who knows? There may be a little Samuel sitting in the wings, who may right at this minute have God's word for the local leaders. We may never hear what God wants to say if we don't give him permission and the platform to speak.

Maybe with the new millennium now started, it's time for

fresh and radical thinking on church. My little slogan is nearly out of date already: 'Kids are today's church, tomorrow's leaders.' I am already witnessing kids being today's church and today's leaders in some places!

11

Church for Children

The gospel according to Levi

In Mark 2 Jesus tells us about sewing new cloth onto old material and also about putting new wine into old wineskins. Before we continue to think about the old passing away and all things becoming new, let's examine these statements in a bit more detail.

First the cloth. We used to believe that Levi jeans were the only jeans that had a life of their own. Most other brands (apparently) would eventually end up by being practically given away in the charity shops as they grew old, faded and torn, but not original Levi's. The more scruffy and torn they became, the more they made their wearer feel sexy, modern and trendy, or so the commercials tried to make us believe. They went on to show us that Levi jeans were never thrown away: when their life eventually did come to a sad but predictable end, they were reverently buried to the sounds of a New Orleans jazz band.

That may be a load of sentimental rubbish, but the fact remains that many believed this make of jeans did seem to mature with age and tears and holes were sheer class. Me – I never claimed to be trendy. If I wore my Levi's and a hole appeared, I am afraid, like most things in this book, I chose to desecrate tradition and sew on a patch. But then came a problem. If I was to sew a new denim patch onto those classic faded Levi's, they may look good for a while, but once out of the washing-machine the cloth would stretch, and the new denim would be far stronger than the old. I would end up with a much 'holeier' yet a much less sanctified pair of jeans than I started with.

The new is costly

Maybe when we are thinking of our church meetings, it's time to stop trying to compromise and mix the old with the new. Maybe the old and new are incompatible. One is not necessarily better than the other, but the old must not be allowed to stop the new from happening. Historically, the new has always pushed through, but usually at great personal cost. In the fourteenth century, both John Wyclif and Jan Hus – and later, in the sixteenth century, Martin Luther and others – believed that it was not possible to patch up the abuses of the Roman Catholic Church of their day. The new had to begin.

In the eighteenth century John Wesley didn't patch up the Church of England – Methodism needed to be the new part of God's ongoing plan. Around that time, Robert Raikes decided to get a team to educate children outside of the established church meetings, and probably one of the greatest revivals for children began under the heading of Sabbath School. At the turn of the twentieth century, the Jeffreys brothers and others saw the need of a new cloth to allow the public manifestation of the supernatural gifts found in the book of Acts, and along came the Pentecostals.

The church has known constant change over the years, and though not all of it has been inspired by God, and not all of it has proved to be good, constant change is very important. To be involved with bringing in the new can be very costly. For the heroes of old, it meant losing their friends and families, their reputation, and for some, ultimately, their lives – that's what it means to follow in the footsteps of the Master.

Getting rid of the real enemy

We know that the scribes and Pharisees in Jesus' day thought they were doing the will of God by sticking rigidly to the rules, laws and traditions. These people were full of religion.

Every generation has seen these sorts of people thinking they were led by God, but actually involved in doing the opposite. They seem to exist to hinder any new thing that God wants to do. I am not talking about any new idea that *man* has, but about those things that *God* wants to do. The way they do this is by stubbornly defending traditions, and verbally persecuting any who dare defy them.

I believe that some of these modern-day Pharisees have now infiltrated church life and can be found seated in some of our gatherings today. Without doubt, something is hindering the advent of a real revival. In my opinion, one of the main oppositions facing the ongoing church today does not come from outside the church, but the enemy is within, and can be found in those who are dogmatically trying to stop the old from going and are refusing to let the new come. Hatred, anger, immorality, drunkenness and violence are not our biggest enemies. Religion always will be, just as it was the influence of religious people that put Jesus upon a cross.

So perhaps instead of continually condemning the obvious, I think it may be time to aim our words at the real enemy and try by the grace of God to lovingly get some of these religious attitudes out of the church. This, however, is a very hard thing to do, because many of the most modern and 'lively' churches have already allowed religious tradition and legalism to become part of the foundation of their faith.

New skins for new wine

Are we going to spend the rest of our days trying to patch up a children's work which in many cases is just copying a 200-year-old model, and which is losing hundreds of children from our numbers each week? Or are we going to spend time asking Jesus what the new is and then lay our lives on the line to help see it come about?

In the days of Jesus, wine was kept in leather skins, not bottles. The new skins were very flexible, and they needed to be, because the new wine was still fermenting and the gases put massive pressure on the skins. The older the wineskins, the more hard and inflexible they became. To put this volatile new wine into a rigid old skin would mean disaster. A minor explosion could easily happen, causing both the wine and the skin to be destroyed.

I think very few of us would question that today is a day of new wine. The Holy Spirit is flowing freely in all denominations, but that has not always been the case. The pioneers of Pentecostalism, the Jeffreys brothers and their followers, knew persecution because they believed that Christians could be baptized in the Holy Spirit and use the gifts today, but along with the suffering they saw revival.

As the years went on, and as other denominations started to change their thinking, some Pentecostals seemed to assume they had exclusive rights to the Holy Spirit. When I was a Pentecostal pastor, older saints in my congregation often made it clear to me that they believed the Holy Spirit dwelt with us and not the other denominations in the town. Pentecostalism seemed to become a name for a denomination, instead of being taught as a powerful experience that was available for all believers from all backgrounds.

As the Pentecostal churches became less popular, the house church/new church/charismatic movement came into full flow, with people leaving their previous denominations to begin or join one of these exciting new groups. But alas, history continued to repeat itself. It was not long before many new churches became smug and superior, and acted as though the Holy Spirit really only attended their meetings. Many became exclusive and would not work with other churches in the area unless they were in charge. It was at this point, thanks to the late John Wimber and many others, that suddenly some of the sleeping denominations started to come back to life. For the first time in centuries, some experienced queues longer than a Disney fun ride outside their buildings, waiting to get in and be filled with the Holy Spirit. This was a shock to many, and now I find people leaving the new churches and returning to well-known denominations. And so it continues.

On reflection, it seems that any church or denomination that considers itself elite or superior, when thinking about the power and presence of God the Holy Spirit in their people or their meetings, will end up with moral or leadership problems, splits and divisions. Instead, humility and treating others as better than ourselves is a great corkscrew for those who want to really experience the new wine.

But where's the big bang?

Over the years, we have been excited by thrilling tales of revival. We have read stories of God in action on earth that have sent exciting shivers down our spines. The new wine seemed to be constantly flowing. So where is the great explosion from on high? It's like watching a firework that has been set alight but refuses to do anything but fizz. Obviously God is ready, but maybe we are not.

But when revival comes, what then? Following the Welsh revival, it did not take too long for the pubs that had been converted into Christian bookshops to be transformed back into nightclubs. The towns and villages, where sinners once were consumed by guilt and ran to a church building to repent, have long since drifted back into immoral pleasure-seeking strongholds. Although the wine was fresh, the skins were old.

In revival times, the lost experienced a brand-new life and a brand-new reason for living. Full of new wine and excitement, these new Christians had to become part of an old meeting structure with many legalist traditions. To 'be church' they were now told they had to become part of an old religious culture that not only had little relevance to the modern world in which they lived, but also had very little in common with the church that the Saviour who saved them began. They had to try and live the exciting new life of a Christian inside a dusty, rigid, old skin that had been handed down to them not by Jesus but by their religious ancestors many generations ago.

Let's remind ourselves once more: Jesus is the same yesterday, today and for ever. The Word of God does not change, but church, as someone correctly stated, is a living organism and not a dead organization, so it should be in constant change. When we come to children the same principles apply.

What's in a name?

In many local churches, we have what we have strangely named 'para church' meetings. This name is generally given to all meetings that are not directly overseen by the local church leaders. For most churches, Sunday school tends to be looked upon as part of church, but other children's meetings are 'para'. I am not sure what 'para' really means, but here are a few dictionary definitions: beside (church); beyond (church); resembling (church); defective (church); subsidiary to (church); informal (church); Yugoslavian monetary unit (church)... I think we can rule out the last one. Take your pick as to which one fits your situation, but I think we can safely say that whatever it means, it's something separate to what we call church.

We call our children's meetings: Pathfinders, Crusaders, Christian Endeavour, Boys' and Girls' Brigade, Kingdom Kids, Transformers, God's Gang, Lighthouse, Covenanters, Adventurers – and so the list goes on. In reality, as we see elsewhere in this book, if two or more children are gathered together to be with Jesus – even if no adults are present – we have church. We have no reference at all in Scripture to 'para' church meetings.

Our problem is that because we have named the Sunday meetings church, or even Sunday school, we consider all other meetings to be inferior to the big ones on the first day. Again, does the Bible or tradition teach this? When Jesus looks at all the various meetings going on throughout the week, and sees any age of people gathering to be with him, I believe he sees them all to be of equal importance.

Sadly, very few church leaders believe this. The Sunday meetings, which they are often leading, are unquestionably portrayed as the most important meetings of the week and the ones everyone should make their priority to attend. This thinking has penetrated our children and youth leaders. Their agenda is to give the children a good time in the week and then to try and persuade them by every means possible to turn up on Sunday as well. It's not until a child shows a regular appearance on Sundays that other Christians will accept them as a true believer.

What is children's church?

Church is two or more Christian people of any age gathering together with Jesus. If our midweek clubs, whatever we are calling them, are not achieving this, then perhaps it's better to close them down. Some may be thinking that they would not dare to consider their children's meeting as church, because as well as teaching them about Jesus, they have a lot of sports and games. A lot of Jesus' life as 'church' was spent not just praying and singing but in eating, drinking and having fun with his friends. If footballs had been invented 2,000 years ago, I believe Jesus would have joined in and kicked the ball about with the children, too – perhaps not with sandals on, though!

We have thought for hundreds of years that one meeting called church on a Sunday will suit everyone from every background. We have thought that when people become Christians they also become 'all one in Christ Jesus' and end up identical in looks and behaviour. Because we all love Jesus, we assume that we will all like the same music, we will all want to meet together at 10.30a.m., and we will all like to be preached at for 45 minutes. Jesus changes our hearts and gradually our sinful lifestyle, but he made us who we are, and he made us all unique. We need different ways of being church – not just one way.

So church does not hinge around one or two meetings on a Sunday. Church and church meetings are taking place every day of the week. The question can then be asked whether, if children go to a church gathering that is especially suitable for their age group on a Friday, they need to attend on Sunday as well.

Of course they don't need to, but if they choose to come along, and enjoy it, they will want to come again. If the meeting is not appropriate for them, they will not enjoy it, and will not want to come again. I want children to really enjoy being part of church, and if this means that they just attend that Friday church aimed at them ... brilliant! Children can still be Christians if they never attend a Sunday meeting, but, like adults, they must realize that they cannot be a church by themselves – they do need to regularly meet up with those of like mind.

A leader's job is to bring church into the community, to reach as many different cultures in as many different ways people can understand as possible. Children's workers should be trusted and be given authority by their leaders to go and reach as many children for Jesus as they can, wherever, whenever and however.

Let's look at when we meet.

This the Lord's day

Sunday is traditionally known as the Lord's day. Why? Well, it's day one in the week, it's supposedly Resurrection day, and so on. More of its history in another chapter.

Most leaders would teach that this is the day when we should encourage people to rest, unwind, spend time with the family and hopefully spend time with Jesus. In the average congregation about 10 per cent of the people do all the work each Sunday, while 90 per cent come along expecting all the 'entertainment' to be ready and laid on for them.

For some children's leaders, this is one of their busiest days in the week. The schedule goes something like this: up early to make sure their own family have their breakfasts and get dressed properly; sort out lunch; rush off to the building; set out the chairs; get the visual aids ready; read through the teaching notes; check the songs, and then the children arrive. What follows is hopefully a blessed but often stressful one to two hours. Then the children go home and they tidy everything away again. By this time, many children's leaders are exhausted.

Rather than spending the rest of the day relaxing with family, friends and God, they either sleep or are grumpy and irritable with the family around them, bearing no resemblance to the spiritual and serene children's leader witnessed by the children just a couple of hours ago. Many can't wait for Monday to come around, so they can have a day of rest at work!

Nowadays, a lot of children's meetings happen on Sunday morning, to coincide with the adult meeting. Some children's leaders are still sadly treated as babysitters. If that is all they are doing, I suggest the parents pay them at the appropriate rate. Others see this as a good opportunity for training the children, who usually have Mum or Dad just down the corridor. To make the most of these meetings I suggest that whenever possible we should try and get the adult speaker and the children's speaker to speak on the same passage of Scripture. Of course, communication of the Scripture will be vastly different in different age groups, but at least when the members of the family eventually get home, each will know what the other has been learning and a good bit of verbal interaction can follow. If you have a children's meeting on Sunday, you will still need other days for evangelism and to build a closer friendship with your children.

Building relationships

As children's leaders, our main aim is to build a relationship with the children, and as we do this they will begin to open up to us and start really listening to what we are sharing with them. I could never build a relationship with my own children if I only saw them for one hour a week. We need to know all our children by name, as well as their favourite football teams, hobbies, and so on.

I once visited a large private school, where many of the children were boarders. Over the summer period, every member of staff had pictures of the children who would arrive the next term, plus details about their interests. When the child eventually arrived, feeling very insecure as they watched their family disappearing down the driveway, they soon noticed that every teacher knew them by name and was able to converse with them on subjects that were relevant to them. To be recognized and have people know your name brings in a lot of security and is a great way to develop a relationship. If school teachers feel it right to dedicate that much time to welcome hundreds of new pupils each year, how much more important is it that we really make time to know the children who make up our church?

But the big question still follows: Is Sunday the best day to hold our meetings, when we have seven days to choose from?

Choose the best day

Wherever Jesus went, he seemed to fit his meetings around where the people were, or become part of what they were doing. Nowadays, all ages, including those who are not yet saved, have to build their lives and their Sundays around us. We tell them when we meet and if they can't make it, it is hard luck on them; they will be the ones who will be missing out. We will not change our meetings to fit in with their timetables.

Sunday is a strange day, especially the morning. Have you noticed how even the busiest city street is quiet before the shops open at 10.00? People walk everywhere, instead of running, for just a few hours, and life slows down a little. I can go for a walk on a Sunday morning, and it is the only time that people will actually stop and enjoy a conversation without forever looking at their watches. The time when people are willing to talk just so happens to be at the time when there are no Christians around to talk to them. Why? Because we are all in our meetings.

Each sunny Sunday, we glance at our next-door neighbours sitting relaxed in their garden, drinking coffee, while we rush past them, screaming at the children who do not want to get in the car and go to the meeting. I believe there are more arguments in a Christian home on a Sunday than any other day of the week. I wonder if we had our meeting on another day, or at another time, we would not only feel more relaxed as families, but also get many more opportunities to share the good news of Jesus with people who are willing to listen. Some might say that there is still Sunday afternoon, but I'm sorry – by lunchtime the momentum has built up again. The shops are buzzing, the streets are crowded and the world has got back into top gear.

Finally, on Sundays, it really is the very worst time for children's meetings, as it is one of the main times when children from broken home situations have a chance to visit their other parent. We should never put the child in the position where they have to choose between a meeting and a parent.

Let's start using other days and nights. Someone told me recently they moved their children's meeting from Sunday to Friday and attendance trebled instantly!

The rich and the poor

It's not always advisable to put middle-class children from Christian backgrounds together with estate kids, and that is not because one group is superior to the other – they are all needy kids, but they do have *different* needs. Try and plant two separate children's churches, one being in the community hall on the estate.

A friend of mine called Bill Wilson has the biggest Sunday school in the world, centred in a very needy area of Brooklyn, New York. Bill and his team take children by bus to a large venue and hence this mega children's church thrives. The team also visits the children's homes on a very regular basis. Many around the world are adopting this model, which is great news, but please remember two things. First, Bill Wilson is not a method, he's a man of God who has given his whole life over to make sure this succeeds, and at immense personal cost. It's not just buses, drivers and workers willing to put a few hours aside each week, but total commitment that is needed. My fear is that some will get very excited about a project like this, but after a while will find reasons why they cannot be so committed or will just want to move on to the next new thing and leave many children and families stranded and dumped. This is a brilliant evangelistic initiative, but it must be seen as a long-term project that needs a lot of prayer and planning and will build up over many years. Luke 14:28 is about discipleship, but I think it still applies.

Is there anyone here who, planning to build a new house, doesn't first sit down and figure the cost so you'll know if you can complete it? If you only get the foundation laid and then run out of money, you're going to look pretty foolish. Everyone passing by will poke fun at you: 'He started something he couldn't finish.' (Taken from *The Message*)

Second, don't forget there are also millions of children around us who are not neglected street kids. These kids from middle-class homes live their lives in front of a computer screen, and seem to be much harder to reach. I just pray that we don't all literally jump on the 'bus wagon' and forget about them. I have yet to hear of revival reaching these types of children, but I know I will soon – if we don't forget them.

Aim high, take risks

Many of us aim our meetings at the 'not so interested' element because we don't want to lose them, but by doing this we often ignore and don't fulfil the expectations of the children who really want to learn more. These children also need our attention. We need to organize special training programmes, as a lot of these children, within weeks not years, could be leading the meetings instead of us.

At one of our camps, where we had 300 ten- to twelve-year-olds, I tried this out. First of all, we invited any of them who wanted to be part of our prayer ministry team to arrive at the tent 30 minutes before the meeting, to give us time to pray over them. Then, on one evening, when everyone else had arrived, I asked all the children to stand in horizontal lines right down the tent. Leaders and the newly appointed prayer team just walked slowly up and down the line praying for the young people. There was only one rule: none of us was allowed to stop walking, as I was teaching them to pray not just as individuals but as a team. By the time we reached the far end of the tent it was like a battle-field – bodies everywhere, as the Holy Spirit had touched them.

One lad, who was not a Christian, didn't have a clue about what was happening. One of my leaders explained as best he could and then asked the lad if he would like to be prayed for. He argued that he was not a Christian, and my leader responded by telling him that it didn't matter; God wanted to show his power and presence to everyone. After a few words of prayer, the boy fell to the floor and stayed there for ten minutes. When he eventually got up, he was rather dazed and wondered what (or who) had hit him. The leader explained afterwards, and rather than rushing in with the evangelistic appeal, he wisely told him to go back to his tent, think about what he had heard and experienced, and come back the following night to let him know his thoughts. The following night, he came back and gave his life to Jesus.

I feel it is sometimes good for people to see and experience the power of Jesus before they choose to follow him. I was once in a very rough area and had a lot of young lads who did not like singing and seemed to have no interest in anything that either I, or God, wanted to do. Putting the guitar down I called the leader of this little gang over and told him that I was going to pray for him. Amid all the giggles, he walked forward. After a few seconds of prayer, he called out to his friends to come over and be prayed for. 'It's weird,' he shouted. 'When this bloke prays for you, you get a really strange feeling right down inside you.' They, too, allowed me to pray for them. None got saved that night but they left knowing that prayer was not just words.

After praying for our 300 ten- to twelve-year-old campers, we still had sports and activities outside the tent, but we left a prayer team inside for any who wanted prayer at any time. There was a constant flow of those wanting to be prayed for, and after prayer they would return to their games. I wonder if they played a lot better? We never told them that to be prayed for was more spiritual than enjoying their activities, for on this camp both were important, and I believe that Jesus was enjoying both of these along with the children. It did prove to me, though, that we really are living with a very spiritually hungry young generation around us. Let's make sure that the children who are spiritually hungry get filled and not put all our energy into those who as yet have only a very small appetite for the word of God.

The preach

I come from a background where I am used to silence when someone is giving a talk, and when I was at school I was taught that any noise would be a distraction to my work when studying. Nowadays, children live in a world full of sound and noise. There are very few places where you can live and not hear the constant sounds of cars, buses, lorries, trains or aeroplanes. Even inside the home, many children need to have a television on, or music playing in the background, while they study, and their results are proving that for some this breaks all the old silence rules and does seem to enhance their work.

With this in mind, when preaching to older children, I sometimes have the band playing quietly all the way through my talk. On one occasion, the drummer just gave the rhythm of a heartbeat while the talk took place. Did any of these background sounds detract from the message? Far from it. We have seen amazing responses after these meetings, and the children even seem to remember a lot more of what was said than if they had tried to sit or listen in silence. Some were actually a lot more distracting and distracted when it was quiet. Try it – believe me, children actually can do more than two things at once.

An idea

Everywhere I go, people complain that they do not have enough people wanting to work with children, or enough resources, musicians, and so on. At last, some denominations are losing their superior attitude and beginning to see that the local church does not consist of just those who sing and pray under their roof, but is made up of all believers in their area. Although it's good to feel a commitment to a local group, we need to learn that it's part of God's plan to help to resource those around us who may not have the gifted people that we have.

Here's an idea that may work in some areas on Sundays. First of all, hire a venue that is not linked with any local church, for instance a school. Children's leaders from all participating denominations can pool their gifts and resources, and work together to give a really good meeting for the children. The parents can drop off their children and then can go and enjoy their meeting in their own church gatherings, returning to collect their children about an hour or so later. This way, children's leaders from all different backgrounds can enjoy working together, and it takes a lot of pressure off the Sunday. While the adults can still enjoy the style of meeting they are used to, the children get the best resources that are available in their area. Midweek children's meetings can be held back in the smaller local church groupings.

The best meeting of the week!

The timing of a meeting for children in the church need not be dependent on the length of the adult meeting. I believe that having the same set time of meeting every week can in itself become very boring. Have you ever considered not shortening but lengthening it? I was recently with a church where the children's meetings started at 10 a.m. and finished at 4 p.m. We had three 45-minute praise sessions that included teaching, interspersed with outdoor games and indoor crafts, and of course a picnic lunch together.

I think children get fed up because we are so predictable, especially on Sundays. When they arrive, they know that they are just going to sit and listen for the duration. Let's include indoor and outdoor activities, and expand our programme lengths.

Summer club every week

Have you ever considered why summer clubs are so enjoyed while Sunday schools are not, even when you have usually got the same people leading them? One reason is that we have managed to kick religion out of the clubs, but we cannot get it out of our Sunday meetings. To make them non-religious means that we are still going to teach the children about Jesus, but, as we did in those summer clubs, we will also have treasure hunts, competitions, teams, and we are really going to make a great day of it. Will it take a lot of hard work? Of course it will. So if you really are going to commit yourself to working with children, please don't take on any other responsibilities in church life – you just will not have the time.

In brief

- Look at the children around you.
- See the different groupings.
- Find the best time, day and venue to hold your meetings.
- Whatever you call your meeting, and whatever day of the week the children attend, keep reminding those who belong to Jesus that they are part of his church and this is a church meeting.
- Try to get out of the mindset that Sunday meetings are more special than weekday ones.
- Make extra time to teach and train up the new young leaders.
- Let them know the power of God in everything they do.

12

Church for Different Cultures

Stretching the wineskins

But why should we stop with just children's church? If we really are going to be relevant to the different cultures around us, maybe we should have many different meetings and give people the choice as to which one they want to attend, and also which one is most relevant to their unsaved friends.

The youth skin

As I write, we have a very successful youth church in Chichester, run and overseen by young people. Its early days began in our local university. The president of the Christian union felt that his job was not just to arrange meetings for Christians; he felt that the union had to be relevant to those who were not yet Christians. So he arranged all sorts of events, which proved to be more successful than those being organized by the official student union. As his reputation for good organization grew, so did his influence, and in a matter of time he changed roles and was elected president of the student union.

Now this newly appointed president also happened to be a member of our local church, and it seemed common sense to him and the youth leaders to use his influence to plant a youth church in the university itself. The ideal venue to hold the church meetings was in the student union bar, and the best time to hold it was Sunday night at 6.30p.m. Unlike most churches that have chosen this time so the congregation can finish their tea and be home in time to put their small children to bed, the youth church chose it because 6.30 was happy hour – which meant that the half-price drinks would ensure there would be a full turn-out of students at every church gathering.

They used rock bands instead of organs, and discos instead of choirs, plus modern dance and expressive drama, and, due to the anticipated verbal abuse and heckling during any sort of preaching, all talks would be finished in a matter of minutes rather than hours. A strange service in an even stranger environment, but young people became Christians through it.

The new Christians were very quickly added to a youth group or cell, where they would be trained up by other young people in the ways of God. This worked well, because church came to the youth culture, and the young people were spared from having to go to a church building and fit in with old rules and dress codes. They could enjoy their sort of music and people, and hear the teachings of Jesus in a non-threatening environment that they felt at home in.

The icing on the cake was that they never lost their unsaved friends. Many think that the expression 'leaving the world behind' means leave your culture, dump your friends – and even parents, if they are not Christians – as all these things may be a bad influence and drag you down. From now on, you build your whole life around the nice Christian family we call church.

This is not what Jesus taught. He said leave your sin behind, stay in relationship with other believers, but also stay in the world and be salt and light in it. Some Christians I know never want to have anything to do with the unsaved. All their friends are church people – even the electricians, plumbers and builders they use are members of their local church. They live as though contact and friendships outside of Christianity will taint them. Being part of church helps us to stay spiritually strong and equips us to be shining lights to our best friends around us, who may still be living in a dark world.

Youth church is for youth

So a youth church will normally meet at later times, the volume will be louder, the lighting will be darker, and the meeting will not be so much a sit down and listen event; it will be more of a flowing in and out event. Remember, many wanting to attend will be addicted smokers, so if they disappear outside the building every now and then, it may not be because the talk has upset them.

I visited our youth church just a few weeks ago and was told I had the choice of two different styles of music to help enhance my praise. I started in the main auditorium where an excellent band played, but I (of all people) felt that after one song it was time to move on, as my ears found it so loud I was scared of becoming deafer than I already am. With this in mind, I entered the other hall, where they were using DJs and decks. Here I lasted even less time, as the pounding bass of the dance tracks made my head and stomach feel they were not attached to the same body.

At this point, it's usually time for us oldies to complain, criticize and say, 'What a waste of time all this noise is,' but I would never dare do such a thing. I've just got to face facts: I'm too old for youth church; I realize this style of meeting is not for me, but I also realize it can be just the answer for many of today's generation. It was wonderful to look around in both these halls and see young people who would normally be drunk, doped up or worse, praising Jesus. The main aim of the youth church leaders is to present the biblical message of Jesus by using visual and creative methods to those who have no idea – or the wrong idea – of what Christianity is all about.

I have been in churches where it is announced that the youth meetings are for anyone aged 9 to 99. It's little wonder that only the 99-year-olds turned up. Praise God those days are gone. Youth church is for our youth to reach the youth.

Accountability

Youth church does need an accountability to older leaders, who will probably never attend the actual meetings but will have constant access and input to those leading it. In the past there have been some horror stories where this has not happened, but let's not write off the whole concept because of the few mistakes. Let's learn from them, correct the faults and allow this wineskin to develop under the leadership of our godly young people.

Release them

Although we do a lot of talking about releasing the young ones to get on and lead, many older leaders find giving over this responsibility very hard to do. They feel that they must oversee and attend every meeting, and sadly often end up as being corks in the bottles. We must trust our young people, and even allow them to make mistakes.

In Victorian England, an eleven-year-old boy enjoyed reading theology books, and at 15 he was preaching in churches. At the age of 17 he was pastoring a church and by 19 it was the largest church in England. For 30 years, he preached every Sunday to crowds of around 10,000 people. Charles Haddon Spurgeon was special, but not unique. I believe there are many more young Charleses waiting to come through, but the older generation so often chooses to block their way.

What other culture groups are there?

The student skin

Although our youth church began by meeting in a university, it was open to all young people. A short time ago, I spoke at our student church. This was very different from the club culture church just mentioned. We sat in a room above a coffee shop, and while we all drank wonderful, real coffee purchased from the cafe below, I spoke. This was a meeting where music definitely was not the main attraction: talk, debate and interaction, plus a constant pilgrimage downstairs for a 'top up' were the important ingredients.

The more regular Sunday meeting skin

Although some churches I know choose not to meet on Sundays, preferring to have their meetings midweek, to leave Sunday free, it goes without saying that there is a place for a Sunday church meeting for those who feel this is the best day for one of their gatherings. The only problem with this is, as we saw earlier, many have made this meeting the superior one. So people are left with no choice, and many from different ages and cultures will never choose to attend this type of meeting.

At home, we do have meetings most Sundays, but tend to alternate the timings of them. It's sometimes in the morning, sometimes in the evening, but never both. When the meetings are in the evening, this allows those who want to have a 'lie in' to rest on in peace, and many Christians seem very appreciative for that extra bit of sleep.

Because of the time and day, this meeting is mainly supported by Christians who prefer to sing along to more 'Simon and Garfunkel' style praise, rather than club or rave music provided by the youth church. In the evening, we are not pushed for time, and we are more free to minister and pray, and may spend longer in meditation.

Nearly all the children attending will be from Christian back-grounds and will be taken out and given a special meeting of their own, which seems to be the norm for Sunday meetings in most local church gatherings. Some tell me their children stay in for what is referred to as the 'praise and worship time', to which I always reply, 'Yes, but do they?' When they say, 'Do they what?' I ask them 'Do they praise?' In other words, are they 'worshippers' or are they just playing with their watches, totally uninterested and desperate to leave and go to their own meetings?

So often, the music during this time is not geared for children, as many musicians I have met hate playing children's songs. They somehow feel these songs are embarrassing, and beneath them and their musical capabilities. Why are the children there if the musicians refuse to give them what they need and the children are hating it? My advice is either change your musicians, or their attitudes, or don't drag the children into an adult meeting at all. Let them stay in the hall and enjoy praise songs that have been written with them in mind. If you have no musicians, it's just as effective to use CDs with backing tracks. I use them all the time, so I know they work.

Bible study skin

There is also a great need for Bible teaching. At most of our different meetings this teaching is very simplistic, so the youngest Christian attending can understand what is being said. Sadly, the real thinkers and students, both old and young, are very rarely allowed or encouraged to get to grips with the true depth of the word of God. They are never trained up to be Bible teachers unless they attend theological college.

Another meeting we could hold, therefore, is an in-depth Bible study which is led by a Bible teacher rather than a preacher, to train others up. Here we could discuss the various viewpoints on creation or the end times, and search the Scriptures together, even though we may not conclude with a dogmatic statement. We have a lot of studious children and young people who have no ambition to play the guitar or drums, but would fit very well into this training group.

Senior citizens skin

How about our more elderly saints? Do we really expect them to behave like born-again teenagers and enjoy dancing around to the modern songs? I am old enough to remember the evolution of church music over the past 40 years. It started with hymns being sung in church meetings and children's choruses being sung in youth groups. Then, in time, special 'after meetings' were arranged. Here, at 8.00 p.m., anyone with any life in them would gather for an hour just to sing short songs known as adult choruses.

As new churches sprang up, led by people who had left the traditional denominations, some put aside the old hymnal as they discovered *The Redemption Hymnal*, which the Pentecostals had been enjoying for years. They thought it wild and radical, as it contained some very lively tunes reminiscent of old drinking songs. With new church came new songs – thousands of them – and it wasn't long before the old hymns were becoming unfashionable, and they were dropped, along with the hymn books that had now been replaced by the overhead projector.

Today, many new songs have become longer, more complicated and certainly less tuneful than many of the old hymns, yet the old hymn has not made a comeback and is very rarely sung in the majority of the new churches. Now some of our senior citizens are 'on fire' for God, but do not wish to be young and trendy. They love the old hymns, which they consider have a lot more depth and content when compared with the modern 'nursery rhymes'. They also enjoy the more formal, gentle, quiet meeting that only lasts for an hour.

But few modern churches allow older people to be older people. So often the attitude portrayed is that 'if they don't fit in and like the way God's shown us to do things here, they ought to leave and join that traditional old church down the road where they *would* fit in'. This is nonsense. If we make room for a youth church, we must also make room for an older people's meeting, where they can invite their friends. If young people cannot fit into our traditional church culture, we are wrong to imagine that all older people are going to fit into a middle-aged church culture.

I have met many leaders who have made disparaging comments about their older congregation just because they cannot or will not appreciate the modern trends that they are trying to integrate into their meetings. Yet, having talked to some of these wise old 'stick in the mud' saints, many of them have better attitudes and seem a lot more godly than their leaders.

This age group enjoys meeting fairly early on a Sunday morning. So let them have the traditional church gathering time. We have six-and-a-half days to fit all the others in. Remember, although these are older people who are literally living in an older skin, they can still enjoy the new wine. It is as hard for the older ones to change their traditions and understand our so-called modern meetings as it is for our modern leaders to change their traditions and understand that meetings do not *have* to be on a Sunday, do not have to last for three hours, and young people need releasing not repressing.

Good old mums skin

My mother is part of the same local church as a popular, but also very loud, band. She is getting on a bit. She is even older than me, and being an evangelist she knows that even though she personally loves modern music, some of her older friends will not appreciate the loud sounds and the rhythmic music. Under the direction of the leadership, she now has church on Thursday mornings in different ladies' lounges. Scripture is read and discussed, prayers are prayed, and of course a lot of tea is drunk. Yet another new skin and yet another church gathering.

Different coloured skins

One time when I was in Germany, I was enjoying myself speaking to a group of white middle-class Christian adults, and became very distracted by a wonderful smell invading my nostrils from another part of the building. While having a coffee break, I asked my translator where that wonderful smell was coming from. I was then told that the Sri Lankan refugees also used another room in the building for their meetings, but it is cultural for them to eat curry at each of their meetings. That really is a culture I could get into!

I remember that wonderful aroma proved to be a temptation that had to be yielded to. I finished my meeting quite abruptly, crept discreetly into their room, and, hoping not to be noticed and forgetting my skin was bright white, joined them in praising God – then joined them in eating the most wonderful curry. It's not surprising that our Sunday meetings never touch the Asian culture surrounding us. All we have to offer at the end of our meetings are economy biscuits and cheap instant coffee. If we want to reach different nationalities and cultures we may need to get the curries out after each meeting . . . or maybe we really believe that when their lives are changed, Jesus will also change them into coffee-and-biscuit Christians, like us.

Cell skins

A cell is a small group usually made up of no more than a dozen people that meet weekly. There are children's cells, youth cells, adult cells and some churches are successfully running all-age cells. Whether a cell group sticks rigidly to the four 'Ws' mandate (welcome, worship, witness, word), or is just a new name for a house group that has been going for years, for some boys, girls and adults this is their favourite type of church meeting.

Not everyone likes to meet in large crowds; some prefer the smaller, intimate grouping, where it is more informal and can be a lot more friendly. Others, of course, love a large gathering but don't enjoy the smaller one. The cell group is still looked upon as just a midweek meeting and not real church. That is why everyone is still expected to attend real church on Sunday. Jesus is present with those two, three or twelve gathered together. In this group they are taught, they pray, they praise, they share, they even eat and drink together – in fact in many ways it is much more like the church that Jesus started than the Sunday meeting.

I wonder why they are not allowed to choose between this and the Sunday meeting if they so desire? Many would choose to go to both and some wouldn't, but surely we should respect these choices and not treat people as 'not so spiritual' because they don't like a certain meeting. No one should be bullied, forced or manipulated to go to a meeting. We go because it's our choice and we want to.

To sum up: new skins; lots and lots of different skins meeting on different days and at different times; choices galore; people attending as many or as few as they choose; but somewhere in all these different skins is one that each person will fit into, even those who have just become Christians. The Sunday morning is not the main meeting or church, all these meetings are as important as each other, and all are church.

If we believe this, it will be like the church has exploded: church will reach many communities and cultures, being sent out from a central base. Many leaders believe in church planting but fail to see any they have planted. Maybe they should take another look at all the other meetings they have going on all around them throughout the week – I think they may be pleasantly encouraged.

How about the skin overseers?

I know the big question will arise over the issue of who is going to lead all these meetings. Well, of course, many are already doing it, and doing it well. Where there are gaps, new leaders will need to be trained up and older ministries released. It is not going to put a lot more pressure on the already overworked full-time worker. Out of the 90 per cent spectators who attend our meetings, we must be able to encourage some to lend a hand and take up some responsibility.

An overseer's job is not to run, organize or even try and attend all these satellite meetings, but to oversee the leaders they have commissioned to go into all their worlds. Because these leaders have been trained and trusted, they must be given a freedom to develop the church as God shows them. However, they must stay accountable for personal input, advice and protection. Overseers and leaders need to be good friends and meet together regularly.

All this does leave two big questions. Could there be a time when all the church meets together? Of course, we could have a monthly 5.30 p.m. Sunday meeting, where everyone is invited, although we know not everyone will come for various reasons.

This would be a celebration, starting with music, followed by preaching and ending with prayer and ministry for those who needed it. Many children could attend this, but if they start getting sleepy, the parents can take them home. To force a child to stay who is overtired and miserable and is desperately crying out for their bed will not be a blessing to anyone.

More skins – less unity?

The other question is, 'Does dividing up the body like this take away unity and togetherness?' I personally believe that unity is not built at meetings. Most of the time everyone is on their best behaviour, facing the front, sitting next to family and friends they like. They avoid, or just say a polite hello to, those who, for one reason or another, they do not want to get close to – and a meeting is an easy place to hide from those you do *not* want to talk to. A meeting does not necessarily bring people closer together. Meetings are a small part of church life. One hour for some, a few hours for others, in a seven-day week.

Real church unity is found in socializing together. Age and cultural barriers stand out in meetings, but when we eat, drink and are merry together, these barriers are broken. Look at the Lord Jesus himself: every 'church' meeting he attended hardly brought people closer together, in fact they usually caused minor riots. I am sure he was quite relieved when he was excused from the synagogue, which was a place where he would never find unity.

I think if I had been given three years to save the world I would not have done it the way Jesus did. There would be no time for socializing, friendships, personal conversations or blessing children. I would be rushing around, panicking, feeling that I must preach my message 24 hours a day, seven days a week. Yet Jesus found time to make close friends, visit people's homes, eat and drink with groups and individuals, attend parties and weddings, because people were always more important than meetings. If you don't believe me, check out that Good Samaritan story once more. Even with the responsibility that Jesus was carrying, he knew how to enjoy life. I am glad that heaven is likened to a banquet and not one of our Sunday services!

Some of us are so busy preparing meetings that we never have time to sit down and really get to know people, but if Jesus did it, so must we. I have often sat with people who I know do not want to form a friendship; they just want to question, counsel or interrogate me. This is not the way to build a relationship, yet I wonder if that's how the people we talk to and consider to be our friends think of us.

Building friendships can happen on a small, intimate, family level, as you open up your home and invite different age and culture groups into where you live. You will discover in discussion that there will be aspects about church life where you will differ in opinion, but you will also discover that you have so much in common you can talk about and participate in.

This can also happen on a larger scale, as a church organizes treasure hunts, barbecues, times at the seaside, or the picnic in the park, and not just for the children or the youth – this is for everyone. It really is a time when all ages and culture groups can be together and a unity can be formed. The children play games with the youth, the youth talk about studies and work with the middle-aged, the middle-aged learn about life from the senior citizens, and the senior citizens listen to the stories of the children.

This can happen as you seek and find. If you want unity, you must be willing to put yourself out. Go and find where other cultures and age groups meet, then join them for a game of pool and get to know them on their territory. Don't always expect them to come to you. And remember, you are there to befriend people, not counsel them.

We call this side of things the social, and the meetings the spiritual, yet, as we have seen, the so-called spiritual lasts for less than one per cent of our week. Social and spiritual should all be spiritual, because we have been reborn by the Spirit of God. We need church administrators to organize days together. As with meetings, not everyone will attend all of the time, but many will, and many will also bring unsaved friends. Church unity does not come by 'attending meetings' together, but by having fun together and really getting to know and love each other.

To sum up

A meeting on a Sunday becomes meetings of equal importance every day of the week, and all stay accountable to local leadership. Many of us agree with church planting, but fail to realize it's already happening as different ages and different cultures are enjoying the presence of Jesus throughout the week.

A very important skin

You may have noticed I have deliberately left out one other skin that needs a very different sort of meeting, which very few seem to get right. I have decided to devote the whole of the next chapter to the family or all-age skin.

13

The Family Church

Definition of words

All-age celebration and family service are, to me, the same thing. In this chapter, I am not just talking about nuclear families; I am talking about all ages in God's family.

Hard facts

I wonder what happened to the family service – the time when all ages of the family could meet together to praise, worship, learn, and also enjoy each other's company. And I wonder if there ever really was such an event. Most of what passes as a family service today is not worth pursuing and has the smell of total disaster about it. Family services are often just adult meetings with the children's slot somewhere between the second hymn and the notices. After the smaller ones have sung the action song and watched the pastor cut his tie in half as a visual aid to his talk, out come the comics and toys because the rest of the meeting will be a total 'snore and a bore' to them.

In a survey I carried out with 300 ten- and eleven-year-olds, well over 50 per cent of them could not stand the family meetings, but 80 per cent really enjoyed the meetings that were put on for their own age group. In this survey, I also discovered that only one-third of their Christian parents would regularly pray or read Scripture with them; half of their church leaders never spoke to them as individuals, and 8 per cent had never been spoken to at all by any of the main leaders of the church.

Every week? Forget it!

The family service is the hardest meeting to organize, and to prepare an effective one takes many hours of thought, prayer and planning – far longer than the time it takes to prepare for what we would call a normal service. Twelve years ago, I would have been pushing everyone to meet weekly as families, because Jesus often set the example of keeping all ages together. As much as I still personally would love to see this happening, my eyes have been opened as I have travelled around, and I have had to have a rethink.

One of the reasons for my rethink is that I have noticed that no leader has anything like the power or all-age communication skills that the Lord Jesus had. If each week we saw the bread and fish multiply, the blind see, the deaf hear, and dead people come back to life, the children's comic would never be opened. Even if we only heard inspired stories about sowers, feasts, wandering sons, and buried treasure, again the toys would probably never come out of the bag we brought them in. Although many would claim that Jesus is present at the meeting, his presence is not quite as obvious to children today as it was to the children who listened to him in Israel 2,000 years ago.

Another reason is that I have observed very few leaders have the patience or even the desire to minister to all ages. When visiting speakers visit, how many want to spend time with all ages in the church and how many feel their gifting is just for adults, or just for youth and children? If the leaders do not have a real heart to keep all ages together, and are unwilling to change their normal programme and make it appropriate for the children gathered, the family service has little hope of ever fulfilling what it sets out to achieve.

A third reason is that, as I mentioned earlier, this meeting takes longer to prepare and organize than any other meeting, and few churches have the time to spend every week to make it the exciting and creative event that it should be.

Do it well, or don't bother at all

I would advise, without any hesitation, that if what you call a family meeting is really predominantly an adult meeting, please don't let those young ones (or, indeed, the old ones) sit and suffer each week. Give them alternative meetings to enjoy, before the leaders get into trouble with the Trades Description Act. As I have gathered statistics, I have discovered that this is the least popular meeting with children, and that makes me sad, as it's the meeting I most have a heart for.

Even if your children say they enjoy the meeting, ask them what they enjoy about it. Often it is not the songs, teaching and presence of the Holy Spirit; it's more the chat, kicking a football and messing about with their mates, while the adults ignore them and enjoy their time with the Lord. Now I am not saying this is wrong, but it does seem a bit of a waste of precious time, as this hour could be spent more effectively with them in their peer groups being trained up by people who really do care for them.

So if you cannot put on a family service well each week, for whatever reason, perhaps it may be better to put all your efforts into making sure that you can put a really good one on a little less frequently.

This is a very important meeting of the church

I still believe that children and adults need to meet regularly together, and that is why I spend most of my life ministering to all ages at the same time. But it's different for me, because this is what I have specifically been called to do.

Children will learn a lot by watching adults, and, as I continually try to prove, adults can also learn a lot by watching children. Let me give you some reasons: the children need to have a chance to contribute to the whole congregation, whether their gifting is musical, preaching or pastoring; they will learn more by being allowed not only to observe 'the experts' and how they do it, but also to work alongside them and be taught practically; the best football teams are the ones that have a youth training programme, which not only teaches the youth theory and how to play against other lads of their own age, but also gives them a chance to play against the first team and see the skills and the standard that will be required of them in the years to come.

Now I'm getting older, my body has demanded that my sporting life be changed from football to golf, and to be honest I get a greater satisfaction finding one lost ball that someone else has lost in a pond than I do in getting round 18 holes in less than 99 strokes. (This has no parallel to Jesus and the story of the lost sheep, by the way.) I have noticed this, however: I play my best golf when I am playing with someone who is very good. For some reason, this seems to lift my game, as I have to watch them and learn from how they play, and because they do not allow me to chat away, as I would normally when playing with someone at a similar standard to myself.

I wonder how many leaders realize that 90 per cent of all the future ministries that will be needed in their fellowship are already in their children's meetings. If they don't give the children the opportunity to blossom and develop, they will put all their talents into careers, business and making money, which in time could take their minds and hearts off God. Contrary to popular belief, imported adult ministries are not necessarily God's ideal, and not necessarily the best.

Example to those outside

I also believe that we need to be an example to a world which, on the whole, has lost its way regarding the family unit and in being able to communicate and befriend others outside its age and generation. Children and parents so often have little communication between them, and teens and parents have even less. Children are quite rightly encouraged not to talk to older people on the streets, because we live in a perverted age when people are roaming our streets with the sole intention of kidnapping our children and using them to satisfy their own evil lusts and desires. Not a day seems to pass without us reading or hearing about some maniac who has destroyed a young life.

In other places, however, we have the other extreme, where many older folks live in fear and cannot go out of their homes because gangs of children are waiting to mug and rob them. I'll never forget the time I was in Manchester doing a mission, and, as I went for a walk outside, I saw an uncontrollable mob of young boys and girls walking down the street destroying anything that got in their path. Later that evening, while we were praying in one room of the building, they crept in and stole the whole public address system, part of which happened to be screwed to the walls.

When I was in south Wales doing some street evangelism, I met some tiny children who, for the whole time that I was singing and talking, just stood there shouting the most obscene swear words that I had ever heard. In another venue, I remember doing the whole concert with the organizer not being present. The reason he could not attend was that he had spent the whole hour-and-a-half chasing a few older kids who had taken his car and were 'joyriding' around the building that we were in.

Tragically, the age gap in church life is following society's trend. The children, through what they have read, heard or been taught, fear and have little respect for older folk, while the older folk feel exactly the same way about the children. How many Christian meetings have you been to where the young and the old trust each other and enjoy each other's company? I'm afraid that at the majority of meetings I have been to, people either stayed with their own age group or spent time with those they already knew quite well. They certainly did not go out of their way to make new relationships with people from different generations.

It's common sense that if we always split the family up and keep the adults in one room and the children in another, it is not going to help this problem. Far from it: it is just going to widen the gap even further. We must have regular times when all ages of God's family can be together, so that they can be taught not only how to communicate with each other, but also how to love, honour, trust and respect each other.

Is the family service the answer?

Is just bringing all the ages together regularly really going to help? After all, most congregations do this either for a short time each Sunday morning or maybe for a whole meeting once a month, and the truth is that very little has changed. The simple answer is 'no'.

If we want to have a real family service, we must be willing to alter our traditions and change the whole meeting around, so that it is enjoyable to the boys and girls as well as the adults. I want the children to look forward to these times together. But are we willing to make the necessary changes, and are we even able to? Let me talk through some of the changes I've discovered that have been helpful. Please remember that very few people find change easy, and it will mean a lot of give and take and patience from the middle-aged and older folk, who should, of course, be the more mature.

Let's start right at the beginning on how things tend to be, but not necessarily how they should be. Here is a little, overdramatized fictitious story about a family, a Sunday morning, and a typical monthly family service.

The Crumbles

The Crumbles family are having breakfast. Well, when I say the family, that does not include Jimmy, because he, despite the numerous shouts of, 'This is the last time I am going to tell you,' from his mum, is still reading comics in bed. Talking about Mum, she, as usual, is trying to do 101 things at once. In one hand she has the potato peeler for preparing the Sunday lunch, in the other hand is the hair-dryer for drying her hair, and her mouth is full of cornflakes. It's true that a woman's work is never done, especially on a Sunday. I wonder if she believes that this is her day of rest.

Now Dad, on the other hand, spent five minutes at the breakfast table, but unfortunately his half-drunk cup of coffee has turned tepid and is rapidly congealing, due to the fact that he has been on the phone for the last ten minutes to Mrs Bloggins. She only rang up to ask for a lift to the meeting, but she has ended up relaying to him her life history, for the umpteenth time.

Darren and baby Sarah are, however, at the table, but Darren has just accidentally tipped the cornflakes all over the floor, in an effort to find the free plastic sword and sorcery model of the hideous hulk from hell, while Sarah is discovering just how far a spoonful of rusk will travel when flicked in a certain way with her spoon. Amid all the reigning chaos, they are trying to prepare themselves for the Sunday morning meeting, which is due to begin in half an hour.

Today is a very special day, as they have decided to try a different church meeting they have seen advertised: a monthly 'family worship' service, where all ages are welcomed. It's not that they don't like their own service or want to be disloyal; it is just that they feel it important to spend time enjoying God together as a family, but their leaders don't seem to see any point in holding family services. Anyway, that is not the burning question; the burning question is will they be ready in time?

The answer to that is, yes, albeit with much wailing and gnashing of teeth. Our intrepid family does manage to get to the building on time – well, ten minutes late actually – but, unbeknown to them, everyone comes late due to the fact that the leaders' watches are obviously always ten minutes slow and they always start late. On the doorstep are two very large men, whose mammoth-sized grins a Cheshire cat would covet. They are not minders, armed guards, sentries or bouncers: no, they are the welcoming committee.

Now, as to which member of the family they welcome first depends on whether the husband or wife is the obvious leader of the family. If in doubt they have made it a rule to go for the larger of the two. The only time this rule may get broken is if the lady is extremely attractive: then she would automatically get the priority. Different doormen have different welcoming customs: some shake hands, some embrace, and some even kiss, but they tend to only give their brotherly kiss to the good-looking sisters. These men, though, discover Mr Crumbles first and shake him firmly by the hand, booming out in loud voices those somewhat worn out words: 'Welcome, brother.' This means, of course, that the doormen don't know the Crumbles family name, and are too embarrassed to ask what it is, in case they have been before and they have forgotten it.

Then Mrs Crumbles gets a similar welcome. The warm welcomers have been unaware of the presence of any children, until one of them falls over baby Sarah's pushchair and the other treads on Jimmy's foot. 'Oh,' they exclaim, their smiles rapidly fading, 'we see you've brought the children with you. How nice.' Then, in true Crufts style, they go round and pat all three children on the head.

The doormen remind the children that they are about to enter the house of God, so they must be opposite to everything that God made them to be: that is, they must keep silent, sit still, and show no external signs of happiness or else they will be dumped back in the Sunday school cells where children really belong. Baby Sarah, though, is still banned. She is too young to be considered a member of the family of God, and anyway, a lot of money has been spent to soundproof a room at the back of the building especially for her age group. A sort of large fish tank window has been installed, so that all the parents are able to see their children crying without hearing them, and all the tinies are able to see their parents paying no attention to their screams and tears.

Once Sarah is out of the way behind closed doors, left in the capable hands of a retired spinster affectionately named Auntie Helga, plus a few teenagers who want to skive the meeting, the rest of the family creep into the cold building and find a spare hard wooden bench. Here they sit quietly, waiting for the leaders to enter from the closed door on the right-hand side of the platform.

All is quiet; you could hear a pin drop. The silence is only broken by occasional 'tuts' that echo around the room, as the odd mother tries in vain to smuggle an infant in, or one of the children present drops a pencil or whispers to his mum that he wants to go to the toilet.

Eventually the leaders arrive, and apart from the initial welcome, which includes a special hello to all the children present, it is hard to work out how this is any different from a normal adult service. 'Let us all begin by praising the Lord together.' This is hard for the Crumbles to do, bearing in mind the events of the morning so far. Dad is wondering if he has locked the front door of the house; then, when he convinces himself that he has, he starts wondering if he has locked up his car. Mum, meanwhile, is wondering if she has turned the oven on, and hopes that baby Sarah is not being too much of a nuisance. The boys are not so much worried about how the meeting is going to start; it is more important for them to know when it is going to end. For any of the family to switch straight into an expression of praise is an impossibility.

The first song is a favourite, but it contains the word 'resplendent'. As Darren tugs his dad's jacket and asks him what it means, he is met with a severe, 'Be quiet, Darren. Now is not the time to be asking questions like that. I will tell you when we get home.' What his dad really means is that he doesn't have a clue either, but when he gets home he will look it up in the dictionary.

As well as difficult words, the children are also faced with difficult tunes, and some of the songs even sound to them like they don't have any tune at all. Darren thinks this is another point worth bringing up, so he turns to his mum this time and asks her why the song has no tune. She replies that the tune is not important, and he should just concentrate on the words.

After some prayers, which seem longer than Samson's hit list, and the reading of what seems like Psalm 119 from the Amplified Bible, everyone sits down with anticipation as the children's spot is about to happen. 'And now,' says the leader, 'a special song for the children.' This is the most predictable part of the service. Everyone except the Crumbles knows that if hymn books are being used, they will sing 'All things bright and beautiful' and if they are not, it will either be 'How did Moses cross the Red Sea?' or 'Who's the king of the jungle?'. This is the one and only silly time in the meeting when people can be themselves, act like idiots and join in with the actions from songs that have very little spiritual content. The songs are introduced as 'oldies but goldies', but Jimmy, having sung them every week in his own Sunday school since he started, thinks that they would be better named 'oldies but mouldies'.

It is during this song that many of the older folk start to relax as they watch the children enjoying themselves. Some of them even start making funny noises, like 'Ahhh' and the odd one or two even manage a faint smile. But all too soon for the wrinklies, and not soon enough for some of the children, the song has finished, and the courageous few that adventurously stood up to do the actions are now told to sit down again.

A blackboard easel is ceremoniously carried onto the platform and a large board with green felt is placed on it. The preacher then comes forward to give a special talk to the children. He has decided on Zacchaeus as his subject, as he feels it is easy for the children to understand, and anyway the local Bible bookshop only had this story left in their flannel-graph section. Apart from Darren whispering that they heard this story the week before in their own Sunday school, old and young sit back waiting for the show to begin.

Sadly, a good adult preacher is not always a good communicator with children, as this preacher proves. As well as using long words, he has a boring voice and little personality. He does have a good sense of humour though, but again it is an adult sense of humour, and while the adults are, metaphorically speaking, rolling in the aisles, the children just look bewildered and wonder what is so funny. The only thing that appeals to Darren's and Jimmy's sense of humour, and gives them the giggles, is when the bits of felt keep falling off the preacher's board and go floating down to the floor, but Mum tells them that it's not funny and to be quiet and listen to what is being said. Being a good preacher, he sums up with three points at the end. Unfortunately he lost the children's attention a long time ago, so the points tend to fall on stony ground, as, by now, have most of his felt figures.

A short prayer for the children is the signal that the meeting has now finished for them. It may as well be the benediction. Out come the *Beano* and *Dandy* annuals, *Postman Pat*, and the special offer mammoth colouring and activity books. The children know that they have at least an hour to kill, and the sensible ones have come well prepared.

There is, of course, nothing wrong with what follows: more

long songs, more long prayers, another extra-long sermon, followed by more long prayers and a final long song. If a survey is held for the adults on what they think of the meeting, the honest ones will say that everything could have been a lot shorter. Those not so honest, however, will put any flaw down to the children being present.

As the meeting concludes, the Crumbles family pick up little Sarah from the collection point of the crèche. She is in a terrible state, having cried for Mum for the last hour, and even Auntie Helga's seemingly endless supply of sweets has not taken her mind off the fact that she wanted her mum.

On the way home, the two boys are irritable and start fighting. They have sat quietly for so long that they are desperate to let off steam. Dad tells them to behave themselves and reminds them where they have just been and what a good meeting they have just had. 'I thought it was boring, and I don't want to go back there again,' Darren and Jimmy say together, with such good timing that it sounds like it has been rehearsed.

Both Dad and Mum decide not to talk to the children about the family service any more; after all, it was a privilege for the children to be invited into the adults' meeting, and they convince themselves that deep down it was doing their children a lot of good. For the children's sake, they also decide it will be good to go back each month, and whenever Jimmy or Darren moan, 'Oh no, we're not going to that boring meeting with all those old fogies, are we?' the reply is, 'Don't complain; it's wonderful that we can go and worship the Lord as a family.'

Oh, and as for baby Sarah, she does eventually get used to Auntie Helga, but as she gets older she also needs ministry for rejection. Here endeth the story.

A typical family and a typical service? I hope not. Wildly exaggerated? I hope so.

Preparation advice

As I have mentioned earlier, if we are going to hold a family service and not the disaster you have just read about, it needs to be done well. Please allow me to give you some simple preparation advice.

1. Aim the whole meeting at the intelligence level of the seven- to eight-year-olds. Those under eight will be able to understand most of what you do, and those over eight will not only understand it, but in time will thoroughly enjoy it.
2. Encourage parents to sit with their children wherever possible and 'adopt' any left on their own. The meeting itself will not just be centred around blood families: everything that is done will be for everyone to participate in together, as this is a meeting for the broader family of God.
3. Unless the Spirit of God does something very special, aim for the meeting to last no longer than one-and-a-half hours. If the leader keeps his eye on the children, he will soon see when it has gone on too long.
4. If any babies get the shrieks, teach Mum or Dad to nip outside the door for a few minutes until the child has quietened down. In an emergency, the occasional biscuit or sweet works wonders, although this is only for extreme cases. I would tend not to encourage it, because the child can cotton on to the fact that every time he shrieks in a meeting he gets a biscuit. It doesn't take long for babies to learn when they can make a din and when they need to be quiet.
5. This is not designed to be a Bible study, and you will not have the time for great exegesis, and we all know that there are plenty of other nights in the week for that. Nearly all churches have midweek meetings specifically for deeper study for the adults. Sunday is still often the best family day, although sometimes the morning is not the best time to meet.

6. The offering: if the service is to be evangelistic, it is best to leave a box at the door, which both your regular adults and children will soon get used to finding. If, however, you choose to take up an offering, take it near the beginning of the meeting. Otherwise, the children's money will end up rolling all over the floor, just when you don't want it to.

7. Toys: you will need to teach your parents that certain noisy toys may not be suitable for tinies in a family service. Remember that what to you may seem common sense, to others is far from common and even further from sense. Define everything clearly – it saves a lot of trouble. Hopefully, in time the meeting will be so exciting that it will not be necessary for any toys to be brought at all.

8. Toilets: do ask the parents to make sure that the children have been to the toilet before you all settle down, then you will know that they can last for at least the next hour, if not longer, and the parents won't be trundling in and out of the door all the time with them. With small children and toilet training I understand this is difficult, but it is sometimes more thoughtful to the other people in the meeting if parents can sit at the end of a row, and their child wears soft-soled or quiet shoes, so that going in and out does not become a major distraction for the whole meeting.

9. Discipline: amid all the fun and noise the family service is not a mad house; it is a special time together. Parents need to be taught to correct their children, and no child should be left running wildly around the hall, especially not at the front and on the platform. There is nothing worse, or more of a distraction, when you are trying to sing or speak through the microphone, than to have little Jenny swinging from the stand, with her parents oblivious to or even smiling at your plight. This one requires a lot of patience; it will take the parents as long to learn their role and responsibility as it will their child.

I guarantee that in the long term all these hints are worth working at.

Ingredients of a family service

At one time I would have given a blueprint on the order of a successful family service, but I will not do that any more, as every leader needs to pray about what should happen in their meetings, and what creativity they should use. I will, however, give you just a few hints of what might be helpful to include.

1. As people enter, have some cheerful music quietly playing: a CD is fine because you do not want prayer or a song and dance at this stage; it's a time for people to mix and talk.
2. In the welcome, do tell everyone what time you expect the meeting to end. Parents need to know this. If you choose to continue to minister after that time, tell all those not involved that they are free to go and get some coffee.
3. After an opening prayer, it's good to mention the theme of the meeting, and give a Bible reading. Encourage different age groups to participate in the prayer and the reading.
4. If you are going to use music, and remember you do not have to have music at every meeting, sing some well-known praise songs that people enjoy singing. Often the musicians only play the songs they like, or the trendy ones of the moment. I suggest you put out a survey to all ages. Ask them to write down their favourite song and their least favourite song. This can be helpful in the selection process.
5. Intersperse praise songs with fun action ones. Don't have a chunk of more adult songs followed by a chunk of children's ones – mix them up well. With action songs, don't force all the elderly folks to join in: just allow them to smile and enjoy watching the younger ones.
6. During this time of singing, include some interactive activi-

ties to break up the age groups. I sometimes call out three people who have brought a Bible with them, three people who keep a diary or filofax, and three people who possess mobile phones. These would be children and adults. The Bible people read out their favourite Bible verses, the diary people tell us about their most special day this year, while the phone people tell us who out of all the Bible characters, except Jesus, they would love to have a one-to-one with.

7. I also may ask if anyone feels they are called to be a preacher, and look around to find a simple visual aid, like a towel or a candle. I then ask what Bible story comes to mind as they look at the object, and ask them to preach to us all for a couple of minutes using the visual aid.

8. You could also introduce a special guest. In our congregations, we have many people who work in uniform. Get your fireman, nurse, policeman, etc., to appear fully kitted-out and after giving them a big entrance, let the children ask them questions about their job. Then the leader can ask them questions about their faith. And, of course, you don't have to limit this to uniformed jobs.

9. You will need a brief Bible story with visuals. Maybe a drama or dance could accompany this. After a Bible challenge, which all ages need, play a quiet, reflective song, or gentle music to allow everyone for a minute or two to meditate and think about what they have just heard.

10. If you choose to have a family prayer time, make this creative. For instance, if you are going to pray about growing closer to Jesus, you could give everyone a sunflower seed to take home and plant as a reminder. Maybe the theme is sheep: wrap a piece of cotton round the children's wrists and tell them that as they look at it throughout the day, it will remind them that the Good Shepherd loves his sheep. Teaching about being a big family of God is a great time for everyone to make paper chains and link them all together,

and, as they are all linked together, to pray for unity. You can think of hundreds more I am sure, and there are books devoted to worship times. None of them need cost the church a lot of money, just a bit of thought.

11. The whole meeting needs to be fast-moving and informal: a meeting where people look at their watches and cannot believe that the time has passed so quickly. This meeting has plenty of time for smiles, which makes it very seeker-friendly.

12. Finally, remember God made you in his image and that means you are creative. This is the best meeting to allow your creative skills to run wild. Let me tell you about some of the creative meetings we have had.

Creative madness

At one meeting, the theme was hitting the target, using David and Goliath as our biblical story. Some of the artistic young people painted bits of Goliath on different cardboard boxes, so when they were all assembled on top of each other we had the full 3 metre giant. The children, with help, assembled him on the stage. It was only then that I saw that the very creative young artists, without my knowing, had put a blown-up photograph of my face on the box where Goliath's face should have been!

Then in walked three of the church's best golfers, all dressed like they were competing in the Ryder Cup, pulling their clubs in the trolleys behind them.

The congregation was divided into three, each with one of the golfers as their champion. The golfers each had three chances to chip a special light-weight golf ball about 4 metres in the air to hopefully land inside the box that made up Goliath's head.

It was a hard task. The crowds cheered, but only one golfer managed it, and the champion did a triumphant lap of honour while carried on the shoulders of the other golfers. I then spoke on hitting the target that God has for each one of us.

When the subject was laughter, I chose Isaac as my central character, because that is what his name means. We started by showing some very funny video clips and then some of the children mimed a dance to the very old but very funny song about the laughing policeman.

On Mothering Sunday, we had a quiz where we gave out sheets with photos of nine famous mothers, including Elizabeth Fry, Catherine Booth and Susanna Wesley. The mums in the congregation were given the nine names and had to put the right name by the right photograph.

Noah's ark is a great theme, but show the children exactly how big the ark was. Set the chairs out in the shape of the ark, and as people arrive they will spend the meeting sitting in the ark. This is harder to do if you have fixed pews! Then explain that the actual ark was ten times as long as this – or whatever measurement is appropriate to your building. Point to the ceiling, having measured its height first, and explain to the people how high Noah's boat would have been. This will show everyone visually just how massive Noah's ark was.

Artwork and clay can also be wonderfully used. Try taking your shoe and sock off and placing your foot into some damp clay. A tiny child then puts their foot inside your imprint. This gives a picture of the big and small, and the small being safe, surrounded by the big. While on feet, one of the most simple yet special activities is when some of the adults are told to take off their shoes and the children are asked to go and stand in the shoes of one of the adults. As they stand in the adult's shoes, the owner of the shoes prays over the child. Again, simple but very effective.

Before your family meeting, spend time with God: ask him to make you creative and to give you new ideas for communicating. This meeting really is worth making the effort for, and to do it well does take a lot of time and preparation. We mentioned cultural church in the previous chapter: should this be a meeting which everyone is encouraged to attend?

The youth

In my opinion, as with the other meetings, this is no more or less important than any of the other wineskins. It will appeal to some and not to others; it is for those who want to be there. I would, however, give it a real push for the teenagers to attend, for two reasons. The first is godly teenagers are the best role models for our children, due to the small age difference. This is the age group our children look up to, and teenagers need to know that they have a responsibility to help to train up their little brothers and sisters. The other reason is that some of the youth have never been cared for by a father and mother: they need the family church, and it will give them a security that they will not find at the youth church. Many will probably attend both meetings.

It is also ideal as an evangelistic meeting. I have noticed that the unsaved of all ages do find the lack of pressure to conform and the fun and informality of this meeting very acceptable.

It's a lot of work ... but it's worth it

I am sure that with perseverance you can make this the most popular meeting with all ages, but beware: you may have some or all of the following difficulties to face.

1. Leaders who want you to fit in with their normal order of service.
2. Older people who find children distracting and noisy.
3. Middle-aged people who want more adult songs and fewer children's songs.
4. Parents who do not want to be with their children.
5. Singles who feel left out.

6. Musicians who cannot stand playing children's songs.
7. One- and two-parent families who struggle to keep any control over their four children.
8. Teenagers who find it all too babyish.
9. Children who would rather play football.
10. Babies who just want to scream.

Well, who said it would be easy? After seven long walks, and some trumpet sounds, even the solid walls of Jericho fell down. Surely no churches are as thick as those walls – are they?

14

Ancient and Modern

Good news, bad news

When a child becomes a Christian, it is so often a case of, 'What do you want first, the good news or the bad news?' The good news is that the Bible teaches in 2 Corinthians 5:17: 'Therefore, if anyone is in Christ, he is a new creation; the old has gone, the new has come!'

The bad news is that the first time they join up with other Christians for a meeting they will discover that, although they are new creations, the old is still here and the new is not only yet to come but seems light years away. They will be taught that 'brand-new people' must not only learn about 'old time religion' but must also learn how to live in it.

Please hear me out: I am not for one minute saying that all trappings and traditions are wrong, and we should ban the lot of them. On the contrary, not only do many older folk enjoy them because of their upbringing, but they also find that they enhance their spiritual lives. The point I am making is, do we really need to inflict them on our up and coming generation of the twenty-first century? Traditions only become wrong when someone insists that nothing – not even God – can change them.

Ancient history

Let me put it another way: history is important to where we are now, and it is valuable to look back and see how the Lord has moved us on with the times, but do we really want to seem, to the average non-believer, to be living in the past and doing some very strange things, which are not going to bring them any closer to the kingdom and are not the essentials taught in the Bible? Are we not wasting our children's time by teaching them things that bear no relevance to the Bible and their society, when we could be teaching them things that do? Are we going to lose many of these children in their teenage years not because they don't want to be associated with the Lord and Scripture, but more because they don't want to be allied to religious traditions which they really have no desire to introduce to their unsaved friends? I expound my thoughts on this in other chapters.

Seven traditions

For the rest of this chapter I want to look at seven of our traditions. Some are biblical but sadly have become ceremonious and very difficult for a child to understand, and others are ceremonious which we have to make appear biblical but don't particularly want our child to understand.

My observations are that all of the following have produced questions by children, and all need to be talked through and clarified in a very simple way, to save them a lot of confusion later on in life. It is important, however, that we as adults also seriously think through the questions so that hopefully we will have some answers and definitions for them that not only make sense but are also biblical.

1. Dressing up

I always looked forward to being ordained because I knew that I was then entitled to wear a clerical collar. This is better known as a dog collar, or a ring of confidence. Apart from always enjoying dressing up, it also got me noticed and everyone recognized that I was a man of the cloth, even though wearing this did not necessarily make me a man of God.

In every religion throughout the ages the 'spiritual leaders' have always chosen to dress differently from Mr Average. There are two obvious reasons for this, the first being, as I've just said, so that they can be recognized as a spiritual leader. The other is the same reason that policemen wear varying numbers of stripes and different shaped hats, to show their rank and position.

To many children the church has become a joke, not because of who we believe in but because of how our leaders look. We know how the unsaved see the church: like a caricature of a short, balding man with strange spectacles and long robes covering a large stomach. We have become the impressionists' and comedians' dream, but personally I do not find it very funny, because at the end of the day they are not only mocking the odd vicar, they are subtly undermining our children's respect for the church and its leaders.

It is worth noting, as we try and explain the place of liturgical garb to our young people, that although the priests in the Old Testament may have worn it, the Son of God did not. He chose to look like a normal person, and that is why he so easily mixed with and related to ordinary people. Jesus showed both his leadership position and spirituality not by the clothes he wore, but by who he was.

It is also worth noting that the apostles, who became the early church leaders, never bothered about dressing up and looking different, but with all the miraculous signs and wonders going on you couldn't really miss them, could you? They also were easily recognized as men of God. I find it impossible to imagine Simon Peter, while in Rome, ever wanting to exchange his fisherman's clothes for lavish robes and a mitre. The popes that followed

Peter not only did not follow his example of dress, but many did not follow his example of humility and anointing.

It was when Emperor Constantine made Christianity a state religion in the fourth century that the religious wardrobe became available. I am sure it is more than just coincidence that at the time the church had become law and the initial fire was starting to be well-controlled the leaders started to look to clothing, not anointing, to portray their positions. I have always tried to teach children the truth of 1 Samuel 16:7 which was referring to a young boy called David: 'The Lord does not look at the things man looks at. Man looks at the outward appearance, but the Lord looks at the heart.' Clothes and position are not things of great concern to God; what is important is how much you love him, and that is shown in how much you are obedient to him. Although I have met a lot of children who feel that in time God wants them to become leaders, and who may well benefit from theological training, unless they change their minds with age, very few would want to enter a denomination where dressing up is obligatory. They too see it as unnecessary.

2. Bible translations and paraphrases

I was looking through some new children's books a short while ago and was amazed to see that in a brand-new edition, the scriptures quoted were in an 'olde worlde language' that had its heyday way back in the seventeenth century. When I asked the sales lady why that was, she told me she felt that it was vital to use this original, archaic language, so the children could see that the Bible was different from any other book. What a strange argument. Here we are talking about God-breathed, inspired truth that has lasted near enough since the beginning of time, but to make it stand out from other books it needs to be written in old-fashioned English.

When I was a young child, someone kindly bought me two books, one of the Old Testament and the other of the New

Testament, but all the stories were in colourful cartoon strip. I read those books time and time again, and am convinced that as a child they gave me a wonderful overview of the Bible contents, which I can still remember today. All I want is to see children reading and learning from the Bible. I am not too bothered which translation or paraphrase they use in their early years.

I was privileged to hear Dr Kenneth Taylor (who paraphrased the *Living Bible*) a short while ago, and was knocked out by seeing what a wonderful and humble man of God he is. I've read some reviews of the *Living Bible*, which hammered him and went as far as to say that a paraphrase like his could never be used by God. It was interesting to hear that the main reason it came into being was that his children found the Authorized Version and the Revised Standard Version hard to read, so he put the Scriptures into his own words in a way they could understand and appreciate. Now millions all over the world have benefited from its easy, readable style.

Don't misunderstand me; I am not recommending that every parent now tries to be a Bible translator, but reading Scripture to a child from any translation does not necessarily mean that it is doing the child good. The child, like Philip's Ethiopian eunuch friend in the desert (Acts 8), needs someone to explain what the words actually mean. At our wedding, when I knew that unsaved people were going to be present, I had to fight tooth and nail to get the minister to speak from the *Living Bible* and not the Authorized Version. That, I may hasten to add, was nothing to do with choosing a more accurate translation. It was just because it was his personal favourite version, which probably happened to be loose leaf and had his sermon notes in.

As I write, many teenagers are enjoying Eugene H. Peterson's *The Message*. It's great to see young people enjoying reading the Bible, whatever version they have chosen. Personally, as I've grown older I've found that I prefer to study from the New International Version. Likewise, with children, once they have an overall outline of Scripture from a paraphrase, they may prefer to move on to a translation for greater accuracy, with less browsing and more study. But again, don't expect them to go back to the 'thee and thou' translations, for two reasons: the first is that when they quote Scripture to their school friends, they need to use today's language to be understood; second, some of the modern translations are a lot more accurate than the 1611 favourite.

3. Denominations

God has made us all very different, both adults and children. We enjoy different ways of expressing our praise and worship; we hold different emphases on different scriptures, and we have different forms of church government. Children need to be taught that the church is a body of believers and not a denomination. I don't believe the Lord is too interested in whether we are Baptist, house church, Church of England or Brethren, but I know that he is interested in how much we love and honour each other. Please do not encourage children to think that your denomination is the best and has all the answers. Teach them that although there are differences, all denominations have strengths and weaknesses and need to learn from each other.

There are two very different church groupings near us and it is very interesting to note that some of the leaders' teenagers have chosen to join the other church, not because they didn't like their dad leading, I would hasten to add, but because they felt more at home with the type of ministry and structure of the other group. Their dads, being good leaders, didn't mind. They were just excited at the fact that their children were going on with the Lord.

As your children get older, don't tie them down to denominational loyalty, as this could be yet another way of losing them. Respect their differing views and opinions, even if their only motivation for change is that there are more people their age of the opposite sex at the other place. Just be thrilled that they are going on with the Lord and meeting regularly with other Christians.

4. Tithes and offerings

A child sits and waits as a large plate or a nice little embroidered bag is passed along each row, with two men who could easily be employed by Securicor standing at each end of the row, to keep the bag moving. Once the child has dropped the ten pence or two pence piece in, depending on how generous he feels, the two men walk to the back of the church until they get a nod from the leader at the front. Then, with a perfect sense of timing, they slowly and silently walk towards the front, with all the precision of the Grenadier guards on a good day. This twice-weekly ceremony is affectionately known as the 'march of the money-bags'. Here the money is prayed for, and that is the last time the child will see his ten pence or two pence piece. Where do children think it goes? Some believe that, as it has been offered to God, he literally comes down from heaven and takes it back with him.

Children need to learn about giving, but so often they only get the two extremes. One extreme is where people take no thought about money, because everyone seems to have plenty, so they give the smallest amount of change they have in their pockets. The other is where the speaker is practically in tears out at the front begging the people to give an offering so that he can provide his family with a Sunday lunch!

The big debatable question lies in whether tithing is still the principal to teach our children today. As a pastor, of course I thought it was a very important principle: after all, if people didn't give, my family and I humanly speaking would go without – and sometimes we did. But biblically it seemed that as all the tithes were brought into the storehouse, some of these would go back out to the needy people and widows and orphans. Today we are told to bring all our tithes into the storehouse sometimes just so we can build a bigger storehouse. When it comes to supporting the needy around us, it seems that has little to do with the tithes donated to the local church: the members then have to find extra money to help needy family and friends around them, or else face the wrath of 1 Timothy 5:8 and be labelled as worse than the unbeliever.

We must be careful that, just like the issue of the Sabbath, we don't try and combine Judaism and New Testament Christianity and just use the bits of Judaism we find beneficial. It also is not a very fair way of giving, as £10 from the person who only earns £100 is worth far more to them than £100 from the person who earns £1,000. Also, I know some people who proudly tithe their weekly income but don't feel that they need to tithe the large amounts of cash they have hidden away in investments and stocks and shares. Then it gets even more complicated when you are instructed to tithe to your local church, and any other worthy cause (that may be even more needy and desperate than your treasurer's bank balance) has to come out of extra giving on top of that. I know a lot of local churches have thousands of pounds sitting in their bank accounts that will not be touched, as it's being held back for a 'rainy day'. It's hard to tell people to tithe if that money is just going to sit in a bank collecting interest.

I have been approached a few times by people asking if and how much I tithe, insisting this is all part of accountability. I feel like telling them to mind their own business, as how I work out how much to give is between me, my wife, some very close friends who advise me, and God. I am not convinced this is something to be shared around with everybody. Maybe I'm just old-fashioned, but I'm a bit of a Matthew 6 person and don't want to tell people about my 'acts of righteousness'. I'm happy not to let my left hand know what my right hand is doing. I will stick with verse 4: 'so that your giving may be in secret. Then your Father, who sees what is done in secret, will reward you.'

Jesus and the New Testament hardly mention tithing, except when pointing out the hypocrisy of the Pharisees, so if it was no big deal to the early church, I guess we should not make it too big a deal today. Of course, giving to our local church is vital for its continued existence, but this should not be done under law, guilt and oppression. It should be done because we love our local body and trust our leaders. Many feel that to teach a legalistic 10 per cent is not the best way, or even the biblical way, to encourage giving. I think some stick with the 10 per cent rule because that, at least, means people are guaranteed to give something. If 10 per cent is not taught, I think that some leaders live in fear that their people will give a lot less, or even not give at all.

Tithing may not be a big deal, but giving away our money and possessions is a very important New Testament principle. To my mind, Jesus superseded the 10 per cent legalism by saying in Luke 14:33: 'In the same way, any of you who does not give up everything he has cannot be my disciple.' We cannot be a follower of Jesus without giving up everything, including our money, until it hurts and we feel the pinch. I teach children that in fact we own nothing, because when we gave our lives to God, we also gave him everything we own. God, though, has allowed us to have possessions and money on loan, which we are to oversee and be good stewards of. With this in mind, even children should be encouraged to sacrificially give away a portion of their pocket money, and also be informed regularly why their local church is a special cause to give their money to. Churches and leaders do not live on thin air, and as they are not only caring for us, but spending many hours with the local community, we have a responsibility to help support them and their families.

We are told in 1 Corinthians 9 that those who preach the gospel should receive their living from the gospel. In 1 Timothy 5 we are told that 'the elders who direct the affairs of the church well are worthy of double honour, especially those whose work is preaching and teaching'. The worker deserves his wages. So I guess if our elder is toiling hard we should give him twice as much, and if he is not maybe we should halve his wages! We must always be on the alert for God to tell us to empty our bank accounts, give away our stocks and shares and pass on to others some of our most treasured possessions. He often seems to say this to keep us living by faith and trusting his provision, and so we won't just rely upon what we have stashed away. Giving should be no big deal, as all that we have is God's, so we are just giving back to him what he already owns. The Bible instructs us that it is also important to give cheerfully. So many times I have told those collecting the money to accept nothing from anyone unless they are smiling. This, of course, is a heartbreaking exercise to the church treasurer. Generally he is more concerned about receiving big cheques than seeing big grins.

Maybe 2 Corinthians 9:6 sums it up best.

> Remember this: Whoever sows sparingly will also reap sparingly, and whoever sows generously will also reap generously. Each man should give what he has decided in his heart to give, not reluctantly or under compulsion, for God loves a cheerful giver.

Children need to be taught that giving must come from the heart; and incidentally the way to a man's (and child's) heart is not through their stomachs; it's through their wallets.

5. Baptism

I have always considered that the many hours of debate people have over the amount of water one should be baptized in is missing the whole point of baptism. The whole of the New Testament points to the fact that we should believe and then be baptized. We are making a statement before God, and before everyone listening, that we have finished with the old sinful life, buried it, and have now risen again with our Lord Jesus to live out a brand-new, clean life as a brand-new, cleaned-out person.

At what age, then, should children be baptized? This is a very hard question and I am not sure if I know the answer to it. My personal feelings are that both salvation and being filled with Holy Spirit do require a response from the child, but they are both gifts from God. They don't need to understand everything that is taking place; a lot of what is happening will be revealed to them as they grow older and get to know God and Scripture better. With a believer's baptism there is a difference. The person being baptized is not stating his death and resurrection through the eyes of faith: it is a thought out, understood commitment that he is making. So although I would not dare to put an age limit on it, I do believe that it has to be a response from the child, not the parent or children's worker, and the child needs to understand the words he is saying and the commitment he is making.

By the way, there is nothing in the Bible that says it has to be a leader or ordained man doing the baptizing. I am looking forward to the day when Christian parents baptize their own children: this would solve a lot of problems because, with their leaders' approval and before all the congregation, they are taking the responsibility for their own children – which is the way it should be.

6. Communion, or breaking of bread

Again, this wonderful feast of remembrance and thanksgiving should never exclude believing children, but it does need explaining to them in a very simple way.

Teach them that it is not the bread and the wine that is holy or anything special; it is that we are remembering the pain and the agony that the Lord Jesus went through so that we could be made right with him. Explain that we have an illustration in front of us: the bread being the body of Christ that was broken, and the wine being his blood that was shed to make us clean. Explain that this is no morbid feast and that we are not cannibals or vampires. To some children who have been allowed to watch horror films, these thoughts seriously come into their minds whenever eating the body or drinking the blood are mentioned. Tell them it's a time to remember what Jesus went through and to be thankful that he not only died, but he rose again from the dead and is one day returning to earth so that we can be with him for ever.

If at all possible, it's best that parents sit with their children, or take responsibility for any young friends they have brought along, while this is done in a meeting. This way they can explain what is happening. It needs to be made very clear, though, that this is a special feast for believers. It should not be taken lightly and just given to every child. The breaking of bread doesn't have to only take place within the confines of a meeting: we as a family have also enjoyed just sitting in the countryside with some bread and drink and giving thanks to Jesus for all he has done for us.

Let me finish by saying again that this need not be a solemn time, but it certainly is a special time and must be taken with true respect and reverence. We must impress on our children that this, above most things, is no joke. They must not take it lightly, but as the invitation to come and join in this remembrance feast has been given by the Lord Jesus himself, they must not be frightened to accept the invitation and to come, eat, drink and be thankful.

As I mentioned earlier, let's stick to teaching the children what the Bible teaches. It will take them all of their lives on earth to learn just some of that. Any unnecessary stuff we try to include, although it may not be outwardly harmful, will prove distracting and a waste of time in an age where the Spirit of God has so many vital things to teach these young ones. Please hold on to the old if you want to, but don't try to pass it on to the new generation.

7. Christmas

I do believe there are certain things that those who are not Christians have distorted, destroyed, and put their own meanings to, and Christians have allowed this to happen. There are things that are God's and they are worth reclaiming. For instance, the rainbow: God's reminder to people that he will never flood the world again. Many Christians will not include the rainbow in their visual aids or talks, as it is now considered 'New Age'. This is nonsense, for surely the rainbow belongs to God and we must not let anyone hijack it. The same applies to crystals, stars, the sun and even the human body – which are all part of God's wonderful creation and belong to him.

But some things may not be worth wasting our energy reclaiming because the question has to be asked, were these ever God's to begin with? People say we need to put Christ back into Christmas, but I am not so sure that he wants to be part of Christmas. Let's look at the facts. Although I am sure none of the following applies to us, Christmas for many is a season of over-spending, greed, jealousy, commercialism, over-eating and drunkenness, often leading to immorality and, of course, bad-tempered parents and miserable children spending hours drifting round the shops spending money that they do not have, thanks to a plastic card.

What makes up Christmas?

1. Winter festival

Way back in the earliest days, primitive man was very worried when seeing the sun he worshipped apparently lose its strength and almost die throughout the autumn months. But it did not take him long to discover that by the end of December it had started to come back to life again. This was a good enough reason for him to dance and sing and invite a few friends around for food and drink.

2. Saturnalia

Years later, the Romans continued the party and called it Saturnalia. When Christianity became the state religion, they did not want to disrupt the old pagan habits, so they decided to abolish the name Saturnalia and change it to a festival to celebrate the birth of Christ, while still managing to retain the old pagan atmosphere and customs. I guess some hoped that it would stop people worshipping the sun – nowadays they worship everything except the Son at Christmas.

3. Father Christmas

The tradition of Father Christmas began 1,600 years ago, in memory of a Christian bishop called St Nicholas who gave money to starving children. I don't think he had reindeers, a strange red and white outfit, dropped his gifts down chimneys or travelled down each year from the North Pole, however.

A few Christmases ago, I was invited to a very go-ahead, lively church group, to perform in a Saturday concert and then stay on to speak at the Sunday meeting. On the Saturday I announced that on the Sunday I was going to expose what Christmas is really all about. This caused an uproar: it was as though I'd said I was going to speak on Adam and Eve and everyone was expected to turn up wearing fig leaves. Some parents refused to come to the Sunday meeting because they were frightened that I was going to reveal to the children that fat old Father Christmas was not a real person.

Why do Christian parents tell such a blatant lie? Some children get mixed up between Father Christmas and Father God, and it's easy to see why. If we take away the 'mas' we are left with the words 'Father Christ'. As some children grow up and learn they have been deceived and Father Christmas is just a fictitious character, some also assume Father God is. In this day and age do we really want our children to believe that a strange man is going to break into their house, and maybe even into their bedroom, on Christmas Eve?

I was talking to a young person the other day who told me that when she was young she was horrified every Christmas Eve at the thought of this. If we must pursue the Father Christmas lie, why not just tell them that Daddy or Mummy is going to pretend to be Father Christmas and during the night will creep into their bedroom and fill their stockings up with some lovely presents? Surely we don't really think that our children believe there is only one Father Christmas? After all, they have met a different one in every different store for the whole month of December. And while I am sure that most of these men are genuinely kind, I do sometimes wonder what sort of character is hiding in that costume waiting to sit a child on his knee. Maybe I am just too suspicious – hopefully nowadays they all have to be police-checked.

4. The Christmas tree

For many centuries, every year the yule log, often a whole tree trunk, was dragged into the castle or manor house by all the local community and lit by the charcoal of the previous year's log. Once alight, still very much a symbol of the rebirth of the sun, the eating and drinking began and the mummers (a group of masked performers) presented symbolic plays.

It was 1,200 years ago that St Boniface, who was a missionary in Germany, started putting gifts on fir trees with the sole intention of stopping the people from worshipping the trees. When Queen Victoria married Albert, who had been brought up in the north German tradition of Christmas trees and Father Christmas, he imported these customs to England. Nowadays, of course, there is no sign of worshipping the Christmas tree; in fact we have so little respect for it that we think nothing of felling a whole pine forest just so we can enjoy a real tree in our lounge for a couple of weeks before the wilting needles cover the floor and the poor dead tree is thrown in the rubbish bin. We try and make it a Christian symbol by sticking a star or an angel on its top, but a lot of people think a fairy is more appropriate and they are probably right.

5. Christmas carols

These have been merrily sung for 500 years, and many have very strange lyrics. I recorded a Christmas carol album a few years ago and it was quite a job to find enough carols with good biblical lyrics to fill up all the tracks. In years gone by, people would enjoy going 'a-wassailing' over the Christmas period. This would involve staggering from door to door with a wooden bowl full of ale or wine. A carol was sung, and then the very merry singers would drink to the health of the poor unfortunate house-holder who not only had to endure this intrusion by the drunken rabble, but also had to pay them so they could afford to buy some more booze to fill up their wooden bowl before they moved on to persecute the next household.

6. Turkey

This poor unfortunate rather ugly-looking bird does not spend too long living on God's earth. Like myself, the one season it does not look forward to is Christmas, but for a different reason. When all around him are rejoicing with mouths drooling and knives and forks at the ready, he lies waiting to be eaten on a silver platter, having suffered the indignity of having all sorts of seasoning unceremoniously inserted inside him. The turkey flew in from Mexico 400 years ago – before that we enjoyed pig, but that proved to be a boar.

7. Christmas cards

Cards were only for the wealthy 150 years ago. Now we all buy them. Most Christians either choose the hundred mixed ultra cheap bargain box, or, for close friends, sentimental cards with a pseudo religious picture on the front. We see the totally unreal nativity scene with Mary and Joseph looking like they have just stepped out of Hollywood, the animals looking like they have all been bathed and blow-dried, and the stable cleaner, tidier and more hygienic than a maternity hospital. Many others choose to invest their money on cards with pictures of old Father Christmas, snowmen, holly and ivy, drunken people supposedly enjoying themselves or even filthy adult-only cards that are displayed in stores at eye level to most small children. Nearly every topic is available and they get more expensive every year.

Cards today, though, are more than a greeting – they seem to be a sign that you love someone. So every year more money goes to the card shops and the postal services as longer and longer lists are made. Friends are desperately waiting to receive your card and you will be filled with guilt if one arrives from someone you have not sent one to. In local church life so much rejection can come about if you forget to send a card to a fellow member: relationships can be broken all because someone did not receive a silly bit of paper in an envelope with sentimental, slushy words inside.

We hang these expensive bits of paper around our rooms for a couple of weeks, then the financially careful people put any that have been written in pencil, or have not been signed, into a special box for redistribution the following year, while the rest of us throw them into the rubbish bin, to keep the Christmas tree company.

What about the birth of mankind's Saviour?

Surely it must cause great confusion to our children when we try and mix up all the above strange customs with Jesus. As I said earlier, I would question whether Jesus would particularly want to be involved with any of the above. Such customs have nothing to do with him or his birth, and certainly we have nothing written in Scripture to say that Christmas or Easter should even exist.

I'm not a killjoy – there is nothing wrong with enjoying a festive season. It's a great time to give gifts, enjoy parties and have fun together. There's nothing wrong with that, as long as we do not go to excesses, and we know that every day is still 'the Lord's day' and every day for the Christian should still remain a time for worship and praise. The wonderful birth of Christ does not really need a day or a season to be set aside for it – along with his death, resurrection, ascension and Pentecost, it is an event that should be remembered and celebrated throughout the whole year. Let's prove we do not live by old traditions and let's enjoy singing 'Away in a manger' in August.

The observant will have noticed that I have made no mention in this chapter about Christians who encourage their children every year to enjoy celebrating burning a guy who tried to blow up parliament, or those Christians who allow their children to remember All Hallows' day with trick and treat, witches and pumpkins. Of course it's not my place to judge anyone, but between you and me, I do sometimes wonder if they actually possess even a paraphrased Bible!

15

Old Issues, New Thoughts

Change is here to stay

With all the renewing, refreshing and restoring that has been happening, many Christians over the last few years have come into a new freedom, which has brought with it changed viewpoints on various important issues. But with that new freedom we have somehow managed to add a lot of new regulations over issues which, in today's Christian culture, are thought of as unacceptable, but which the Bible is a lot less dogmatic about. Are these added regulations putting chains of bondage on the church and restricting the freedom that Jesus died to release us into? Or maybe the opposite extreme is right – maybe we should stay as we are and not allow new thinking and changes. For some, a change of opinion is at best a sign of weakness and at worst a sign of compromise and backsliding. Is it best to abstain from anything that may trip up the weaker brother and seems to have even the slightest smell of the world about it, and to say no to sin and everything that could cause people to sin?

It's important to respect different opinions, but the following questions must be asked: Will the liberated know when to stop before becoming identical to the unsaved in the world? And will the old school ever be willing to sit down with children and explain why some of their views not only contradict certain scriptures, but also may even be subtly insinuating that some of the things Jesus said and did were far from helpful for the 'weak' around him?

Personally, I see the Christian life as a journey, and as we learn more about God and about Scripture, so our thoughts, actions and even what we teach our little ones will change. However, not all changes are for the good, and certainly not all changes are for the bad, but when we alter or redefine our views on certain subjects, these need to be explained to our children. So, are these changes making us more liberated, or more liberal? Are they setting us free from the old laws and traditions that bound us up, or giving us more 'rules' to obey?

We know that all sin is wrong, but have we classed things as sin when the Bible does not? Let's look at a few issues that need rethinking, because our children deserve well thought out answers on what is right and what is wrong. I have deliberately tried not to tell you what you should or what you should not teach, although in the very way I write, I think that you may be able to judge my opinions, but remember these are only my opinions – you have to find your own. I have written the next two chapters to provoke your thoughts and get you to discuss these real problems that our children face today. Hopefully you will be able to approach all these issues with an open mind and an open Bible.

The Lord's day revisited

In Chapter 9 we have looked at the name of the day, and how the so-called day of rest is often the day of exhaustion for many children's leaders. Now let's look back over the past 50 years and see how our thoughts and actions have changed in regard to the 24 hours that many call the Lord's day.

Dressing up

When I was a child, I always enjoyed dressing up. My cowboy outfit was my favourite attire. But on Sundays, my mum chose my fancy dress for me. Every Sunday morning I was forced into a hot, itchy suit, to go to church meetings. I was reminded that if I ever stood in front of royalty I would want to look my best, so how much more important to dress up if we are going to meet with the King of kings.

Views today have changed. Today I realize that I am in the presence of the King of kings every minute of every day, but instead of permanently wearing a suit I only wear one for weddings, funerals and meals at exclusive restaurants. Man may look on our outward appearance, but God looks at our hearts. So on Sunday most people nowadays wear what they like.

The big switch off

I remember the time when Christians were very selective about what TV programmes could be watched on Sundays. I would be allowed to watch the 'God slot', the news or, as a special treat, programmes about wildlife and nature. But that was it. There was no place for unholy viewing on the holy day.

Today, the television has become an adopted member of most families. Some children love it more than they love their parents, and many parents pay more attention to it than they do to their children. Today, Sunday afternoons are dominated by Christians of all ages feeling no guilt as they peer at hours of sport, catch up with their latest depressing soap story, and even watch programmes about how much antiques are worth.

Leisure time

I remember the time when Christians never bought newspapers on Sundays. They would not be the ones to make the newsagents break the fourth commandment, but they would always buy the

Monday paper, which involved thousands of printers, journalists, and editors working all day on the Sunday before!

I remember when buying an ice-cream on a baking hot Sunday afternoon was a sin, but buying fuel for the car was allowed in an emergency. I remember when Sunday afternoon was a roast, which all the family ate together, and tea was neatly cut triangular sandwiches with fish paste in the middle. Today, many of us – not knowing what time the morning meeting will end – eat a McDonald's with our little ones at lunch time and a curry when the children have gone to bed in the evening.

I remember when long walks were the Sunday afternoon Christian activity and sport took place on Saturday. Today, many parents miss the Sunday morning meeting because their child is playing in a local football team.

I remember when I was forced to go to three meetings on Sunday, and that did not include the meeting in the evening. Nowadays, Christians feel that one meeting on Sunday is enough, and for some even that is too much.

I remember when only Christians involved in essential services, or who were farmers, worked on Sundays. Nowadays, some openly say they have to work on Sundays to be able to make ends meet and to provide for their loved ones; others say that in all honesty they just like having the bonus money that working on Sunday provides.

One day or fun day?

Sunday has now become a very different day than it was half a century ago. We have Sunday trading, both inside and outside of church buildings, DIY shops and places of sport and amusement to visit on Sunday afternoons, eating and drinking establishments open day and night, and most Christians seem to quite enjoy it. Some feel we have gone backwards by not standing firm and fighting to keep Sunday special; others would say that, with all the facilities open and available, Sunday has become even more special. You have an opinion and so have your children – whatever it is, communicate this together.

The biggest question

In the book of Revelation we find the apostle John exiled on the island of Patmos. At this time one of the most evil Caesars, Domitian, was in power. Although the mad Caligula claimed to be God, and the crazy Nero didn't much fancy being god, the so-called sane Domitian really believed he *was* god, which made him even more dangerous than the others. All Christians who dared question his divinity would face persecution and death.

Every week, Emperor's Day would be celebrated when Domitian would expect everyone to think about and worship him. It's in the first chapter of Revelation that we have the first and only mention of the Lord's day. If the wicked Caesar chose a day on which people should worship him, how much more should there be a day in the week set aside to worship Jesus? But now comes our big problem.

Goodbye Saturday, hello Sunday

Up until then, both the Christian Jews and non-Jews seemed happy to stick with tradition and make the Sabbath, which was the last day of the week, the one special day to hold sacred. Suddenly, with no apparent new instruction from Jesus or any biblical explanation or reference, the early Christians made one of the most radical moves in church history. They dropped the Saturday and made the first day of the week, Sunday, their special day.

The Sabbath was, of course, remembered for being the day that God rested after creation, but the Sunday became at this point of time even more special because it was the beginning of the new creation and the Resurrection of the Lord Jesus. From the second century until today, Christians have decided to abandon the Sabbath altogether and just celebrate the Lord's day.

Do we need a day of rest?

In John 5:16–18 we read of how Jesus broke the Sabbath laws
and got into trouble for not only continuing his work but also
claiming that God his Father had continued to work as well, even
on the Sabbath. He then seemed to go even further in Matthew
11:28–29 by saying, 'Come to me, all you who are weary and
burdened, and I will give you rest. Take my yoke upon you and
learn from me, for I am gentle and humble in heart, and you will
find rest for your souls.' Matthew, Mark and Luke all tell us that
Jesus referred to himself as Lord of the Sabbath. The book of
Acts and Colossians 2 refer to the day called the Sabbath, but
with no instruction about it. In Hebrews 4, a book primarily written to Jewish converts who were being tempted to try and mix up
Judaism and Christianity, we get another mention of the Sabbath,
but it's mainly about encouraging us to enter into God's rest.
There is a very strange silence from every other book in the New
Testament, as none of them mentions anything about the
Sabbath. It does seem, as you study the words of Jesus, that he
seemed to be telling everyone that it was not a legalistic rest for
one day a week that was needed but resting in him seven days a
week.

By Jesus referring to himself as the Lord of the Sabbath, the
fourth commandment was not cancelled out – it was simply sur-
passed by the reality of Jesus.

No rest for the righteous?

Between the second and fourth century, the Christians had no
day of rest. The Sabbath was gone, and as Sunday was a working
day, they were expected to work, along with every other Jew,
Roman and so on. They did, however, hold meetings of worship
and communion each Sunday, either very early in the morning
before going to work, or after sunset, when work was finished.
But there are no biblical references to suggest that Christians

must or even should meet each Sunday. This was something that the early church chose to do. With the few hours we work each week nowadays, compared to the many hours they worked in biblical times, do we really need a whole day of rest, or do we need to learn that our rest will come in staying close to Jesus? So often rest for the Christian consists of sleeping, and sitting for hours in front of a TV screen, but this sort of laziness can lead us into becoming lethargic and visionless. If we choose to meet on Sunday, perhaps we should follow the early church's example and meet at the crack of dawn. This would leave us the rest of the day to do all sorts of different things that we normally do not have time to do, like serving others and spending time with our families or showing the love of Jesus to those who are less fortunate than we are.

Have we come full circle?

In the fourth century the forever compromising Emperor Constantine started to reverse what the early church had begun. For reasons of popularity, he instigated and legalized a day of rest, and as he had no thoughts of reinstating the Jewish Sabbath, he decided it would be good to make the Sunday a day where people didn't have to work.

As we look back over the years since then, we can see that church leaders of the past centuries have been slowly but surely completing the full circle by changing Constantine's day of rest back into a compromised Jewish Sabbath, along with many new rules and regulations. It seems the freedom and release that the early Christians found by not being in bondage to a Sabbath or a day of rest now needs to be rediscovered all over again.

If Jesus really is in himself the completion of the fourth commandment and we, along with the early church, no longer believe in celebrating a holy Saturday or a Jewish Sabbath, where is our biblical foundation for teaching our children that Sunday is a day of rest or – for that matter – any different than any other day of the week? Neither Jesus nor any disciples endorsed that Sunday should be kept special, but tradition has. And what makes this wrong is that it has become a tradition not just set in stone but set in granite! I think some of our fears are that if we don't set apart a day to be holy, we will stop being a holy people. We need to keep a day set aside for God or else church as we know it will die.

Perhaps in time our children will get it right. Perhaps they will want to live in a godly freedom like the early apostles; perhaps as they enter leadership positions they will stay free, holy, and choose to keep all seven days special, and, like Acts 2, make a time every day to meet together. In churches where revival has broken out, this often seems to be the norm, and I guess the majority of us believe that when revival comes our children will be right in the thick of it.

Is nothing sacred?

What about the music and worship? There was a time when rock music was labelled by Christians as demonic jungle music: only classical and sacred pieces were for real Christians to enjoy. Then some movies were released depicting the lifestyles of some of our favourite classical composers and we were thrown into confusion as we discovered that some of them were even more depraved than the Sex Pistols.

I personally do not believe in the sacred and the secular. The dictionary definition of sacred is 'exclusively devoted to a deity or to some religious ceremony, holy and consecrated' while secular is 'worldly, temporary and not within the control of the church'. God is holy, music is not, and most songs written by Christians nowadays are not within the control of the church – they are within the control of the music publisher and the copyright licence.

Music is just sound, a noise that reaches the ear, and the possessor of that ear then decides if the sound is enjoyable or objectionable. How can noises be good or evil? Is the skylark sacred and the foghorn secular, or is the pipe organ sacred and record scratching secular, or the trained voice of the opera singer sacred while the highly untrained voice of Ishmael . . . ? I think we'll leave it there.

Waxing lyrical

Some would say that the lyrics reveal whether a song is sacred or secular. Does that mean that if someone who is not yet a Christian writes a song with Christian lyrics that makes it a sacred song? Or if a Christian writes a song that has no Christian lyrics, does that make it a secular song? I remember many years ago a friend of mine who was a very devout Christian musician sang a love song to his wife in a concert, and because there was no mention of Father, Son or Holy Spirit in the lyrics, the lights came on and the leaders stopped the concert in disgust.

Maybe a sacred song is a song with Christian lyrics written by a Christian, but what if the composer claims to be a Christian but sadly worships his music more than he worships Jesus? It can happen. We also have to face the fact that some of the songs written by Christians are very average. Notice I did not say awful. Can a song be sacred and a pain to your ears at the same time? At the time of writing I have released about 32 albums, which means I have written hundreds of songs. I don't really think that I would like any of them to be classed as sacred, as even 'Father God I wonder' was written while I was in the shower.

The one thing I will never be able to work out is why I can listen to so many songs written by Christians and God simply does not speak to me through them. Then every now and again I hear a song that has not been written and performed by someone of the Christian faith, and not only does it send shivers down my spine, but God really inspires me through it.

I suppose if God can use a jawbone of an ass, he can use any human jawbone. So in my opinion there is no such thing as sacred and secular music, but there is such a thing as music that God enjoys and music that he does not.

What are they really singing about?

It's not the noise; it is not even always the lyrics: it is the message behind the music that we adults need to look out for. What is this song or singer trying to push at my children: immorality, perversion, drugs, arrogance, lawlessness, rebellion, and so on? Music plays a very big part in a young person's life; that is why parents and children's workers need to have some idea what they are listening to, and that means occasionally listening to your least favourite radio station, watching those tedious pop programmes and reading those music mags that often seem like they have been written in a foreign language.

Singspiration

So can a person be inspired by God when they write a song? I certainly hope so. I believe that God wants to inspire his children in everything they do, creative or otherwise. Some Christians come up to me, push a scruffy piece of paper in my hand and tell me that 'God wrote this song'. Of course it's not my place to disillusion anyone, but I wonder if God really wants to be associated with bad spelling, bad rhythm, and a tune borrowed from someone else's repertoire. I wonder if I will ever open up a songbook and see written by the title 'words and music by God'. That would really give the publisher a major problem when they had to post off the copyright royalty cheque.

On a personal annoyance level of between one and ten, very few things related to my music reach ten, which for me is boiling-point. But one thing does: Christians write to me and say that God has given them two extra verses to my song 'Father God I wonder'. Why don't they leave my song alone? If I felt it should have three verses, I would have written three verses 15 years ago. So if you are one of these songwriters who get inspired to 'improve' other people's songs, please don't. Use that inspiration instead to write a brand-new song of your own.

Quick changes

Music is not what it was. Forty years ago, musical trends took years to develop; today they take months or even weeks. So if your child is raving about a singer whom you consider to be harmful, often by the time you have got round to explaining your viewpoints, they too have got fed up with them and have now got into something completely different. You will need running shoes to keep up!

It's great that nowadays we have so many Christian bands playing every type of music, but with all this choice of what we consider to be good quality, godly entertainment, your child may still prefer some weirdo from the top ten. Don't be too surprised. Many of us did the same when we were their ages, and we have not turned out too bad – have we?

The screen test

Remember those movies many years ago that were X-rated and scared us to death? They have now become comedies to our children. The scariest bit to them is the lion that roars at the beginning. Taste and levels of fear have changed over the years. The only thing that tends to scare some children is real life.

So are our children influenced by what they watch on the box? Of course they are. Most would spend more hours per week listening to the voice of the television than they would listening to a teacher, pastor, parent, or even a friend. If the truth is known, for many of them their best friend is the television, so of course consciously or subconsciously they will in time listen and live out what their best friend is teaching them.

The ten commandments of the small screen

1. Thou shalt understand that it is now normal for a boy and girl to sleep together as soon as they feel the sexual urge. Thou shalt not consider it right to use self-control and wait till marriage.

2. Thou shalt participate in violence and be allowed to release all pent-up aggression and anger. Thou shalt not be non-violent or a peacemaker unless thou art a wimp.

3. Thou shalt verbalize obscene words and use finger actions at any time. Thou shalt not consider small children and others around you, who may be offended by such outbursts.

4. Thou shalt find true happiness if thou art highly intelligent or have great wealth. Thou shalt never be satisfied if thou art content to just accept what thou are or what thou havest.

5. Thou shalt enjoy eating and drinking to excess – this is a normal part of growing up. Thou shalt not try to aim for moderation.

6. Thou shalt argue with thy parents and teachers, as it is character-building. Thou shalt not try and obey those in authority over you.

7. Thou shalt need to be good-looking, or very thin, to be attractive. Thou shalt not be satisfied with the way or shape God made you.

8. Thou shalt put thyself first then all other things will work out fine. Thou shalt not think others as important as thyself.

9. Thou shalt change thy husband or wife whenever thou findeth a more suitable one. Thou shalt not work to retrieve a marriage or take the 'till death us do part' promise too seriously.

10. Thou shalt mock Christianity and portray all Christians as being immoral, desperate or non-intelligent fools. Thou shalt never consider that they have discovered the answer to life and want to share around good news.

Watch it

Today our children face entertainment on a screen for many hours a day, whether it's at the cinema, or in the home with television, videos, DVDs or computer games. Many of us would love there to be a listing engraved in stone, in the handwriting of the Ten Commandments, of movies and games that are suitable for Christian and especially children's viewing and playing. Some have tried to do this, but even the so-called biblical films such as *The Ten Commandments* and *Moses: Prince of Egypt* are written with the multi-faith audience in mind and contain biblical discrepancies.

As with music, we have to literally keep our eyes open and see what is popular. It is not for the church or children's workers to dictate the good, the bad and the ugly – that is the parents' responsibility. But we can advise and give helpful guidelines, and then leave the final responsibility with the parents, because that is what God has given to them.

Throw out the TV and computer?

Do I feel it's best not to own a television or computer? Personally, no. I think it's best to teach our children how to use them. There are some programmes that are very good for our children, and if you don't have a television they will only go and watch it at their friend's house, where you have no control over what they are viewing at all. We need to teach our children that they are little worshippers and they need to prayerfully consider what they watch and also to remember that Jesus is watching the programme or playing that game along with them. None of us would want to watch or play anything that would make Jesus unhappy, would we?

We must teach them how to walk out of a room, how to change channels and most of all where the off switch is. An alternative is to subscribe to a Christian channel. This may be an answer for some, but personally I would rather Christian children had the choice of all channels and were enabled to choose for themselves not to watch programmes that they felt were unsuitable.

Trend followers

In the 1950s we had the teddy boys, with their tight, light blue jeans and quiffs. In the 1960s we had the mods with their parkas, cropped hair and scooters, the rockers with their studded leather jackets and Harley Davidsons, and the hippies with their kaftans, bells and 'peace, man' terminology.

In the 1970s we had the high-heeled glam rockers and the aggressive skinheads, followed by the infamous haircuts of the punks. The 1980s and 1990s brought in the stylishly attired new romantics, and even the yuppies, who felt naked if they did not have a filofax in their hand.

The twenty-first century has brought in tattoos, aggressive looking shaven heads for any man who thinks he is going bald, and a mobile phone for anyone who is old enough to read the numbers 1 to 9.

In every decade, everyone wants to be different, yet so often everyone ends up looking the same. I often wondered why men wear ties – they really are a complete waste of time. They don't keep you warm or hold your trousers up; in fact they don't do anything except perhaps make a man feel smart, well-dressed and that he looks good to other people. Pride maybe, or just another fashion statement from a different generation?

Christian trendies today

Many Christian young people are just the same, but now they seem to start to follow the trends not long after they are out of nappies. Check out the number of toddlers wearing clothes containing the latest designer labels. But we should remember our young ones find it hard with school friends. They are the odd ones out because of their beliefs and standards; they don't want to add more misery and persecution to their lives by also having to look the odd one out by their nerdy appearance. We must try to understand how hard it is for them. Like music and pop stars, trends come and trends go . . . very quickly.

Keeping it under wraps

We do need to teach, especially our Christian girls, that they do not need to follow the world's motto: 'If you've got it, flaunt it'. Tight-fitting clothes and low-cut tops will certainly not offend their weaker brothers, but without doubt it will also not be the incentive that boys need to 'keep their eyes' on God. It's not heavy rules and regulations young people need preached at them – that is a sure-fire trigger for rebellion. Just a gentle little chat about sensitivity in time may do the trick, but be patient.

The right label

Designer clothes are so expensive, yet fashion dictates we all wear them. At our youth church a while ago, they had a meeting where no one was allowed to come in any designer clothes. I would imagine for some this was very hard to do – non-designer clothes in their cupboards would have been very hard to find, and I half expected some to turn up with a blanket around them. At the meeting, the leaders explained that designer clothes were commercial exploitation as they were over-priced and ended up just making richer people richer. Young Christians will always want to follow trends; that's OK, so long as following Jesus is more important. The question is, after the meeting did any young people change their opinion or their clothes? I wonder.

Parents: the good news is, if your children still choose to follow the designer trail, many of these clothes can now be purchased at your local charity shop at a tenth of the original price – and, once washed and pressed, hopefully, none of their friends will know the difference. The only trouble is you will have to shop without them tagging along, as most teenagers would not be seen dead walking out of that sort of shop.

Rude or prude?

When I was a child I never saw any tops or bottoms of the female anatomy. These were secret parts that were to be revealed to me on my marriage night. Nowadays many parents walk around the house naked, share baths with their children and don't have any hidden body parts. What was once rude to look at is now considered part of God's wonderful creation.

The teenager no longer needs to buy certain magazines off the top shelf to satisfy his pubic curiosity, for what he has not seen in the home he can easily see on the local beach or on television. But on the other hand, I was reading a classic old children's book recently with very old illustrations, and was amazed that all the mermaids were proudly showing off their curvaceous breasts and nipples. This would never be seen in our bookshops today. All the latest children's books would always have their mermaid figures discreetly covered by long blonde hair hanging just in the right places.

I have also seen parents who show no embarrassment at walking around the art gallery and watching their children stare up at Raphael's *Three Graces* because that's art, but if that was a ten metre full-frontal colour photograph of three nude ladies, or, worse still, a much smaller black and white photo of one nude lady found on page three in a tabloid newspaper, that would be disgusting.

Nature's way

Nineteenth-century missionaries made women in the southern pacific wear more clothes – although it gave them no more dignity. Today they think it terrible when they see European tourists sitting on their beaches with little or no clothing on.

I remember stumbling upon a nudist beach in France while on holiday with my family. It was a totally non-erotic experience, and at times I thought quite ugly. However, it didn't put me off my food, and as we were hungry, rather than walk for miles we sat down and ate our croissants while the children looked around, pointing at various bits of people and giggling. We carried on eating and tried to ignore their observations. Within ten minutes there was no more giggling, no more embarrassment, and the children played on the beach, went swimming and were oblivious to the naked people all around them.

I am not recommending that we all become naturists, but I did get a vision of what Eden or maybe the new earth will be like. Here were people of all ages, all shapes and sizes, not caring what they looked like, or dressing up in expensive clothes to outdo those around them, but just being themselves in their pre-Fall attire. There is no show of wealth or class when all we have on is our skin, and strange as it may seem, I could sense no feeling of sexual promiscuity, vice, lust, or immorality. The next day, we found a normal beach where everyone was partially clad, but here I could sense and see sexual promiscuity, lust and immorality very clearly.

Other cultures

While the Americans are very much clothes-on people, the Europeans can't seem to wait to get them off. I heard an amazing story about a church in America that loaned their hall to a group of Swedish teenagers to sleep in, while they were visiting to do some local evangelism. The pastor nearly died when he walked into the hall early on the first morning and discovered the males and females not only sleeping in the same room, but also walking around talking to each other with very little clothing on. There was no immorality, but for this Swedish group, who were so used to seeing nudity, and the pastor who was obviously not, there was a slight clash of cultures.

A musical friend of mine was about to begin a tour of Norway. When he and his keyboard player arrived at one of the leader's houses on the first night, he was surprised when his host leapt out of all his clothes and invited my friend to spend the evening with him sitting nude in the sauna eating sausages. While in Scandinavia I was approached many times to do the same, and was offered the additional pleasure of slapping my naked body with a tree branch while sweating. I turned down the invitation – I think I'm allergic to trees!

On one of my trips to America, I was guest speaker at a large Christian conference centre. It was very hot one afternoon, so I decided to join the other guests in the large pool. It was then the lifeguard approached me and, looking me up and down, said I was not allowed to use the pool dressed as I was. I had no idea what he was talking about, until he mentioned I was wearing speedo's, which I discovered meant swimming trunks, and men had to wear shorts. When I asked why, he told me they were provocative, and when I asked whether he really thought a middle-aged, overweight person like me was going to turn the ladies on, he said, 'Well we do have some very odd ladies here this week.'

By contrast, a few weeks ago, in a town in mainland Europe, I was told that shorts were not allowed in the pool – only trunks. In my travelling ministry, I either have to do a lot of research before I arrive in each country, or take a very large suitcase, with a variation on each attire.

Nudity in the Bible brought on various reactions: let's look at a few.

Revealing characters

In Genesis 2–3 Adam and Eve, after sinning, did not want God to see them naked.

In Genesis 9 a drunken Noah lying naked was not a pretty

sight, and obviously embarrassed his sons.

In 2 Samuel 6:14 King David, not naked as some think but doing a praise dance while only wearing a revealing hip length, tight-fitting sleeveless tunic, seemed to only embarrass his wife and not the entire house of Israel – which proves that she was the problem, not David.

In Micah 1:8 the prophet Micah saw nothing wrong with presenting his message while barefoot and naked, but Habakkuk 2:15 says 'Woe to him who gives drink to his neighbours . . . so that he can gaze on their naked bodies.'

Finally in Mark 14:51–52 a young man, probably the writer of the Gospel, was not going to stay around naked when the only clothing he was wearing was seized while he was following Jesus.

Nothing to hide

So nudity is not sin, but again we must be aware that in certain situations it can lead to temptation and sin. In some cultures you will be frowned upon if you take your clothes off; in others you will be frowned at if you keep them on. The naked body is God's masterpiece of creation, but not all naked bodies are beautiful to look at. Nude art and photography are very creative but can also be very provocative. Again, it is not for me to dictate what we teach in the home and wear on beaches, but just remember that what you are revealing to your children now, they may be revealing to others when they are teenagers, or, on the other hand, it might put them off altogether.

Body talk

When the children were tiny, we introduced them to jewellery and thought nothing of it. Now they are older and may want to add a ring to their jewellery collection, but it seems holes can be pierced in every part of a person's anatomy to accommodate the item. To see a ring in certain places can be quite attractive; to think about a ring in certain other places is quite revolting.

I feel it's a bit extreme to think of a tiny hole pierced through the ear as mutilating the body, but it really comes down to why a person wants to wear that ring. If it's because they feel it makes them more attractive, then fine. If it's out of rebellion, that is not so fine.

I remember years ago I had just finished an extensive and exhausting tour, and when I arrived home I talked to Irene about having a ring in my left ear. She agreed I should give it a go, to see if it would suit me. Well, I went to the chemist and a hole was banged out of my ear, which reminded me of my farming days when I used to do the same thing to label the pigs and calves. I now realize the pain I inflicted on them. I was then given a stud and told all the rules of how to stop the hole closing over, how to stop it weeping or bleeding, and other advice to help my new operation be a huge success.

I wore it for a while, and of course had a few comments aimed at me by Christians, ranging from 'Wow, I like your earring' to 'How can you be a Christian with a ring in your ear?' If I faced a very aggravated person, I would just quote Judges 8:24 (it was the custom of the Ishmaelites to wear gold earrings) and that would usually totally confuse the argument and move them on. As a musician, I did not get half the critical comments about my appearance that I did as a preacher. If I stood on a stage leading praise, an earring was much more acceptable than when I stood in a pulpit preaching a sermon. Strange standards.

As I explained earlier, I was not wearing an earring to make a statement. I just wore it because Irene and I thought I looked good wearing it. Why did I stop wearing it? Was it because I felt convicted? No, I'm afraid not. I stopped wearing it because it was too uncomfortable in bed and I could not be bothered wasting time fiddling about each morning trying to find the hole to put it back in.

Did my boys follow my example? No, they just thought earrings were for ageing trendies trying, without success, to hang on to their youth – like their dad. Adults are forever criticizing young ones and their fashion, but us oldies do a lot of unnecessary things to our bodies and also wear some odd garments. Before we have a go at the younger generation, it may be good to examine ourselves.

Razor sharp

History tells us that from way back to our early ancestors, man has had an obsession about scraping away the hair that grows on his face. In ancient times, men used clam shells, sharks' teeth and sharpened flints, so they must have been really desperate to be beardless. Why do we do it? Is it just because we think we look better without the face fungus that grows naturally? Is it because subconsciously we want to look more feminine, or do we do it because our wives refuse to kiss us if we don't?

We know Jesus wore a beard, so if we really want to be like him, shouldn't we all grow beards? Many men have never questioned why they shave, and a lot of these shavers are the ones who would throw up their arms in horror at the thought of a male Christian mutilating his ear by having a tiny hole made in it. Surely to choose daily to deliberately swipe a blade on your facial skin, realizing that at some stage it's very likely that the razor blade is going to accidentally cut into that skin so it bleeds, must be self-inflicted mutilation in anyone's books.

As we get older, for some reason less hair seems to grow on our heads. Instead, it starts growing out of our ears and nostrils. Just as we considered our visit to the hairdresser would take less time, they now occupy that time by ignoring our heads and trimming away at other parts. We eagerly judge the young lads on the way they look, but why do we spend so much time concerned about our appearance?

But it's not just the men. What about the women? Why do

some women shave their armpits? And how about that barbaric custom of leg waxing and eyebrow plucking? What is the reason that ladies spend so much effort in getting rid of unwanted hair? Is it to please their husbands or boyfriends or do they think they look better clean-shaven? It's easy to criticize young girls who try and follow fashion, but can't we see that many of them are just following the example of older Christian ladies?

Put those stones down

Just a few things that maybe we 'oldies' need to look at. Before we throw our stones at young people who are slaves to modern fashion, it may be good first of all to look in a mirror, then look in our own cupboards and wardrobes, and finally try to think back to when we were their age – if we can remember that far back!

16

New Thoughts, Old Issues

Food for thought

I realize I am taking this scripture slightly out of context, but Jesus says in Matthew 6:

> If you decide for God, living a life of God-worship, it follows that you don't fuss about what's on the table at mealtimes or whether the clothes in your closet are in fashion. There is far more to your life than the food you put in your stomach.... (Taken from *The Message*)

Since the Bible tells us to take no thought for what we eat or drink, it's strange that much of our lives is taken up with discussing and highlighting these very things. Many Christians have now become health diet freaks, who spend more time counting calories, fats and E numbers than they do counting the lost who live around them.

Nobody will argue with the fact that exercise is important to stay healthy, together with a reasonably balanced diet, but some Christians spend more time reading diet sheets, and the small print on the side of a baked bean tin, than they do reading their Bibles. If we endorse this 'live to be thin' image, then some of us may be subconsciously influencing our young ones to see themselves as overweight, and we will see many more of our beautiful children wasting away with anorexia. We want to pass on to them the sense in healthy eating but not fanatical food obsessions.

If people choose to be vegetarian, I respect their choice. But I don't respect those who try to push this viewpoint onto others, as though this is God's perfect plan for a more spiritual way of living. If you are faced with one of these people, it's worth discussing with them why God put certain teeth in our mouths, especially designed for eating meat. Then ask them why the loving father gave his wayward prodigal son the best food possible: a fatted calf, not a nut cutlet. And finally, why Jesus himself decided to cook a fish meal for his friends after the Resurrection by the Sea of Galilee. It seems that all the closest friends of God in the Bible were meat eaters, but so, I guess, were all his greatest enemies. In other words, it's not that important.

The devil's brew?

In Britain, throughout the centuries, the church and beer seem to have been almost inseparable, and for a classic example of this we just have to look at the Middle Ages. A different ale was brewed for each special occasion. There was child-ale sold to celebrate the first-born, christening ale, marriage ale, bride ale, and even a brew called give ale to be drunk at someone's death in order to give the deceased a cheery farewell. Often you will find the old church building very near the pub, so after the service the congregation would reunite just down the road for a much less formal gathering.

Although all this may sound like harmless fun to some, the downside was places like Norwich Children's Hospital, where in 1632 two gallons of beer were included in the weekly ration for each child. After 1690, a drink far more harmful than beer arrived from Holland: this drink was called gin. In 1836 there were 46,000 places where drink could be bought, and in some towns that was a public house for every 20 families. Due to massive competition, some pubs changed their image and became gin palaces. They were even known to have organs so they could play Psalms on Sundays. Children became alcoholics at a very young age, and the saying was that a person could be drunk for a penny, dead drunk for two pennies.

It was around this time that the powerful temperance movement came into being. It began by encouraging drink in moderation, but later pledged total abstinence, claiming that alcohol was 'the devil in solution'. In 1847 the Band of Hope was formed, whose members would visit Sunday schools, and, by using magic lanterns, show slides to the children in lurid colours, portraying what a drunk's insides looked like.

The Church of England opposed the extreme temperance movement and could not agree that alcohol was 'the devil in solution' because there were so many references to wine in the Bible. Even Christ drank wine, and, just like today, the temperance movement had answers to satisfy themselves but in no way conclusive enough answers to change the minds of those who disagreed with them – or those who knew their Bibles.

During the majority of the twentieth century, very few Christians, apart from the Anglicans and Catholics, would openly admit to drinking alcoholic beverages, except maybe the baby who unknowingly had a wee dram in its medicinal water to help it belch, and the odd pensioner who had a nip of sherry for medicinal reasons before retiring to bed.

For years the medics have told us that drinking in excess will inflame our stomachs, scar our livers and damage our brains. Nowadays, however, we are told moderate amounts of alcohol can be good for us, and I quote from my medical dictionary: 'It can encourage the appetite, reduce fever, stimulate hearts, help relaxation from tension and can help some people sleep at night.'

Today, in the twenty-first century, many alehouses are now family restaurants, and many Christians literally 'take no thought' about drinking alcoholic drinks. Drink is not an issue to me. Some would not be seen drinking 'because the weaker brother might stumble', and at certain times I can understand that viewpoint. But most of the time the weaker brother turns out to be the so-called stronger one, who is determined to push the anti-drink campaign onto everyone else.

Wine is fine, beer is queer

I respect people who are teetotal and I respect people who are not. I find it strange that some Christians think that it is OK to drink wine but not beer, especially as wine is usually a lot stronger than beer. I even met a leader once who said he only drank wine, which didn't count! Children do need to know why we do, or do not do, certain things, and this is an issue that must be talked through, because once they get to those teenage years, or even sooner, they will come face to face with a bottle.

A drop of the hard stuff

Just to say alcohol is evil or that no one should ever touch the stuff is not good enough. It's good to read all the scriptures that warn us about the dangers of drink, but before outright banning and prohibition comes into action, it may be good to keep a balanced viewpoint and also examine, read and think about scriptures like the following. Proverbs 31:6 says 'Give beer to those who are perishing, wine to those who are in anguish,' and Psalm 104:14–15 tells us 'He makes grass grow for the cattle, and plants for man to cultivate – bringing forth food from the earth: Wine that gladdens the heart of man, oil to make his face shine, and bread that sustains his heart.'

Moving into the New Testament, we need to explain why Jesus would brew 180 gallons of the best wine to give to people who were already merry. Some teetotal believers may say that he turned the water into non-alcoholic wine – in other words, clear water to coloured water – but that, I suggest, is depreciating the miracle. Instant fermentation of the very best wine would have taken a long time. The wedding party was amazed that Jesus could do this instantly.

Furthermore, we read in Matthew 11:19 and Luke 7:33 that although John the Baptist was teetotal, Jesus seems not to have been. He himself declared that the Son of man came eating and drinking and he was criticized as a glutton and a drunkard.

Then, of course, we have 1 Timothy 5:23, in which Paul instructs his young disciple to stop drinking only water and use a little wine because of 'your stomach and your frequent illnesses'. Interestingly, Paul was recommending wine here, rather than prayer ministry or healing – not many churches that I know would offer this sort of advice!

Not shaken, but stirred

Now, I've not put in these scriptures to change people's viewpoints. If they need changing, the Holy Spirit will do that. Our children do need biblical instruction on a subject that is still one of the most controversial in church life. It's hard to find scriptures that say to drink alcohol is a sin, but there are some that speak of drunkenness (Luke 21:34–36; Ephesians 5:18; Galatians 5:21). We do know by looking around us that it can bring out violence in some, loosen morals in others and after a 'skinful' all drinkers soon lose control of their actions, speech and memory. So, for a subject we are instructed to 'take no thought about' this will always be one of the most contentious and talked about issues in church life when thinking of our young people.

Children's leaders need to think it through, but beware of being too dogmatic either way, as some parents are likely to disagree with your opinion, whatever side of the fence you come down on. Parents who dogmatically tell their teenagers not to drink may well find they react, rebel and drink in excess. Those who tell them to 'drink in moderation' will probably be accused of encouraging drunkenness. Whatever we say to them, eventually they will make up their own minds, and whatever we advise, we will always have our critics to tell us that we gave them the wrong advice.

Workaholics

Just in passing, does it not seem strange to you that Christians think there are few things worse than being an alcoholic, yet they seem surprisingly smug when someone refers to them as a workaholic? Surely one is not worse than the other: they are both serious addictions and both involve habits that are going to be very hard to break. They both affect not only the individual, but cause pain and neglect to the family, and the untreated outcome of both is likely to shorten their lives. I would like to see more preaching on the dangers of workaholism, followed by ministry and counselling. Maybe when we realize the seriousness of it, we will start to feel a sense of shame instead of pride.

Gambling

I remember the days when it was considered a sin to own a pack of cards – even if all you wanted to play with them was snap! When my children were young, they used to bring some raffle tickets home from their school, and the profits would go towards a worthy cause. I remember telling my children to take them straight back and to tell their teacher that their daddy was a Christian and does not believe in gambling. I cringe with embarrassment at that now, and think I would die if I ever saw the teacher.

Nowadays many Christians enjoy raffles, the National Lottery, and in America some churches even arrange special family outings to the casinos in Atlantic City and Las Vegas.

The stakes are high

I was in a meeting a while ago where the Bible teacher had taught on the evils of gambling, making special reference to the National Lottery. A while later, the National Lottery offered him some money to help restore their building, which of course was gratefully received. I wonder what would happen if a member of a strict anti-gambling church won a million pounds on the Lottery and offered to tithe £100,000 to the local church. I wonder if the church would accept so-called dirty money. I could be wrong, but after praying over it to make sure that it was clean, I think most leaders would snap it up as a gift from God.

I am also hearing of Christian organizations that are now applying for Lottery money to help fund them. Some members of our church have just held a week long play scheme for children with special needs in our building, and both the National Lottery and the local council helped to fund it. Lottery money seems to be donated to all sorts of strange causes; personally, I would much rather see it go into Christian work.

The Bible says little against gambling. I realize that, like alcohol, work, cigarettes, coffee, television, computer games, chocolate and painkillers, it can be addictive. The Bible does not say 'thou shalt not gamble' and so I do not feel I can teach against it in an absolute way, but as with all the above, obsession is dangerous.

By the way, you may have noticed that I have discreetly not mentioned stocks and shares as being a bit of a 'gamble', as I know that would really upset quite a few Christians who are totally against gambling!

Language barrier

This is a very strange one. What makes a swear word a swear word? Is the answer simply that it's a word that the majority of the culture of the day finds offensive? Let's look at a scripture that talks about 'filthy language', which is the nearest expression that we can get to our word 'swearing'. Colossians 3:8 says 'But now you must rid yourselves of ... filthy language from your lips.' Vine's dictionary tells us that the Greek word used here, *aischrologia,* 'denotes any kind of base utterance, the utterance of an uncontrolled tongue', so of course it does not necessarily relate to our modern-day four-letter words.

Curses

Although today when we hear someone swearing we sometimes say they are cursing, the word cursing, when used in the Bible, did not mean using filthy language. Without going into great detail, the word 'curse' has many meanings. Perhaps the most familiar is found in the New Testament in Romans 3:14: 'Their mouths are full of cursing and bitterness.' This meaning was more one of wanting to inflict hurt on someone.

When we read that Jesus cursed the fig tree in Mark 11, and when Paul tells us that Jesus redeemed us from the curse of the law by becoming a curse, we can see the variations in the usage of this word, but it is still not used for filthy language.

Back to the Bible language

If we go back to Colossians and assume that Paul's statement does even vaguely incorporate what we now call swearing, what words was he talking about, as those words would have been in Greek?

Let's just have a look at certain of our four-letter words that we are hoping our children do not use. It's interesting that none of these go back to Anglo Saxon times, although many have Germanic origins. All of the following words can now be found in the English dictionary, with taboo written alongside them. I won't write them in full, as even reading them can be offensive to some.

The 'S' word. First known usage early fourteenth century. Its proper meaning is to defecate. Used all the time in movies, from PG Certificate upwards.

The 'C' word. First known usage a few years later than the 'S' word. Its proper meaning is the vagina. This is one of the most offensive words in the English language and at the time of writing is not used very often, even in adult movies.

The 'F' word. First known usage early 1600s. Its proper meaning is to have sexual intercourse. An aggressive word that is now commonplace in movies from Certificate 15, but by the time you read this will probably be Certificate 12.

Time changes words

Over the years, swear words sometimes change from being offensive to being acceptable and commonplace. Whereas the above words have taboo written alongside them in the dictionary, the thirteenth-century French word 'damn', which once meant condemnation or deserving damnation, seems for most people today a very tame word. In 1799, when the young upper-middle-class daughter of a vicar, Jane Austin, wrote *Northanger Abbey*, her worst expletive was this word damn. But you will not find this bad word in its offensive entirety in the book; she just writes D– and hopes the reader of the day will not be so offended that they instantly stop reading and burn the book in horror.

Nowadays, we find a similar thing in our daily tabloids but instead we have S– or even F–. These words are usually followed by a sort of apology, which says, 'We will not print the full word, as this is a family newspaper,' but even our children know which word they are referring to.

Let's look at a few other 'bad' words, their original meanings and how they rate today.

The unacceptable becoming acceptable

Bloody is a late eighteenth-century swear word, and very British. Once considered offensive because some thought this word had

Christian roots, I can find nothing to back this up. Brewer says it comes from aristocratic rowdies who were known as 'bloods', due to being foolish drunkards. Nowadays, it is a fairly inoffensive slang word not rated taboo.

Bastard is a thirteenth-century French word, which was very offensive when people took it at its real meaning: a child from an unmarried couple. But today, with such a large percentage of children being born outside of marriage, very few use it in connection with its original meaning, and it is slang rather than taboo.

Fart is actually of Norse or high German origin, meaning to break wind. I've noticed over the past few years that it is now a word used quite widely by Christians of all ages, yet the dictionary rates it taboo, along with the four-letter words mentioned above.

Bugger is a sixteenth-century French word, the original meaning of which was a person who has anal intercourse, and is rated taboo in the dictionary. Many people use this word without having any idea of its original meaning, and it is often substituted for 'bastard'.

The acceptable becoming unacceptable

In the Authorized Version of the Bible, we will find twice the word 'piss' meaning urine. We can also find about half-a-dozen different scriptures which use the expression 'cutting off him that pisseth against the wall' which I believe meant a person's descendants. The word piss obviously did not cause offence in the seventeenth century, and I guess it is still being read by fans of the 1611 King James version now, in the twenty-first century.

I wonder if our modern-day children are missing out by not hearing that very descriptive expression 'cutting off him that pisseth against the wall' read out from the pulpit, because today's modern translations have deleted it altogether without even adding an expression that may be apt for today. But alas, modern translations saw no place for a late fourteenth-century word that probably was of French vintage, and now even the dictionary has put it in the same category as our so called obscene four-letter words and written 'taboo' next to it. What was once used as an everyday word now causes offence.

It was all Greek (Hebrew or Aramaic) to them

So the original Scriptures were not actually talking about any of the English words we have mentioned, and certainly the characters in Bible times would not have used any of them, although I am sure they had slang and taboo words of their own. So, to take us back to our original point, what makes a swear word a swear word?

A very learned friend of mine informed me that the majority of the above words used in the way they are today are either degrading God, degrading parts of the wonderful body God made, or degrading the beautiful act of sexual reproduction. But the question has to be asked, if we used the above words in their *right* context would they still be swear words? The answer I have discovered is that to some people they would be, but to others they would not.

I used to be a farmer, and no one was offended when any of the workers used the 'S' word while cleaning out a cow shed or a pigsty, but if a school party arrived to look around the farm, suddenly the word changed to dung. But what makes one word bad and the other not, when they are describing the same thing? Some even have problems if the word 'bloody' is used in a church meeting, when describing how the body of Jesus must have looked after being beaten by the Roman guard.

Out of context

So, what if we use these words in the wrong context? Does that make them even more offensive? Is it less offensive when we see somebody smile as they call someone a silly little b**** in gentle humour, than when we hear that someone is told to b**** off, in violent aggression? They are both using the same word, yet some would see the latter as more offensive because of the way it is said.

Alternative expressions

So maybe the answer is not to use any of the words already mentioned, and make up some new ones to put in their place. Can we say 'Oh sugar, shoot, rats' or 'push, shove, rack or naff off'? Our children go for a pee, tinkle, wee-wee. We teach them to call body parts bums, butts, tiddly-winks and willies, and, as they grow older, boobs instead of breasts and snuggling, screwing and making love, instead of sexual intercourse. But are these words just as bad as the originals that we would never dream of saying?

Christians often use the oddest sayings without ever considering what the root meaning may be. A leader told me the other day that it was 'hissing' down with rain. Have you ever heard anyone use the expression 'fits and starts' without realizing a couple of letter changes gives you rather different words? Or how about short and curlies, caught with his trousers down, odds and sods, and even knackered and plonker? And how many times have preachers told us to get our fingers out? Many ladies have come up to me over the years claiming to be Ishmael 'groupies'. They never were, and I'm sure if they knew what the word meant, they would never want to be! Now you can even purchase a poster from Christian bookshops showing a picture of some lovely little ducks, with the wording 'Father says ... keep your pecker up'.

Still, more modern-day words appear and we cannot blame the Germans for these. They certainly don't sound very nice, but who is going to be the one to declare them offensive or swear words? We can't leave it to the writers of the dictionary. Words like horny, shag, gonads, roger, blow job, cum, spunk, crud – and next week our children will come home with an even larger vocabulary.

It gives a new meaning to sign language when you see the bent arm salute, or the two finger or middle finger wave: obscene language without a word being said. I wonder if this sort of thing happened in Bible times. Christians have told me in my research that some offensive words said in a Scottish or Irish accent do not sound as bad as when they are said in an English accent, and everyone seems to think that it is far worse to hear a girl use some of these words than a man.

What makes life even more complicated is when I travel to other countries and some words are accepted while others are not, and many have completely different meanings. I remember performing at a youth concert in America, when a very famous English musician and friend of mine, who was also performing, announced that as well as selling pencils and pens in his shop, Ishmael also sells rubbers. The pastor nearly had a heart attack. (In America this refers to condoms not erasers.)

I was on another children's camp in America and was told by one of the leaders that a girl had just broken her fanny pack. I had no idea he was talking about what we call a bum-bag. I also discovered that people in America do not smoke fags. While in mainland Europe, I have taught Christians in my seminars who have learned only a small amount of English, mainly from English-speaking movies. They ask questions in pidgin English, adding some very unorthodox words, assuming they are the words we all use.

Why have I said all this?

The main reason is that not many, if any, Christians dare to write about or teach on this subject, yet it's so important, especially when we are thinking of our children. I remember when we had a local church leader round for a first visit and, knowing first impressions are important, we had tea served in cups, not mugs, and some cake, instead of biscuits, on the table. It was then that one of our children arrived home from primary school, having just learned the 'F–' word from one of his friends in the playground. As he walked into the lounge, repeating this one word over and over again, I could see our visitor was not impressed. It's strange but the more you try and shut your child up, the more intent they seem on saying a word over and over. It was not my child's fault; it was a word he picked up and he had no idea what it meant or how offensive it could be. I made sure he did know the minute our embarrassed guest had gone.

Our children will come home using all sorts of words and we do need to talk through with them why, as Christians, we don't say them. I still cannot define a swear word, because I have discovered that as cultures change, so do words. We don't need to use what is known as 'dirty talk'; we don't need to use words that could offend people; but having said this, parents and children's workers still have their work cut out when it comes to defining these words.

We also somehow need to remind them that it is not just a word that can be offensive but also the way we use words which is culturally unacceptable. Matthew 5:22 tells us that anyone who is angry with his brother will face judgement, and anyone who calls him a fool will be in danger of the fire of hell. Be careful, little tongue, what you say!

Misusing the Lord's name

Finally, blasphemy is comparatively simple to work out. Around 1863 the Revd Charles Kingsley wrote the very clever, if not slightly surreal *Water Babies*. The book is basically an endorsement of Darwin's origin of species for children to understand, although, in my opinion, they would have to be very intelligent children to understand it. He said of the hero, little Tom, that he had never heard of God or of Christ, except in words that you have never heard, and which it would have been well if he had never heard. Nowadays, our children do not just hear these words; they seem to use them as much – if not more – than adults do.

We must teach our children never to take the name of the Lord our God in vain. Encourage them not to say good Lord, God, Oh my God and Jesus Christ in the way their unsaved friends do. These words, misused, should offend us far more than any of the above taboo four-letter words that we have been looking at. Don't try and make excuses for people when they say 'God', because they are using a small g, or because they do not know him. Blasphemy has nothing to do with just Christians and God; according to the Bible, anyone who takes God's name in vain is a blasphemer. Our world is far from holy, but God is holy, Jesus is holy, so let's keep his name holy and never use it as an expression of surprise, anger, or even out of context.

God has given us so many expressive words to use; let's just pray we find a way to teach the right ones to our children.

17

Worship, Praise and Music

Different opinions

I respect the fact that many of my close friends who are affectionately known as 'worship leaders' may disagree with the following paragraphs and consider praise and worship to be interchangeable words. Nevertheless, in the Bible they do appear to be two different words, and in the Greek and Hebrew too they do not appear to be the same.

When teaching children we need to differentiate between the two words, and whatever overlap there might be, I believe the Bible gives them different and specific meanings (just as we saw with interpretation and prophecy). The words for 'praise and worship' have much more significance than the usage and meaning we give them today.

Worship is. . . .

The word worship in the Bible can be translated as follows: to bow down, to serve, to esteem, to make obeisance, to reverence, to revere, to honour religiously, to kiss the hand, and so on.

Time of worship – what's that?

Let's jump in at the deep end. Maybe it's time to drop some of our religious non-biblical terminology, so our children can understand the true meaning of certain words. We have cheapened the word worship by constantly using the expression 'a time of worship' when referring to a singing time included in our meetings. Let's take this phrase out of our Christian vocabulary because it is very unhelpful and confusing to our children. Most Christians today feel worship is only something that happens at a meeting when the musicians start playing their instruments, but as we can see above there is no scripture that directly says worship is singing or music.

Worship must be taught as a lifestyle; it's our daily close relationship with Jesus, it's our reverence for Almighty God, and we should be worshippers worshipping 24 hours a day, 7 days a week. Music has its place and certainly can be linked to worship, but music is not worship.

Worship is not visible

We look round our meetings and so often judge people on what they are doing, and how they are looking or participating during what we call our worship time. I mention this because we automatically look at our teenagers and children in a similar way. Often, when a boy passes the age of ten, he does not enjoy singing songs the way he used to when he was eight. When adults see children looking uninterested and bored during the long sessions of singing, many think that this is a sign they are on the spiritual downward spiral that ends up in a place called 'backsliderland'. Some would even go as far as to doubt someone's salvation if they do not appear to enjoy singing songs to God.

Young teenagers are going through major body changes, which includes strange voice changes in boys. Some are embarrassed to talk, let alone sing, and yet we often put them in a cell group of ten in someone's home and expect them as good Christians to sing their socks off for Jesus. Worship is a matter of the heart. If the young want to vocalize those feelings, that is great; if not, never mind, so long as the heart stays in tune with God.

I remember hearing someone at a meeting of musicians teaching how to sing out rather than speak prophecies. They then encouraged everyone to try it. It was terrible! Some voices were not made to sing solos, and while we listened to sounds that resembled a cat being pulled through a combine harvester, we were also supposed to believe that this was the voice of God communicating with us. We must remember that those who attended the synagogue in the New Testament to worship did not rely upon music; we know this because there were no instruments used and no songs sung in their meetings.

Of course, the Bible does talk about groups of people meeting together to worship. What this means is that these people were able to take their public praise and prayers and use them to express their love and gratitude to God in a real act of inward spiritual worship, just like many Christians do today.

Worship leader – who's that?

The second phrase I suggest we drop is worship leader. Worship leading is not a human responsibility. There is only one worship leader, and he is the Holy Spirit. I often think about the pressure put upon human 'worship leaders'. People arrive for a meeting, many sadly out of fellowship with Jesus because of rebellion and unconfessed sin. The human worship leader's job is to lift them up, get them singing, maybe culminating in these people with their hands in the air, or singing in tongues.

Now we all know that music is a great manipulator and certain sounds and instruments can make you feel happy while others make you sad. Our emotions are often more quickly affected than our hearts by these sounds. For example, if the background music was taken out of some movies, they would not have half their impact; the music that goes with the picture can easily affect our emotions but rarely does it alter our innermost convictions.

So, by the end of our meeting, if people have sung the right songs and really entered into the music, this is usually enough to satisfy many leaders and musicians. But unless there has been a time for repenting and cleansing, many people go out exactly the same as they came in – as non-worshippers.

Praise is . . .

Praise too has a deeper meaning than what we refer to as a 'praise time'. Praise in Scripture often refers to sacrificial offering, confession, to bless, to glorify, and does sometimes involve singing and music.

One meaning for praise is to stretch out our hand to God in confession; yet in worship, as we see a bit later, it's as though God has stretched out his hand towards us, for us to kiss in adoration.

Praise time and praise leaders

As seen above, the word 'praise' has very different meanings. One Greek word, *humneo*, means 'to sing', and we have many scriptures that talk about singing praises or hymns. There is also the word *Psallo* which can mean to twitch, twang or play a stringed musical instrument. From these two words we get 'hymns' and 'psalms'.

So maybe it would be more helpful to change the name worship time to praise time, and to change the name worship leader to praise leader or chief musician, if your church believes that it's important to give people names and titles. This way, children will understand that worship is not a musical time, but praise can be linked with instruments and singing our feelings out loud to God. We can then see what the real worship leader wants to say into all of our lives. For others, it may be more honest to rename our worship time 'a time of singing' and to rename our worship leaders 'people leading us in our time of singing'.

Having said all of this, there is a special place for music. We should remember how powerful music can be: harps can calm demons when played by a friend of God; trumpet sounds can assist in smashing down fortress walls when used in faith by an obedient servant of God.

For a worshipper who is a close friend and an obedient servant of Jesus, sometimes during a time of praise, music and singing, something very special happens to them. But I would not attempt to put those 'happenings' into words, or even expect that all our children will experience such things, although some definitely will.

It was always God's plan that children should be instruments of praise. Psalm 8:2 says, 'From the lips of children and infants you have ordained praise because of your enemies, to silence the foe and the avenger.' And Jesus himself quoted this scripture in Matthew 21, as in that triumphant, yet in some ways sad, procession he entered the temple area and heard the children shouting, 'Hosanna to the Son of David.' Children have a natural ability to praise but, as is so often the case, the environment and the influence of adults have encouraged children to grow up in a way that tends to squeeze this heartfelt expression out of their lives.

Praise and worship is a massive subject, and numerous books have been written on the meanings of these two well-used words. I realize that my including them in just one chapter does not do these words justice. Most of these books on worship, however, have tended to be for adults and use phrasing which few children can understand. It seems that most parents are more keen to encourage their children from a very early age to play a musical instrument than they are about giving instruction on how their child can develop as a musical instrument for the glory of God!

For young children, simple and clear definition is important, and I would instruct them that praise is giving thanks, often verbally, while worship is adoration and sometimes silent. Let us look at these in more detail.

One of my favourite scriptures is 1 Thessalonians 5:16–22. This sums up so much of my teaching to children:

> Be joyful always; pray continually; give thanks in all circumstances, for this is God's will for you in Christ Jesus.
> Do not put out the Spirit's fire; do not treat prophecies with contempt. Test everything. Hold on to the good. Avoid every kind of evil.

When someone comes and says to you that they are not sure what God's will for them is, quote them that scripture, emphasizing: 'Give thanks [praise] in all circumstances, for this is God's will for you in Christ Jesus.' Often when people are needing guidance, once they begin thanking God, their guidance and answers seem to come so much clearer and more quickly.

This whole chapter could be filled with scriptures that instruct us to give praise and thanks to God, proving what a very important part of our Christian life God would like this to be. Sometimes giving thanks to God is hard for Christian children because they have been brought up in this modern generation to believe that the world owes them, and that they deserve all they are given. Through being spoilt, they have not learned the importance of saying thank you and being thankful to others.

Most members of the older generation were trained as children to be courteous, polite and to express their appreciation. With each new generation, this seems to be less and less the case. When children are not taught to give thanks for what they receive, it has a far more harmful effect than just making them rude and impolite to those around them. It also teaches them to be disrespectful and irreverent to God. These children will need to be re-educated before they will be capable of entering into real praise.

Out of the thousands of adults and children I have spent time ministering to, less than 2 per cent would come up and show any gratitude, even though I know that they have enjoyed what I have done. Please don't get me wrong. Although I appreciate encouragement, I have learned to be able to live without it. I really don't need everyone to keep patting me on the back and telling me how wonderful I am, but I do believe an indication of how much we really appreciate God can be found by how much we appreciate the members of his body. It is important that we learn to show our appreciation, and that isn't just by giving somebody a round of applause.

I remember after one praise party two people approached me; one was a tiny little girl who thanked me and told me how much she had enjoyed the evening, and the other was a treasurer, who said nothing but just thrust an envelope in my hand without even a smile. I received more of a blessing from that little girl than however many digits were written on that cheque; I guess it's got something to do with being a cheerful giver.

Actions speak as well as words

Although true thankfulness comes from our hearts, we usually express it by action. Sometimes we pat each other on the back; other times we may embrace or kiss as a sign of our appreciation. At events, if we have enjoyed being entertained, we may clap, shout, whistle, or even stand to our feet to let those who have given to us know that we are thankful.

The Bible also talks about many ways in which people, through movement, gave thanks to God. Here are some in alphabetical order:

Bowing and lying flat on the ground

Therefore God exalted him to the highest place and gave him the name that is above every name, that at the name of Jesus every knee should bow, in heaven and on earth and under the earth, and every tongue confess that Jesus Christ is Lord, to the glory of God the Father. (Philippians 2:9–11)

Then David said to the whole assembly, 'Praise the Lord your God.' So they all praised the Lord, the God of their fathers; they bowed low and fell prostrate before the Lord and the king. (1 Chronicles 29:20)

Clapping and shouting

Clap your hands, all you nations; shout to God with cries of joy. (Psalm 47:1)

Dancing and music

Let them praise his name with dancing and make music to him with tambourine and harp. (Psalm 149:3)

Hands raised high

Ezra praised the Lord, the great God; and all the people lifted their hands and responded, 'Amen! Amen!' (Nehemiah 8:6)

High-energy dancing

David, wearing a linen ephod [cloth], danced before the Lord with all his might. . . . (2 Samuel 6:14)

Jumping

He jumped to his feet and began to walk. Then he went with them into the temple courts, walking and jumping, and praising God. (Acts 3:8)

Standing up

And the Levites . . . said: 'Stand up and praise the Lord your God, who is from everlasting to everlasting.' (Nehemiah 9:5)

These are just a few of the many ways in which people praised God in the Bible, and each one of these had more variations than one could imagine.

Children need expression

My observation of children is that for years they have been suppressed and not taught about the many ways of releasing their praise. Some have learned that praise is just singing a hymn, and think that all that is required for them to express their thanks to God is to stand politely until the countless verses have been sung and then to sit down again. Others have been taught that their praise must be expressed with reverence – which they think means being still and remaining silent – and many churches are actually proud to have installed long, hard, wooden benches called pews which, like the stocks of old, make sure that nobody can move, even if they want to. Some could be very courageous and dance on top of them, but then they would probably be thrown out for hooliganism!

Of course, there is a place for stillness and silence, but don't confuse children into thinking that these are the definitions of reverence, or else you are in danger of writing off most of God's friends in the Bible. Reverence is shown in our feelings towards God and not necessarily in the way we humbly and honestly express them. Little children are naturally bouncy and energetic, and when they do something they tend to do it like King David did, with all their might. I wonder, if we invited David to come to one of our meetings, how many of us would let him preach but never allow him to teach us about how to be really free in our praise.

Some people have told me that I am an extreme extrovert, but compared with David I think I'm a shy, reserved introvert. I do sometimes care what people think of me, but David didn't. All he seemed to care about was pleasing his best friend, and that was God, whom he loved and obeyed. One of my aims has been to restore children's natural expressions to them so they don't have to fit into the reserved and restricted adult mould that we have chosen to bury ourselves in.

You'll never dance alone

I remember going to one church in the Midlands, and while praying about what praise songs to sing, I felt I should do a song which I didn't particularly like. The song encourages people to clap and dance as part of their praise to Father God. As the meeting began, I noticed all the children had come down to the front to get a good view. I started singing this well-worn song, and both children and adults alike just watched me in amazement, standing as still as cement statues, with their eyes popping out in unbelief, as I sang and danced to it.

Before you ask, yes, I was totally embarrassed. I had come to encourage them to praise, not do a one-man *Come Dancing* exhibition at the front. Determined not to give up, however, I played it a couple more times, and on about the third run through I noticed that some of the children had started tapping their feet. Well, this was a 100 per cent improvement, so I thought I would sing this song – which was rapidly getting more boring and repetitive to me – a few more times.

By the fifth time, all the children were dancing and singing, and the adults' feet had started tapping. Some had even started to smile. Always being willing to push a point to extremes, I continued to play this chorus, and it must have been about the tenth time through that everyone began to dance and sing and praise God. In fact, I think I was the only one who had stopped, due to wearing myself out on the nine previous renditions.

No, I do not do this at every meeting, but it was right to do it at this one because through it I learned a few important lessons.

The first was that it was the children who were used to release the adults. It was only as the older folk saw these young ones enjoying praising God that they decided to join in with them. The other important thing that happened was that as everyone joined in together a heaviness lifted off the meeting. People became more at ease and relaxed, and as I preached a little later in the meeting I noticed that because they were more relaxed they were so much more willing to respond as God spoke to them on personal needs and issues.

Children enjoying their praise are not only a blessing to the rest of the church, but also an example of how we older children can be before our heavenly Father.

Let me give you an example

I invariably meet children's leaders who treat me as some sort of 'pied piper'. When I take a meeting, their children respond, but when they take a similar sort of meeting they seem to get nowhere.

I have no magical or sinister powers, but I do believe that children and adults are led by example. I would never teach people to do things that I would not be willing to do myself, and I would not sing praise songs which encourage folk to raise their hands or dance unless I was willing to do it. In fact, I have gone as far as to tell people not to sing certain lines of songs that require certain movements if they won't do them. It is ridiculous to sing words that we don't mean.

Leading by example is important for nearly every area of the Christian life. There is the argument, of course, that the children just imitate and don't understand what they are doing. For many of the very young ones this is a valid point, but I think of what Paul said in 1 Corinthians 4:16: 'Therefore I urge you to imitate me.' To copy what is good and biblical, whatever the motives (or lack of motives in this case), is not such a bad thing. Subconsciously, we all imitate others.

I have observed that if the child is taught well, it is not long before they stop copying and begin expressing praise of their own volition and being very sincere in their actions. Another thing I have noticed with children is that their praise has very little to do with their personalities and temperaments. They, like us, would just use these as an excuse for not being as free as God would like them to be.

Come Together

A Christian musical called *Come Together* was very popular some decades ago, and this was quite revolutionary as it taught people to clap and raise their hands. The only problem was that many in the audiences were not in the Spirit, and it taught people how to be extrovert rather than how to be free in the Spirit.

God does not want us all to be of extrovert character, but he does want us to be so full of Holy Spirit boldness that we are not frightened to do anything that pleases him. The extrovert who is not sensitive to the Spirit of God can be a praise leader's nightmare in a meeting. I have had them in my meetings, and while the loud praise is being expressed they are fine, but as the mood of the meeting changes and the music quietens down and becomes very gentle, our extrovert praiser fails to recognize this and still leaps around, bashing his tambourine like a maniac.

God has made children with different personalities; how boring the world would be if they were all the same. The last thing I would ever want to do is put them in an Ishmael mould so that they all came out as little replicas of me. But I do want to teach them to lose their inhibitions and learn what it is like to be free in their praise.

Back to worship

Hopefully, by now we do not believe that praise is the fast songs and worship is the slow ones. Praise and thanksgiving can be fast music, slow music or no music at all. Worship is what is going on inside, between God and us.

Children so often need a picture to help them understand. One of the Greek words for worship is *proskuneo*. The meaning of this word is simply 'to kiss the hand', and it is used over 50 times in the New Testament. To give children a picture of this, I wrote a song called 'I'll kiss the hand of Jesus', which went like this:

> I'll kiss the hand of Jesus, yes I will.
> I'll kiss the hand of Jesus, yes I will.
> As I see the hole where the nail has been,
> I realize it was my sin,
> That marred those beautiful hands,
> That scarred those beautiful hands.
>
> The hand that held the little ones sitting on his knee,
> The hand that only taught to love and care,
> The hand that rescued Peter from drowning in the sea,
> Was soon to feel the cross that it would bear.
>
> The hand that was tied up for the love that it had shown,
> The hand that didn't resist the enemy,
> The hand that didn't scream as the blunt pins
>   held it high,
> The fingers reaching out to victory.
>
> The hand that couldn't die now writes the Book of Life,
> This hand also shares the bread and wine,
> And Jesus says 'Christian, if you want to worship me,
> Just come and kiss this hand of mine.'

This song helps children use their imagination to understand why we adore our Lord, and just a little bit of what heartfelt worship really is. I firmly believe that children need to know the significance of the suffering and pain of the Lord Jesus upon the cross if they are to really know worship. At one meeting, I spent quite a few minutes explaining this to about 400 eight- to eleven-year-olds. They were so quiet you could have heard a pin drop. After this I sang a song, and without giving the children instruction as to how to express their feelings, I told them to tell the Lord how much they loved him. It was at this point that we all felt the power of God in a very special way, and many of the children spontaneously fell on their knees before the Lord. Some started crying out to God, while others were weeping before him as they considered the cost of Calvary.

I have yet to be in a meeting with adults where there has been such a deep, sincere level of the presence of Jesus. There is no doubt about it: these little ones really know how to praise and are also worshippers.

Song writing

Songs are much easier to write than most people imagine, and I would encourage any children's workers, even if they are only slightly musical, to try writing them.

Before you start composing songs of thanks and adoration to God, have a go at writing a scripture song; they are the simplest. All you need to do is find a short scripture and put a melody to it. It does not have to rhyme, but it does need to be easy to sing. This, of course, has a dual purpose, as it not only teaches the children a new song, but also teaches them scripture. At this stage, involve some of your other leaders, who may not be musicians, to think up some actions or dances, if and when the words are appropriate.

Praise songs do require a little more thought. Writers need to consider what age group the song is primarily for, what they want to convey through the words and music, and what they hope it will achieve for those singing it. The first praise song that people write usually sounds like the following:

> Jesus died for me.
> He died at Calvary.
> How happy I should be.
> Now from sin I am set free.

A good start – factual, accurate, simple, and I'm sure easy to sing. The more you write, however, the more creative and expressive, and the less clichéd and predictable your songs will become. After a short while your song will say a similar thing but in a different way, and may sound something like:

> Lord Jesus, I'm so thankful that you gave your life for me,
> For the pain and suffering endured upon that cross at
>   Calvary.
> The more I think about it, the more happy I should be,
> 'Cause from the sin that once made me its slave,
> I'm released, I've been set free.

There may be one or two words which small children may not understand, but I am a keen believer in stretching their vocabulary as well as their spiritual lives. Rather than use one-syllable words all the time, use longer ones and explain to the children what they mean.

As you progress in song writing you will want to get away from the obvious rhyming patterns and also the 'da de da de da de da' stanzas, and you may end up changing your song to:

> I'm so thankful that you gave your life, Lord Jesus,
> And it's you I want to worship, it's you whom I adore.
> You've filled my life with happiness, since your blood

has set me free,
And the sin that once ruled in my life, will not rule
me any more.

And so you keep working on it until you feel it says what you want, to the age group you want to say it to. By the way, as you may have guessed, I have not spent days composing these three stages of a worship song. It has taken me, hold on, I'll just look at my watch, yes, about ten minutes, and that includes the time it's taken to type it out on the computer, answer a phone call, and drink my coffee. So you can see how easy it is – you've got no excuse. There is a great need for new praise songs which children can enjoy. If we want to keep our children in line with the Bible's advice to sing a new song, we will have to write songs first.

Action songs

Remember, children love songs with instructions of how to praise. Nearly all my recent songs contain music and motion. My sister told me that one day after their church meeting all her family came back to her house for coffee and while the adults were in one room, the children went into the other room to have their own 'meeting'. After a while, she quietly peeped around the door and saw all of them, the youngest aged about two, genuinely expressing their praise to God while joining in with one of my songs. The words just said:

I raise my hands up high,
I bow my head down low,
Then I kneel before the Lord and say I love you.

They did not need Ishmael; they did not need adults; they did not need a band. All they needed was probably the most simple song that anyone could write, plus, of course, the presence of the Holy Spirit.

Songs that speak

Finally, we do need songs that speak into people's lives while they sing them. In 'Father God I Wonder', I wanted people from rejected backgrounds to understand they now belong to a loving family, with a Father who will never let them down. The Holy Spirit has used this song to minister to many such people over the years as they have sung it.

> Father God I wonder
> How I managed to exist
> Without the knowledge of your parenthood
> And your loving care.
> Now I am your son/child,
> I am adopted in your family,
> And I can never be alone,
> 'Cos Father God you're there beside me.

> I will sing your praises,
> I will sing your praises,
> I will sing your praises for evermore.
> I will sing your praises,
> I will sing your praises,
> I will sing your praises for evermore.

Ian Smale.
Copyright © 1984 Thankyou Music,
PO Box 75, Eastbourne BN23 6NW.

Many people ask why I did not write child instead of son. The reason I used son was because I took it straight from Galatians 3:

no Jew or Greek, slave or free, male or female. We are all sons –
and all heirs. As a female, if you find this hard to swallow, don't
worry: the Bible balances it up by referring to males as the bride
of Christ. If you still think your children will not understand my
explanation, just use the word child. I really don't mind, as long
as the song is blessing them and you.

18

Young and Gifted

It was he [Jesus] who gave some to be apostles, some to be prophets, some to be evangelists, and some to be pastors and teachers, to prepare God's people for works of service, so that the body of Christ may be built up until we all reach unity in the faith and in the knowledge of the Son of God and become mature, attaining to the whole measure of the fulness of Christ. (Ephesians 4:11–13)

Talent spotting

I wonder why we wait until children are adults before we start encouraging them to develop their ministries? So often we do not recognize children's God-given talents until they are older, and by then we may well have missed out because they have left the church anyway.

One of the functions of any leader is to see what qualities his people have, and this needs to include the qualities that children possess. Many feel that future leaders for their local churches will be imported when needed, but I'm a keen believer that the vast majority of our future local ministries are sitting in our children's meeting, waiting to be trained and discipled.

Generally, people are not allowed to develop nowadays. Unless they have an incredible natural in-built talent and can preach immediately, they are rarely given the chance to develop. We leaders forget all too quickly how green and inexperienced we were when we first started, and often expect up and coming leaders to be as we are now, not as we were then, before we can accept them.

Performance points

A friend of mine, who has been greatly used by God and is one of the best children's communicators I know, had been through some hard times, having moved towns and joined a new church group. After a time of settling in, the leaders asked if he would like to do the children's talk at a family meeting, which he, of course, was thrilled to accept. Sadly, he felt as though he was on trial and that he ought to try and impress those who would be assessing and judging his performance. With this in mind, he brought out all his best visual aids, but in doing so tried to cram far too much into a short space of time and ended up by taking a long time to communicate very little. It was his one chance – and he blew it; he was not asked to do another talk.

Realizing that the leaders had no faith in his gifting, he soon left that group and joined another, where he is now being greatly used in a less judgemental gathering. I remember when I gave my very first talk: I was given a bit of freedom to do something, and it was awful. But people didn't give up on me – they trained me.

Gifts for all

Every person in church must have a God-given talent somewhere to bless the body of Christ with, and all leaders have to do is find it. The problem is, if it is that hard for adults to find and be allowed to develop their ministries, what hope do our children have? There is no age limit for any ministry at either end of the scale, but the sooner one is encouraged to start, the more chance one has of being proficient when one is older.

One of the great unwritten laws of the church seems to be, 'You've got to prove yourself,' but no one is really sure what that means. I think this statement means that you have not proved yourself until you have done something absolutely fantastic and everyone is 100 per cent behind you and thinks you are great. But how often does that happen in those early days? Could even our elders and leaders pass this criterion?

Even in your local church situation, you are always going to find people who do not like you very much. Oh, they love you because the Bible says they must, but they still don't particularly like you. And also, due to the fact that you have grown up in the church, they still see you as a young boy or girl, even when you are middle-aged. Some folk will never see your potential, and it is so easy after a bit of criticism to become discouraged.

Church leaders need to release people into their ministries and even allow them to make mistakes. They can cover all this as long as the pupil is humble, submissive and willing to learn. Don't you find that there is always someone better at what you are doing in the church? Is there someone better at children's work than you? If there is, that person only arrived at that point through learning, making mistakes and doing it. Why wait until a child becomes an adult before we give them that opportunity? If you work with children, you need to start promoting their talents. Keep your eyes open and begin looking for certain things the children are good at.

Seek and ye shall find

You need to watch for tell-tale signs, indicating what kind of gift or talent there is. Little Johnny might pick up a guitar and only play one chord, but that's a beginning. Don't spread it around, but a lot of my own songs only use another two, and he should certainly be up to my standard in no time.

Others might be more percussive, so you will need to encourage them in that area and let them have a tambourine at some stage. It's better to hand one tambourine to a child with a sense of rhythm, than 20 to children with no sense of timing. When our eldest son, Joseph, was still very young, we noticed how every time music was playing, he would tap along to it with anything that he happened to have in his hands at that time. To some parents, this would just be seen as an annoyance, and the thumping implement would be removed from their child's hand with a verbal warning to stop making that noise or else. We didn't say that. Instead, we bought him a very cheap drum kit, and a few years later he was drumming in my band, in front of thousands of people.

It was a similar story with our son Daniel and his guitar playing, and Suzy and her dancing. All my children have either played instruments or danced for me over the years, so I have been well rewarded by that early personal investment.

Treasure is not just buried on desert islands

Not all children are musical – some may be good at art. Perhaps you were disgusted when you saw them doodling during your talk, but then to your amazement, before you screwed up their masterpiece and threw it in the bin, you noticed that it had shades of a budding Van Gogh. Use them! Just think, it will save you having to do the artwork and posters that you so hate doing. Promote their qualities.

Talent is not always discovered at meetings. It may be necessary to visit the children's homes to find out what they are capable of doing. It's a great opportunity, especially to get to know unsaved parents. On a different level, as 1 Corinthians 12 reminds us, although we may all be able to speak in tongues, prophesy, pray for healing, do a bit of admin, and so on, there are those who have a specific ministry to the church and will major in one particular area, but they will still need help and encouragement.

You need to praise their qualities. We spend too much time talking about the bad things children do: 'They're scruffy and they sneeze all the time. They never clap, never sing, are football mad, and they are always fighting.' If you examine their characters, you will see some good qualities and some fantastic fruit. There will be gentleness in some, indicating a pastoral future; a real kindness in others, which will be shown in later years as a ministry of hospitality.

We must help the children discern what their ministries are. We don't know how long they have on this earth, so let's start to encourage them while they are here.

We can learn much from some of the famous 'children' of the Bible. Unfortunately, you never know how old the child was because the word 'children' sometimes related to thirty-four-year-olds. But here are a few heroes we know were learning and being prepared for their future while they were very young:

An obedient son

Isaac spoke up and said to his father Abraham, 'Father?'

'Yes, my son?' Abraham replied.

'The fire and wood are here,' Isaac said, 'but where is the lamb for the burnt offering?'

Abraham answered, 'God himself will provide the lamb for the burnt offering, my son.' And the two of them went on together.

When they reached the place God had told him about, Abraham built an altar there and arranged the wood on it. He bound his son Isaac and laid him on the altar, on top of the wood. Then he reached out his hand and took the knife to slay his son. (Genesis 22:7–10)

We don't know how old Isaac was, but he was reasonably young. The story obviously gives credit to Abraham, but I want to give credit to Isaac. I think it's amazing.

Let's try to picture what was actually happening. Isaac knew his father loved him and is invited to go with his dad to perform a sacrifice. They go away from home to do it, and after quite a while they get to the top of a mountain, where they are to give their offering up to God. I can imagine young Isaac's excitement.

But as Isaac stands there, he finds himself getting tied up, still not having been told what or where the animal was that they were going to sacrifice. It suddenly must have hit him: 'I am the sacrifice. Dad is going to kill me.' If it had not been of God, that boy would have been filled with every fear imaginable! He did not fight and kick, but I also guarantee that he did not particularly want to die. Isaac was a special young man, already showing the unique, in-built quality of a man of God, even in his early years. Isaac was obedient to God, but it didn't all just happen there and then on that mountain top. I believe he had been well trained and was taught who Father God was. If God said it, it had to be right, even though he may not have understood why. At the same time, I am sure that all sorts of questions would have gone through his mind as his dad prepared him for sacrifice.

Isaac was also an obedient servant to his father. He had a fantastic servant heart and trusted his father's guidance implicitly. He believed in his father. How many children today believe or trust in their parents – even in simple things? It's little wonder that some find it hard to trust Father God as they get older.

A boy prophet

Samuel lay down until morning and then opened the doors of the house of the Lord. He was afraid to tell Eli the vision, but Eli called him and said, 'Samuel, my son.'

Samuel answered, 'Here I am.'

'What was it he said to you?' Eli asked. 'Do not hide it from me. May God deal with you, be it ever so severely, if you hide from me anything he told you.'

So Samuel told him everything, hiding nothing from him. Then Eli said, 'He is the Lord; let him do what is good in his eyes.' (1 Samuel 3:15–18)

I find the story of Samuel very exciting. We know Samuel was a young boy. You may remember how Hannah actually brought him to the Temple and gave him over to God when he was tiny. For a young lad, that must have been quite something to be handed over like that. He had no choice in the matter, but God's hand was upon it, and his mum, with the confirmation of the priest, knew that she was acting in obedience to Father God.

God's hand is on our children as well. It's no use saying, 'Ah well, God's hand was more on those children in those days,' because that is just not true. Samuel had learned to live without parents. In your work with children, you will have plenty of people excusing a youngster's behaviour because he or she came from a bad background, or a broken home. They conclude that because of such a background, the child is going to be disadvantaged and will therefore find spiritual things more difficult to grasp. But that needn't be true. My wife Irene came from an extremely rough and tragic background, from a child right into her late teens, and God totally transformed her and healed her of all that. Her life is a tremendous testimony of God's power and grace.

As mentioned in previous chapters, there may well be some things that you will need to pray through with a child who comes from a tragic home situation, but ultimately he or she has as much chance as any other. Samuel would have known nothing about home life, and yet the Temple was where God wanted him to be.

If people come to you and say that there is a reason for a certain child's behaviour, again, that child might need to be shown more love, but he has as much chance and potential to be used by God as any other child. The minute he feels he is different, he will start to act differently, and more often than not in a negative way.

Samuel heard the voice of God but didn't understand whose voice it was. Poor old Samuel had a rough night and little sleep;

God was not going to leave him alone until he recognized his voice, which was going to be the most important thing in his life as he grew up to be a prophet.

Eli, though, actually taught him how to respond to God's voice, and showed him what to say. Likewise, we need to teach our children what the voice of God sounds like, and how to respond to it. Without instruction and guidance, they can easily become confused and mistake God's voice for either their own ideas or, worse still, that of the deceiver, Satan himself.

I love the way Samuel prophesied. You can imagine this little lad sharing God's word. The boy spoke out what God was saying, even though it was bad news. He wasn't exactly sharing, 'God is with you; God is happy.' He had a message that was going to be a severe rebuke to Eli. Mind-blowing, isn't it? God chose a young, inexperienced little boy to tell one of the nation's spiritual leaders that he hadn't been obedient to God and would be punished. We need to be aware that God can still move a child to deliver such a message.

As we read through the biblical account, we can see that from that point on, Samuel was respected. From early days, you can see the prophetic ministry developing in this young lad. And again, with some of our children today, we should be able to see a prophetic edge in their young lives. My personal observation is that the prophetic ones sometimes tend to be a little rough, wild, and, dare I say, outwardly rebellious? But somehow, if you can see through that tough exterior, you may find someone whose heart is really after God. We need to let the children speak God's word and share what is on his heart. Yes, we oldies will have to weigh it up, but they must have the opportunity to contribute.

A young heart after God

So he asked Jesse, 'Are these all the sons you have?'
    'There is still the youngest,' Jesse answered, 'but he is tending the sheep.'

Samuel said, 'Send for him; we will not sit down until he arrives.'

So he sent and had him brought in. He was ruddy, with a fine appearance and handsome features.

Then the Lord said, 'Rise and anoint him; he is the one.'

So Samuel took the horn of oil and anointed him in the presence of his brothers, and from that day on the Spirit of the Lord came upon David in power. (1 Samuel 16:11–13)

David had no fear. He was a boy who seemed to enjoy fighting with wild animals. The Bible actually says he went out of his way to fight bears! He was a warrior from the word go. That was in his heart. He was out there learning how to protect his dad's flock, and God knew that in a few years' time he would be the greatest protector of his flock the children of Israel would ever know.

He also had persistence. Although still very young, he wasn't put off by his brothers, or Goliath, or even King Saul. David knew God; he was and would remain God's friend. David's ambition was not to be the big hero. He just wanted to stand up for God. Where did he learn all about that? Obviously, he learned from his dad and family; it would have been too late to learn about it on the battlefield while face to kneecap with a giant.

I believe he was a spiritual boy. This sort of God-filled courage did not come instantly; it came from a well-taught background. Goliath was just the chance he had been waiting for to put his teaching and faith into action. Fear just wasn't present in David's heart. He had not considered losing because he knew that God was on his side. Some children think that every time they go to school and church, they cannot win. They lose their persistence and become frightened of all sorts of things, and end up living their lives as failures. They should not have their faces to the ground, but should be taught to hold their heads up high, confident and secure in the God they serve.

A little boy and a big giant; a little stone and a big victory; a little shepherd boy who grew into a great king.

An incredible dreamer

> Joseph, a young man of seventeen, was tending the flocks with his brothers, the sons of Bilhah and the sons of Zilpah, his father's wives, and he brought their father a bad report about them.
>
> Now Israel loved Joseph more than any of his other sons, because he had been born to him in his old age; and he made a richly ornamented robe for him. When his brothers saw that their father loved him more than any of them, they hated him and could not speak a kind word to him.
>
> Joseph had a dream, and when he told it to his brothers, they hated him all the more. (Genesis 37:2–5)

I think Joseph was incredible. I have such great respect for him. He knew what a dream from God was. While Samuel learned the audible sound of God's voice, Joseph knew God's voice in dreams. He not only knew when a dream was from God but he also knew how to interpret it. He was far from perfect, however, and in those early years, he was also a little unwise.

One of the things you will notice when working with children is that they have not been gifted with great wisdom. Wisdom is something that comes from maturity. But just because they may sometimes go beyond their briefing from God, that is still no reason to stop or quench them. We have to be patient with children because they will learn.

Young Joseph was totally insensitive. His dream wasn't a great blessing to his brothers, and there seemed very little need to tell them, even though what he was saying proved to be true. Children need to be taught that when God speaks to them, on most occasions they will need to share what God has said. But there will be times when what God says is personal and, like Mary, Jesus' mother, they need to hold it in their hearts, keep it to themselves and not share it.

Joseph also coped with hatred and jealousy against him. It is very hard for a child to cope with these things, but he did. He was a very lonely child, which was not helped by having a father who spoiled him and treated him better than he did his other sons. Whatever his brothers thought of him, however, Joseph was keen to see them, and was pleased when his dad told him to go and find them.

Imagine being grabbed, beaten up and thrown down a well. If the slightest thing happens to some people nowadays, we not only sympathize with them and ring up for help from the professional counsellors, but we tend to believe they will be dogged by rejection for the rest of their lives. But here was a young lad suffering at the hands of murderous brothers. That was serious stuff for a little boy, but with all the horrendous fears that he must have felt as he was sold and dragged off to a foreign land, he refused to die of rejection. The voice of God had told him that he had a future, and whatever men might do to him, he was going to hang on to God's words, because he had been taught that they always come true.

Some so-called mature Christians today act like babies. You have only to shout 'Boo!' and make them jump and they claim to have a spirit of fear! They could learn so much from Joseph.

Today's children, today's ministers

What a difference it makes if we teach our children that not only does God have a future for them, but the church has one too. If they have something to aim for, they can face all sorts of difficulties in life because they know that ultimately God has his hand on them, and they are given the boldness and power to fulfil that mission.

I remember taking a meeting where a little boy was crying his eyes out. Later, he told me why. He said, 'God has just shown me he will use me in a ministry of music.' That young lad knew it was God speaking to him and that God had just given him a glimpse of his future, and not just how much fun it would be, either.

On another occasion, an eleven-year-old boy said to me that God had shown him he should be pursuing a preaching ministry. I heard later that the lad had started preaching at his church's youth group and that he was brilliant. At our church, we sometimes let the young ones lead the meetings and even preach. I remember quite a few of the children at one of our meetings prepared talks and spoke out to all the church, and very powerful it was as well. At a large family camp, I asked if anyone felt that God was calling them to be preachers. Two ten-year-old girls responded. I called them to the front, handed them the microphone and told them each to preach – and they did. They did not speak for long, but were very good. When they had finished, I told them that preachers never finish by walking off the stage; they finish with some sort of appeal, and if these girls were really preachers, they had better do the same. They did, and many responded having heard the voice of God through these two young preachers.

At the final meeting of the week, adults and children all met in a big barn. I informed the organizer of what had happened and he did the same as I had done previously, calling the two girls up on to the main platform, but this time they preached to 5,000, not 300, and again a wonderful response followed.

We need to start looking for signs of ministries springing up in children's lives, and then supply the right conditions for them to flourish and grow. Most of the Bible heroes were being trained in various avenues of ministry long before they became 'famous' for it. A ministry will take time to mature, so the sooner you start training, the longer time the person will have on this earth to be used in it. Let's make things clear: we are not looking for professional performers, following just hours of practice; we are looking for humble little servants who are waiting and needing to be exalted. Professionalism and performance can so easily bring about pride, but sadly in today's world, life seems to have the opposite problem. Today, so many have so little self-worth that they are under the impression they can't do anything. With God's help, we need to change that way of thinking.

Finally, remember that if we do not allow children to develop their God-given talents for kingdom use, they will have to have an outlet and try to be successful in something else. Sadly, many are likely to pursue personal ambition or making money, and surround their lives with priorities that will end up taking them away from God. Encourage their qualities, make and train up disciples, and let's enrich the church with their potential. It's often a case of use them or lose them.

19

The Children's Worker

Much that I have written in this book I have deliberately aimed at the parent, guardian and the children's worker, and although at times I may have given advice to the parent, this can often overlap to the children's worker. This is especially so where the one-parent family needs some assistance, or the child is from a non-Christian home. I've tried to emphasize that the parent must have overall responsibility, and that children's workers, however much love they may have for a child, have no right to feel that while the child is in their care they are adopting him.

I must repeat again that children's workers should be those who have a heart for all ages but have been given a special talent from God which allows them to communicate, in a very clear yet profound way, biblical truths and their modern-day application to children. They must encourage Christian parents to train the children in spiritual ways, and must not look down on them if the parents don't do their teaching according to the children's workers' manual, if there ever was such a thing. The parent and children's worker form a team, and there must be no competition between them, as they both want to see the child grow in the Christian faith. The parent is like a cake, bearing both the spiritual and the day-to-day responsibilities, and the children's worker is like the icing on the cake – something special, the treat, that will be of great benefit to the children and a great encouragement to the parents.

The Glorie Company

Alongside years of overseeing the children's work in a local church, I also for many years ran an international children's work called the Glorie Company. Glories are characterized as little, smiling people who have springs instead of legs because they enjoy bouncing around a bit. They have large tambourines, and even larger smiles on their faces. Although they are fun characters, they love praising God, and their aim in life is to put him first. They are obedient to what he asks them to do, and also do those things with a cheerful heart, not because they have to, but because they want to and because they love him.

Although children can associate with these little characters, I have also found that teenagers and adults have adopted them, too. This could be due to the many thousands of records and books that we have sold about them, which I have tried to make appealing to all ages of the family.

For both local and national work, I have had to be involved in selecting workers to join my team. Sometimes this has meant finding up to 100 for one event, but I have learned a lot in the process. I would like to share with you some of the qualities that I look for in a children's worker, and hopefully this will not only be a help to those who oversee the children's work, but also to those who are pondering whether this is what God is leading them into.

Selecting children's workers

I must add that I don't expect all my workers to be brilliant in all the following, but I do expect them to be willing to learn and be submissive to me as their leader, who at the end of the day is going to bear the responsibility and be accountable and answerable to local church leaders and others who are organizing the event.

My relationship with my workers is one of friendship, and they know that my aim is to stretch them in those areas they may need to be expanded in, yet I never dishonour them or ask them to do something I would not be willing to do myself. The age of the worker is not important to me, and ages have ranged from twelve years to those over sixty. They have found it to be indirectly as much a training programme and time of blessing for them as it has been for the children. Also, their position in their local church means little while in the Glorie Company, and again I have had everyone from principal leaders from very large churches to ordained vicars. Although they would never end up being mainly children's workers, they came to learn and have their eyes opened to what God could do in children, and were able to take what they had seen back to their local flock.

I don't want to leave out any who are under twelve if what I do can be of help in training them. Although they participate in nearly everything the older leaders do, they don't, of course, bear the responsibility.

As a leader, I also have a responsibility to be honest with members on my team. Having to choose so many helpers, I have sometimes chosen a few wrong people, whose hearts were not really for the children; they may have just wanted to get a free place at the event. With these folk – and I would stress that they are very few and far between – I share with them my concerns and sometimes even have to explain to them that unless certain attitudes change they will be little use to either children or the kingdom. I hate doing this, but as a leader this has to be done. There is a way of doing it which is not totally destructive; a way which gives that person a few positive comments, or even suggestions as to how things can be amended. And even after I have shared with them, I must still impress upon them that this is just my opinion, and if they feel that my analysis is incorrect about them then they have every right to ignore it, but it would be worth their while to talk the whole issue over with their local leaders when they get home.

When choosing a team, we so often have to trust leaders' recommendations, but these have let us down quite a few times. Many leaders send young people to be on our team, hoping the experience will help the person they sent. Of course, we hope this happens to everyone on our team, but their main reason for being with us is not just to receive but to give 100 per cent to the children.

Here, in my opinion, are some essential qualifications for a children's worker.

1. A real walk with God

However much talent and gifting people may have, it will not achieve much if they are not close to the Lord. They may be great at sports and games, music, puppets, storytelling, creativity, and so the list goes on, but those people will in the long term be more of a hindrance than a help if they are not willing to get their lives sorted out. Leaders have been guilty for a long time of giving talented people jobs and responsibilities just to keep them in fellowship, and at the end of the day it has only brought sadness and heartache. The old days of 'anyone will do' to work with children are over. The children deserve the best: those who are all out for God. It must follow, then, that the worker must also be able to know and define the voice of God, but how can they do this unless they are regularly talking and listening to God themselves?

Once a leader has explained biblically how we hear the voice of God, they must follow this with practical sharing that comes from their own day-to-day experience. This is going to be one of the most important things a child needs to really understand. As well as leading them out of the traps of temptation, being able to discern the voice of God will lead them along the straight and narrow path that the Lord has set for them, and save a lot of confusion and heartache.

2. Bible knowledge

The worker does not need to be trained at theological college, but he or she does need to have a good overall view of Scripture, and also know how to study properly the passage of Scripture that they are sharing. Pre-packed children's notes, which are all ready to simply shove in the microwave and then dish out, were never meant to be the lazy way, and although they can give some useful and helpful ideas, they really are only a foundation for people to build on. It is still vital that the worker learns how to use a cross-referenced Bible, knows where and how to discover the setting and context of the passage, and tries their hardest not to add little comments that are not really present.

In preparation for a talk you will probably use only a small percentage of your background research, but at least you learn a lot through your preparation, and hopefully you should have an answer for that difficult question that is sure to be asked. You will feel quite accomplished when you have an answer and you do not have to rely on being able to waffle on until the child gets bored and wishes that they had never asked the question to start with.

3. Ability to stay in charge

Amid all the noise, laughter and fun, a leader's responsibility is to see that things don't get out of hand and that the children are not allowed to become wild and unruly. A leader needs to know how to be firm and serious. Discipline is an important part of training, and children feel more secure in an environment where they know that someone is in charge.

Of course, the use of any physical force on a child is forbidden, and I would be furious if any of my workers thought that they had the right to manhandle a child in a rough way. In my experience, I have found some school teachers in Christian work far too strict, to the point of undoing any good that has been built up.

I personally am not a great advocate of regimented meetings, with children forced to sit on mats, and if they talk or stray off them they miss out on a burger at the end of the meeting. We are not sergeant majors running an army barrack, where we want our children to be scared stiff of us; we are living church, where our love is going to be the emotion we want the children to feel.

A children's club is also not school, and you don't have to carry on the teacher/pupil image. It is very hard for some teachers to drop this after all their training. In cases of bad behaviour, a stern word is enough, and with the thousands of children from different backgrounds I've worked with, it has never been a major problem. Without meaning to sound super-spiritual, I guess this is because I believe that the power of the Lord is present, and also the children don't think about being naughty if they are really enjoying themselves.

Is every child that comes to our meetings sent by God? I don't think so. Ninety-nine per cent are, but I have found the odd one who has no interest at all in God and really seems to have come along intent on trying to destroy what God wants to do in other children's lives. I have no problems in banning an unruly child for a couple of meetings if he or she continues to misbehave and distracts children who want to listen. I would do this firmly but also lovingly. I want this child to come back – but only when they can behave themselves. In Sunday meetings where a Christian parent would be in another part of the building, if a child's behaviour does not improve after warnings, I would ask one of their parents to come and sit with their child for a couple of weeks, and then leave it for the parent to discipline them. I believe a parent should assist and encourage the children's leaders at every opportunity.

4. Ability to set a good example

Whatever else you are when you are working with children, you are always an example, for better or worse. They are going to learn more from who you are and the way you act, than they will from what you teach. I find this quite a challenge.

5. Life and fun

Although there are pressures facing our children, they are naturally full of bounce, life and fun. I believe that the Christian has life more abundant, or lives life to the full. Either way you look at this, it must mean that we too, as God's children, have a life that is fun and exciting. How much life and fun do children see in you as you stand out at the front of a meeting, claiming to be full of the joy of the Lord first thing on Sunday morning? I hear one person who wants to justify their miserable exterior by saying that their joy is deep down, not surface level, and the Lord knows you and loves you. Well, I'm glad to hear that. All you need to do now is ask the Lord to bring that deep joy up to the surface and then I believe you will be more of a blessing to others, and maybe they will love you as well.

It's no use you saying that you love to be with children if they don't love being with you. The classic example is when you ask the children to get into two teams; you will lead one and Johnny will lead the other. It's very embarrassing when all the children, including your own, rush to be with Johnny. Some children will want to be with exciting and fun-loving people; others will want to be with someone they feel they can trust and who won't embarrass them by being too over the top. You need to be able to portray the fruit of the Spirit in your own life in order to have the children's love and respect.

6. Honesty

Leading people should never be a performance. Many a church

leader has failed to communicate with his congregation because every time he is in public view he looks like perfection itself, but in his mind, in his home, and in his relationships with other people, he is a completely different person – a real Dr Jekyll and Mr Hyde personality. I believe that the day of putting on a show just to impress people is over. The average person needs to see his leaders as they really are, warts and all; a person who, like them, has to confess before God his shortcomings and the odd failure, but also a person whose heart is after God.

Even in the Bible, God chose to highlight the faults and sin of his greatest heroes – not so that we could think less of them; no, more that we could relate to them and learn from their faults, as well as the numerous good things that they did.

When working with children, we must not put ourselves on a pedestal which is higher than where we are really at; it is nothing short of a con. There may be occasions when we arrive at a meeting after a very busy or difficult week, or when we may be a bit confused in our guidance. These are the times when, without going into great detail, we need to ask the children to pray for us. We leaders are so often frightened of becoming vulnerable, and yet we love it when our listeners are.

Please understand me here. If you have some major ongoing problem, this must be shared with your church leaders, not the children. It would be madness to confess some sexual sin or spend your whole meeting telling the children of all your woes; the poor little things arrived so happy, but went away so depressed, having had to take on board all your problems as well as their own. I think you know what I am trying to say.

Also, I would never encourage children to relate to their leaders as uncles and aunties. Apart from being untruthful and confusing, they are unbiblical terms. While still teaching respect for those older and in authority, I do believe that respect also needs to be earned. Titles can be a barrier, and I want children to relate to children's workers on a friendly yet respectful level. All my team, whatever age they are, are known by their Christian or nicknames. This they have written across the fronts of their T-shirts or jumpers so that not only can the children remember who they are, but, more to the point, so can I!

If you feel strongly that older leaders should not be called by their Christian names – after all, they may feel embarrassed if a child calls them Horace or Gertrude – may I suggest using Mr, Mrs or Miss, or whatever their title is, which of course the child is used to saying at school. This would still be much more appropriate than the meaningless words uncle and auntie.

7. Freedom in expressing fun and praise

Although it may sound strange to put these two together, I suppose what I really mean is that we need to be people with very few inhibitions, and not just find freedom when we are with the children and lose it when we are with adults. It's no use teaching the children an action chorus and then not doing it yourself, and it's no use trying to hide behind a guitar or piano, because with the little beady eyes of children watching there is no hiding-place.

Also with praise and thanksgiving, if you are encouraging the children to express this through dance, raising their hands, kneeling, and so on, again, it needs to be part of what we do naturally, not just something we teach and encourage others to participate in. If you are bound and inhibited in your outward expression, may I suggest that you pray and ask the Lord to release you, as a lot of this may be due to your past and upbringing? For many, it is quite a hard task to shake off years of inhibition and may take a little while. However, I do believe that with God's help, no matter how much of an introvert you think you are, if you really desire to be free, God will fulfil the desire of your heart.

If it is any encouragement to you, it took me ages to be free enough to express my praise in dance. I made all the usual excuses about how stupid I would look, how I was too fat, too short, and even had what seemed like two left feet, but deep down I knew that my problem was that I was too embarrassed and too scared. I am thankful to God that he helped me through these insecurities, and I know that my work with children would have been a lot less effective had I just stayed with my feet planted firmly on the floor.

8. Ability to use the spiritual gifts, and portray the Spirit-filled fruit

In this book I have talked a lot about the supernatural gifts of the Holy Spirit. May I emphasize that I need to be a regular user of these gifts and not just expect the children to be. I have emphasized the spiritual gifts rather than the spiritual fruit, not because they are more important, but because I feel little is said, written, taught and practised about the spiritual gifts with children. It should go without saying that the fruit of the Spirit mentioned in Galatians 5 as love, joy, peace, patience, kindness, goodness, faithfulness, gentleness and self-control' should be visibly obvious in our lives, for the children to see. In all the wonderful and supernatural ways that God is using us, our growth rate in the Christian life can be calculated and discovered not by how much the gifts are being used, but by how much the above qualities (the fruit) are being cultivated and allowed to blossom and grow.

If you are feeling brave, ask the children if they can see more of the fruit of the Spirit in your life than they could six months ago. Even if one answers that you don't 'lose your cool' so much as you used to, at least you know that the fruit is visibly growing.

To sum up, when talking about setting an example, the fact that we must always remember is that we cannot be leaders unless we lead.

Qualities

Here are eight qualities I would want to see in those who want to work with children.

1. They are not only willing to give to children, but they are also open to receive from them.
2. They have a pure and innocent love for children.
3. They believe that children are not only important in the present, but that they also have a future and they in fact are the future.
4. They believe that children are not an inferior part of the church of Christ, nor the most important people in the church; they are normal members of the body of Christ, and they need to let them know that they are.
5. They desire to equip the children with everything that God has made available to them, so that they can live victoriously in a world that will often be hostile to them.
6. They want to see the children grow in the Christian faith, and by passing on their baton to them, train them up so that in time they will be even more spiritually successful and have achieved more for the kingdom than even the teacher has.
7. They are able to achieve the balance of never forgetting that they are working with children, and always remembering that they are working with young spiritual beings who have a large spiritual capacity that needs satisfying.
8. They must be able to relate to other people – not just children, but people of their own age group. I find it unhealthy when someone is interested only in children and has only children for friends.

Finally, for those who are involved with organizing teams, it might also help you to see the outline in the appendix that my wife Irene produced to send out to our would-be workers.

Why rules?

In hard print this may sound very strict, but clearly defining the rules is important when forming a team of people.

I realize that halfway through the week some will be physically and spiritually exhausted, and some of the worst parts of their characters are likely to start showing. We are prepared for this and many times have been able to pray into workers' lives and see them return home at the end of the week having been transformed in one area or another by the power of God.

Adrian Plass has reminded me that an anagram of Ishmael is 'I lash 'em'. As a leader, my team members may say 'Amen' to that! But I'm sure they realize that underneath this confident, harsh exterior beats the heart of a man who, in working with children, is still very much in the learning process.

The Children Act

As we come to a close, I feel it's important, especially for UK readers, to mention the Children Act. Mention of the Children Act seems to frighten many people involved in work among children in church, but there is no reason why it should. I believe it is something to be welcomed into the church with open arms, for with this act there is very good advice for safe practice when working with children.

Another good source of advice for good practice is the Home Office Code of Conduct, called 'Safe from Harm', which has been written specifically for churches and other voluntary organizations that work with children.

Hebrews 13:17 tells us to obey our leaders and submit to their authority, and complying with the law enshrined in the Children Act is not excluded from this scriptural obligation. Out in the secular world, people working with children are following these rules and guidelines every day, making the world a happier and safer place for children to live, and giving parents confidence that their children are in safe hands. Surely we, as Christians, should be striving to do this too – not just by following the guidelines, but going that extra mile to ensure the safety of children. In other words, we should be doing it better than anyone else, not complaining about the 'bureaucracy', or commenting that we have 'managed all these years without it'.

I am not going to quote the Children Act in detail because there are a lot of publications already available – you can find all the information you need from the PCCA, or from the numerous books produced for different denominations (e.g. *Worth Well Doing* from the Methodist Association is excellent). All I am going to do here is give you the main points to consider when checking if your church is a safe place for your children to be. Hopefully, you will be able to see the reason for all of them. I am very grateful to a friend of mine, Kay Morgan-Gurr, from Children Worldwide for providing me with the following information.

Do you have enough leaders?

The criteria set out in the Children Act are guidelines – the bare minimum to work with. This does not mean that if you meet these criteria you are necessarily safe. You should be taking into account not just the ages of the children, but their abilities, behaviour and special needs. You should also be looking at the environment you are working in, and whether any of your leaders have special needs too.

Do you know your leaders?

It is good to have known your children's workers for at least six months before they are invited to come and work with children. Make sure you ask for and obtain references, give a job description explaining what is expected, and keep things reviewed regularly. Always be careful of 'church hoppers', and contact their previous churches for references to validate their reasons for leaving. Police checks are not generally required in a church setting – but do consider having those in leadership with the children police checked, as this is good practice. We would be dangerously naïve if we were not aware that for good reason churches have been regarded as 'soft targets' by those who do not have the best interests of children at heart.

Do you have a children's policy?

If not, then you should. This is essential in the care of children. It helps to set out your aims and ideas for your children's work, and at the same time declare how you intend to safeguard the children and deal with any incidents that may occur. It also sets out what should happen in the event of any allegation of abuse, naming those who should deal with the situation and how they should respond. Sample copies of the children's policy can be obtained from the PCCA (website is www.ccpas.co.uk), or your own denomination may have one available for your church to adapt to its own needs. The PCCA stands for Promoting Christian Care and Action and they operate the Churches' Child Protection Advisory Service, with a 24-hour helpline on 01322 660011.

With a correct policy in place and operational, any allegations can be quickly identified as real or false and dealt with accordingly. The policy is there for the protection of the leaders and the ongoing work, as well as the children.

What is in the room you use?

If your church building is like most other church buildings around today, then the chances are that the chairs are stacked too high, there are heavy doors that can slam shut, there are uncovered electric sockets and there are corners of tables at a child's eye height. Why not stand in the middle of the room you use and try to think like a child who is the same age as those who would normally be using that room? Where could you trap your fingers? Is there any glass that you could fall through? Is there anything you could bang your head on? If you find difficulty with this, ask a teenager to help you. I have found that they rise to the challenge and are very good at spotting hazards.

Is your equipment safe?

If you use craft equipment, be very vigilant. It is amazing what children will attempt to put up their noses, in their ears or in their mouths. Did you know that a six-year-old can fit 18 jumbo lentils up just one nostril? Yes, I have actually had to sort this one out, although I still don't understand why. ('Because it's there' doesn't really seem appropriate in this case.)

Play equipment should be checked before you use it – every time, not just once a month. Again, bear in mind the ages, abilities and behaviour of the children before attempting any activity using equipment. Make sure that they are able to use it properly, and can be stopped instantly should a problem occur.

If you are using a play parachute, remember that parachutes have an in-built tendency to wrap themselves around any available watches, rings or earrings and then pull them off, causing maximum discomfort or worse. This goes for many other types of games equipment too.

Are you on your own with a child?

If you are, then you should not be. All ratios are expressed as one leader to a number of children. This is a minimum basis for guidance, not an absolute. Even if the ratio is one to eight, and you have eight children, then you should still have two leaders. If you find yourself on your own with a child, then keep doors open, and make sure that someone else can see you at all times. This not only protects the child, but it also protects you against unfounded allegations.

Use your common sense

A lot of the issues surrounding safe practice are basic common sense. The overriding point is to ask yourself if you have taken all reasonable measures to ensure the safety and well-being of the children, remembering that you may be asked to account for this.

If you are in doubt about the safety of anything, then try to think like a child. After all, we were all one once, and it's quite a useful and biblical thing to be able to do. Please don't just pay lip service to the Children Act, but accept it as a useful and positive guide to best practice. Should we settle for anything less?

The end, nearly...

Every book has to end somewhere, and although there is so much more I could say, perhaps I'll leave those thoughts for another twelve years, when it will be time I'm sure for a further update.

Let me conclude by saying that I am even more sure than ever that we are experiencing a unique generation of children. The main reason that some people may find some of the things I have written about hard to swallow is because many of the things I have mentioned didn't happen to them when they were children.

I believe there are two reasons why this new generation of young people is so hungry for God. The first is that they are being prepared for persecution, but they will not fear it. Far from it, they will thrive and grow from strength to strength because of it.

I am reminded of a Baptist church that was holding a family service, and the children were on the platform doing a dramatic production in front of their parents and the rest of the congregation. Afterwards, the minister felt that the Lord wanted to speak through him to all present. As he started speaking, he didn't have a clue what he was going to say, and if he had, I doubt very much that he would have had the courage to say it. He made statements about the children they had been watching on stage; some would be persecuted for their faith, and some would even be martyred. This, understandably, was too much for the parents and close friends to cope with, and many broke down in tears.

It was at this point that all eyes were directed to the platform and the children. They saw an amazing sight. Far from being scared by what they had heard, the children had spontaneously fallen on their knees and were rejoicing and praising God with their hands raised.

Preparation for revival

God is building up and equipping an army where warfare is going to be the norm, and every soldier on the battlefield will learn to cope with pressures and dangerous times. I believe they are being prepared for a mighty outpouring of God's Holy Spirit on the unsaved. Call it revival if you like, but unlike similar happenings of old, they will not only be equipped to see people saved and filled with the power of God, but they will also lead warm, friendly and untraditional church gatherings that relate to all the different ages and cultures that desire to be part of the body of Christ. Those who have been completely outside of the faith will be nurtured without being lost; they will change to be like Jesus and not be forced to change to look and be like 'church leaders'.

As I write this, we are post church empires, post 'Toronto', post gold teeth, post Pensacola; in fact through our human eyes we can see very few 'new things' about to appear on the horizon. I guess this is why it is one of the most exciting times to be alive. What is the Lord going to do next in your community – and is the next thing he does going to be the 'big one' that we are all anticipating?

Spurgeon once said 'God does not expect our children to be good for the sake of being good; he expects them to be good to qualify them to become mighty.' I believe that as children 'break moulds' to follow the Almighty, they will become mighty and incredibly used by God. This book is in a fairly large print so even children can read it, because my prayer is that this book may be just a small start in encouraging parents, children's leaders and our younger ones to start rethinking many things through. I also appreciate that parts of it may be a bit premature for where we are at today, and that maybe its true impact may hit a later generation rather than this one. I finish with the words that I wrote at the beginning.

Just look outside your window and ask yourself honestly how the thousands of lost little ones around you will ever get to know Jesus, or get to love church, if we just stay as we are for the next 2,000 years.

Glorie Company Guidelines

The vision

The Glorie Company came into being through a concept and vision that Ishmael had several years ago.

The objective

The main aims and objectives are:

1. To lead children and young people to salvation through the Lord Jesus Christ.
2. To encourage them to have a continual relationship with him through prayer, Bible teaching and the fullness and gifts of the Holy Spirit.
3. To encourage them to have right attitudes and relationships with each other as Christians, by praying and ministering to each other.
4. To show them that the Christian life is one of happiness, excitement, joy, and is not boring. To make this world a better place to live in, through the influence of our lives by example.
5. To help them realize that though they are young, God cares,

and that they are just as important to the body of Christ as anyone else.

6. To show them they are loved and needed; they are not an unnecessary nuisance, and should never be rejected, ignored, patronized, or neglected by the church.

People were bringing little children to Jesus to have him touch them, but the disciples rebuked them. When Jesus saw this, he was indignant. He said to them, 'Let the little children come to me, and do not hinder them, for the kingdom of God belongs to such as these. I tell you the truth, anyone who will not receive the kingdom of God like a little child will never enter it.' And he took the children in his arms, put his hands on them and blessed them. (Mark 10:13–16)

The team

Ishmael's main ministry is musically orientated, therefore his band make up the nucleus of his team, with Irene, his wife, as administrator/secretary. On large-scale events, an excellent team of people join him, and over the years, under Ishmael's training and supervision, many have now moved on and have become key Christian workers in their own right. Ishmael firmly believes in training others so that they can be used more effectively in their own local churches and in national and international ministry. Those wishing to be on the team must have a heart for children and young people, must like working with them, and ideally see a future working within that age group. Their motive for working on the team must be in that context.

Ishmael stipulates that those working in his team must be born again, Spirit-filled Christians. They should be fairly mature in their faith and based in a local church or fellowship where they have the confidence and respect of their elders, leaders or minister, who would, if asked, be willing to provide a reference to recommend them.

After people have been accepted on to the team, as well as being given all the day-to-day details of the programme, they would also be informed of the following.

Preparation

Prepare yourself spiritually, so that you have lots to give to the children, and don't panic that you may not be up to it, because we will all be there to help each other.

Safety

It is vitally important that you remember that these children have been placed in our care by their parents. They are looking to us to help build up their relationship with Jesus and with their friends. This will, of course, include having a good time.

Safety and security is a high priority. Please do not physically handle the children. You must not pick them up, swing them around, or playfully fight with them. Accidents can easily happen, and we will be held responsible.

The children

Remember that they are on holiday, and they are looking for lots of fun and friendship. Plenty of participation and movement from you as leaders will help them to relax too. Please try to be as happy, pleasant and friendly as you can. The priority is the children; we are here to serve them. Please pray for them and take special interest in their lives individually. They will come from all sorts of different backgrounds. Some will be very shy and may be frightened of being with us; others will be full of fun and mischief. Be patient and keep control.

You

We are sure that it will be a great experience for you, but children can be very demanding. Do use your free time to relax and enjoy each other's company, and try to be aware of anyone in the team who needs practical help or friendship. We are all living in close proximity, so do also respect each other's privacy.

The Glorie Company standards

Over the years, Ishmael has striven to build a team of high reputation. He intends to maintain these standards and profile – to bring glory to God. We are known to have the liveliest children's workers around, and he expects 100 per cent energy and commitment 100 per cent of the time. You will be expected to give hours of bouncing, shouting and ministering during the week.

Ishmael also expects his team to be mature enough to comply with the following three rules:

1. No gossip or criticizing of each other.
2. No barbed humour. There will be no pulling down, getting at each other, or disrespect using cruel jokes or bad humour.
3. No crude or sick jokes.

These things are not 'fun' and are not in keeping with our image, nor do they glorify the Lord Jesus whom we serve. We should respect, honour and encourage each other at all times.

Children's Ministry Teaching Programme

- Do you want to see children develop a personal relationship with Jesus?

- Do you want teaching sessions that are fun, biblical, evangelical and interactive?

- Would you like children to enjoy age-appropriate activities as they learn about God?

If you've said YES to any of these questions, you need the Children's Ministry Teaching Programme.

The Children's Ministry Teaching Programme provides four leader's guides covering ages from under 3 to 13+; KidZone activity books for children aged 5-7, 7-9 and 9-11; MiniKidz and KidZone craft books for children aged 3-5 and 5-9, a magazine for those over 11; a CD of music and stories; and FamilyZone with song words, ideas for all-age worship and parents' letters.

For more information visit our web site
www.childrensministry.co.uk

Children and the Holy Spirit

by Chris Leach

Over recent decades the gifts of the Spirit have been
welcomed in churches around the world. But one area
of church life seems to have dragged its feet: children's
ministry.

Chris Leach understands the nervousness, even fear of
those who work with children. But, inspired by the
levels of faith she has seen in the children themselves,
she has no doubt that we can lead the children in our
care into the fullness and gifts of the Spirit,
appropriately and confidently.

Biblical and practical, this guide will help all those who
want to lead young disciples into more of the fullness
of the Spirit they themselves enjoy.

CHRIS LEACH plays an active role in her local church in
bringing the gifts and fruit of the Holy Spirit to children,
and has a growing itinerant ministry encouraging and
training children's ministry leaders.

CHILDREN'S
MINISTRY

50 Fun-Filled Family Activities

by Ishmael

Fascinating facts, puzzles and activities cover such unique themes as grasshoppers, teeth, wardrobes and baboons!

Ishmael's inimitable style combines with Flix Gillett's lively illustrations to make an entertaining resource for bringing families closer together. Let these 50 activities help your family discover the Bible together in a fresh way.